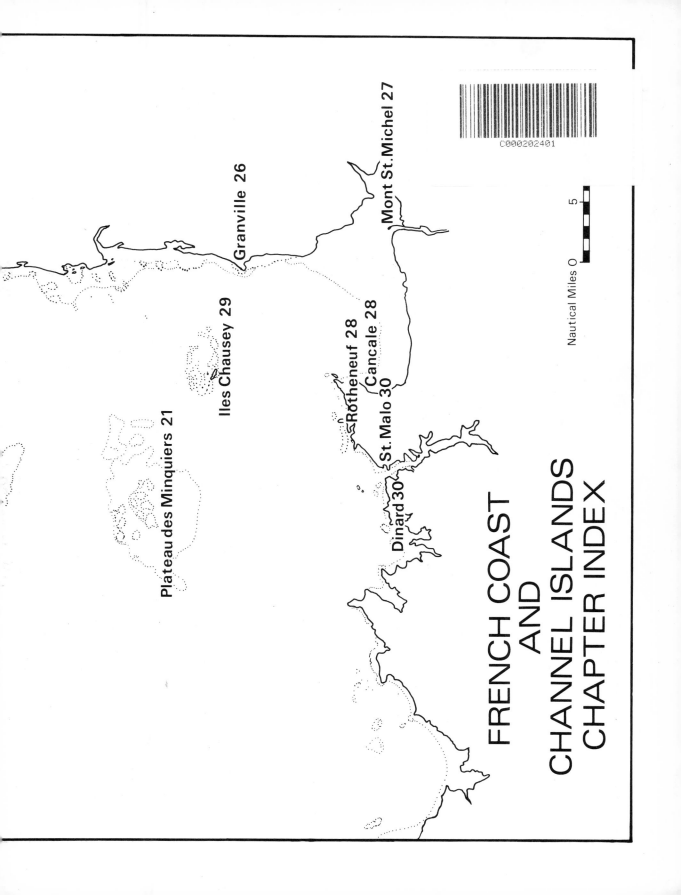

FRENCH COAST
AND
CHANNEL ISLANDS
CHAPTER INDEX

Mont St.Michel 27

Granville 26

Rotheneuf 28
Cancale 28
St. Malo 30
Dinard 30

Iles Chausey 29

Plateau des Minquiers 21

Nautical Miles 0

5

CHANNEL HARBOURS AND ANCHORAGES

Other titles of interest

Adlard Coles Pilot Packs
Brian Goulder
Vol 1: Great Yarmouth – Littlehampton and Ijmuiden – Carentan
ISBN 0–229–11798–8
Vol 2: Chichester – Portland, the Channel Islands and St Vaast – Erquy
ISBN 0–229–11799–6
Vol 3: Bridport – Isles of Scilly and Le Légué – Ushant
ISBN 0–229–11800–3

A major pilot series covering popular sailing grounds in Europe. Every harbour has a two-colour pilotage chart facing comprehensive navigational information. Each *Pilot Pack* is spiral bound for easy use.

Channel Crossings Around Britain
Peter Cumberlidge
ISBN 0–229–11852–6

For anyone planning to set off for foreign waters, this is a completely new style of passage-making guide for 16 open sea routes starting from popular British ports. Pilotage and navigational details, guidance on waypoints, tidal streams, weather forecasts, optimum times of departure and arrival and tactics for poor visibility and heavy weather are given.

Brittany and Channel Islands Cruising Guide 3rd edition
David Jefferson
ISBN 0–7136–3417–0

This popular guide, now fully revised and updated in its third edition, provides invaluable reference for anyone planning to cruise around Brittany and the Channel Islands. The Contentin coastline west and south of Cherbourg is also covered, as are the French Channel Islands and the Brittany canals.

Channel Islands Pilot 4th edition
Malcolm Robson
ISBN 0–7136–5771–5

An invaluable pilot to some of the most perilous coasts in the world. A detailed system of illustrated transit bearings, enables the navigator to find small anchorages and passages which do not appear in more conventional pilots. The islands covered are Alderney, Guernsey, Jersey, Sark, Hern, Jethou, Les Ecrehou and the Minquiers. Additional information includes advice on weather, tides and local sailing conditions.

K ADLARD COLES

CHANNEL HARBOURS AND ANCHORAGES

Seventh Edition

Fully revised by J D Dewhurst, L Peyton Jones and J Woollett

ADLARD COLES NAUTICAL
London

Published by Adlard Coles Nautical
an imprint of A & C Black (Publishers) Ltd
35 Bedford Row, London WC1R 4JH

First published	1956
Reprinted	1962
Second edition	1963
Third edition	1968
Reprinted	1972
Fourth edition	1974
Reprinted	1975
Fifth edition	1977
Sixth edition	1982
Reprinted (with corrections)	1985
Seventh edition	1991

Copyright © K. Adlard Coles 1991

ISBN 0-7136-3418-9

A CIP catalogue record for this book is
available from the British Library.

Printed in England by Clays Ltd, St Ives plc

Caution
While great care has been taken in the compilation of this book, it is regretted that neither
author nor publisher can accept responsibility for any inaccuracies or mishaps arising from
the work.

Contents

General Introduction

When this book was first published the information and photographs were obtained over a period of eight years cruising in the waters described.

Many amendments have been made in this edition, in particular numerous buoys, lights and beacons have been changed. Also abbreviations have been changed and simplified to conform with the new international chart abbreviations. Many of the charts have been altered or redrawn and many new photographs substituted.

Among cruising yachtsmen there is a substantial increase in relatively shallow draft craft, designed to remain upright when dried out. This has made many of the harbours covered in this book much more accessible, particularly those on the French coast. Thus, while the earlier editions were based on cruising yachts of some 1m8 draft, these harbours have since been visited in a bilge keel yacht drawing about 1m, which regularly dried out.

In these days when even very small yachts are fit to cross the English Channel in suitable weather, the Channel Islands and adjacent French coast offer a fascinating cruising ground which, in my opinion, is quite as interesting as the Bay of Biscay and more distant parts. Alderney, Guernsey and Jersey provide pleasant ports of call, although nowadays they are often crowded. For 'rock dodgers' there are countless bays and anchorages to explore. The French harbours are equally interesting, and, whether large or small, each has its own character.

Some yachtsmen used to be deterred from cruising in these waters on account of the rocks and strong tidal streams. An exaggerated impression of the dangers is given by a casual examination of small scale charts. Here many areas appear as almost impenetrable mazes of rocks and reefs, but given a chart on a larger scale it will immediately be seen that the rocks form groups, between which there is plenty of water; and with the aid of the large scale charts it is found that the approaches to most (but not to all) of the anchorages and harbours are by no means difficult in clear weather. Furthermore the majority of the rocks which decorate the charts are well covered at half tide, owing to the large range of tide. Before making a passage it is useful to put pencil circles on the chart around rocks which will be inadequately covered at the state of tide when they will be passed. This enables concentration to be given to the dangerous ones rather than wasted on those which will be covered and harmless except for overfalls in strong streams or bad weather. A liberal factor of safety should be allowed remembering that swell reduces the depth by half its height.

Likewise the streams. Casual references to rates attaining at six or nine knots or more, and setting on rocks, sound alarming to the uninitiated, but the fact is that rates such as these are only attained in certain places, and then only at certain times. Over a considerable area of the Gulf of St Malo the tidal streams are no stronger than in the Solent, although, of course, the range of tide is quite spectacular.

It is true that a steep sea gets up more quickly than in home waters, and overfalls occur in many parts when wind is against tide. For these reasons, when cruising on these coasts for the first time it is wise to choose neap tides, and always, if possible, to avoid the top of springs. I have not attempted to define which harbour approaches may be dangerous because I think the questions are answered by reference to the charts and descriptions. Narrow passages between rocks in strong tidal streams are always risky unless the marks and bearings can be identified with certainty and conditions and state of tide are suitable. For newcomers to cruising obviously difficult harbours such as Goury or Les Ecrehou or for that matter Herm and Sark should not be attempted until experience has been gained in the easier ones. The point is that a single error may possibly bring serious consequences. Auxiliary power is desirable on the occasion of a first visit to enable transits to be followed exactly where necessary without sails impeding vision and to avoid being set on rocks if the wind drops.

To my mind fog or thick weather is the principal hazard of the French coast or among the Channel Islands. It is idle to pretend that it is pleasant to be borne along by the tide on a rock-strewn coast which one cannot see, and in water which may be so deep that it is difficult to anchor. I have found myself in this predicament on several occasions, the worst being when approaching the SE of Jersey from Iles Chausey in thick fog, with my wife and daughter, at a time when I was unfamiliar with this bit of coast, which is the rockiest of all.

To omit mention of these difficulties would be misleading to the reader, but equally it is right to emphasize that in a normal summer there will be weeks of fine weather without fog or gales, when sailing in these waters is a delight to the amateur navigator. The distances between harbours are never great, the tidal streams may be bad masters but by careful calculation can be made good servants. Nevertheless, particular care is needed in navigation and caution in the choice of weather and state of tide suitable for passage making.

K. Adlard Coles

Charts, Tides and Navigation

Chart datum and depths. As early as 1965, the Admiralty commenced adjusting datums in accordance with the International Agreement to the level of the lowest astronomical tide (LAT), which can also be defined as the lowest predicted low water. This alteration is also being made in the Admiralty Tide Tables (ATT) Volume I and in other tide tables based upon them. By the time this fifth edition has been published most of the new issue Admiralty charts for the areas covered, will be available.

As explained in the Introduction, the harbour plans of the English coast from Poole to Weymouth in Part I and for the Channel Islands in Part III of the book have been altered to conform approximately with LAT datum. The theoretical datum on the French coast, in Parts II and IV, is the lowest possible low water. This may be a foot (0m3) or so below LAT datum and varies from place to place, but the datums in ATT and the charts correspond closely enough for most practical purposes. Thus the whole book (except for Christchurch Harbour where the level is impounded by sands at about the level of MLWS) is now referred approximately to LAT datum and the depths are converted from the nearest foot to metres and decimetres to conform with the new issue charts and tide tables.

The low level of datums are of particular significance in calculations of depths in the Channel Islands and on the French coast where the range of the tide is great, because it means that at most states of the tide the cruising man may find considerably more water than shown on the harbour plans. For example, on the St Malo chart the depths at MLWS are 1m3 above datum and at MLWN no less than 4m3 above datum, and these figures can be added to the depths or references in the text as may be appropriate. On the other hand, it is easy to forget that the level may actually fall to LAT datum near the Equinox and nearly as low at other times, so tide tables should always be consulted. Meteorological conditions may also have a considerable influence on the levels which can fall even below LAT predictions.

On the harbour plans in this book the shaded areas show the parts which dry out at chart datum and the dotted line indicates the fathom line (1m8), unless otherwise stated. In some of the harbour plans such as Goury, based on French charts, a rock which never covers may be marked by a symbol like a 'T' with a short transverse, which must not be confused with some form of beacon. Height of land, lighthouses and islets and rocks which never cover are given above MHWS or MHHW. Note that, where the differences are material, the **Visible Distances of Lights** have been amended to conform with the latest charts which show nominal ranges. For further information and definitions, or to calculate geographical ranges (often the more important viewed from the low height of eye in a yacht) see *Admiralty Light List Vol. A.* or Nautical Almanac.

High Water. Constants are given in relation to high water Dover; for example −00 h 15 m Dover means 15 minutes before *high water Dover*. Where appropriate, constants are also given on the nearest standard port, Cherbourg or St Helier. Tide tables for these appear in *Macmillan and Silk Cut Nautical Almanac* or *Reed's Nautical Almanac*, and are, of course, more accurate than working from constants of a distant port. The most accurate method of tide predictions is shown in the *Admiralty Tide Tables* (ATT), Volume I, which is published each year.

Tidal Streams play such an important part in the navigation on the coasts described in this book that frequent reference is made to them and to the more important eddies. Tidal Stream Charts are given in the *Tidal Stream Atlas* for the Channel Islands and adjacent coast of France and in *Macmillan and Silk Cut Nautical Almanac* or *Reed's Nautical Almanac*. These are necessarily on a small scale where it is impossible to show all the local eddies. The streams generally turn earlier inshore than offshore and this feature is particularly marked on the neighbouring French coast, where in the vicinity of the Cherbourg Peninsula eddies exist running contrary to the main streams as much as two or three hours early, and in the Channel Isles (especially round Herm) there are fast running reverse eddies in some parts. Times, rates and directions of tidal streams are approximations as they vary between springs and neap and can be materially influenced by winds, barometric pressures and other conditions.

Abbreviations Tidal

ATT	*Admiralty Tide Tables* (Vol. I)
HW	High Water
LW	Low Water
LAT	Lowest Astronomical Tide
HAT	Highest Astronomical Tide
MHWS	Mean High Water Springs
MHWN	Mean High Water Neaps
MLWS	Mean Low Water Springs
MLWN	Mean Low Water Neaps

Other Abbreviations

Al	Alternating	Mag	Magnetic
B	Black	Min	Minute
Bu	Blue	Mo	Morse
Bn	Beacon	Oc	Occulting
Cheq	Chequers	Or	Orange
Dia	Diaphone	Q	Quick Flashing
F	Fixed	R	Red
Fl*	Flashing	Ra Refl	Radar Reflection
Fs	Flagstaff	Ro Bn	Radio beacon
G	Green	s	Seconds
H	Horizontal	Tr	Tower
I	Interrupted	Vert	Vertical
Iso	Isophase	VHF	Very high frequency
L Fl	Long Flashing	VQF	Very quick flashing
M	Miles (nautical) or land miles as appropriate	W	White
m	Metres or minutes	Y	Yellow

*Gp Fl has been discontinued e.g. Gp Fl (3) ev 15 sec is now the International abbreviation Fl (3) 15s

Bearings. Bearings are expressed accurately in degrees true, and, approximate magnetic bearings, expressed in points, are sometimes used to indicate a general direction.

Sailing Directions. The rocky coasts of France and the Channel Islands change little throughout the years, but alterations may occur in navigational aids, even while this edition has been in preparation. Alterations of this kind are notified in Notices to Mariners and also shown on charts corrected up to date. *Macmillan and Silk Cut Nautical Almanac* or *Reed's Nautical Almanac* gives the necessary information up to the time of going to press. Minor local changes, not necessarily notified anywhere, may take place in leading marks (such as the removal of a chimney or the building of new houses near what had been mentioned as a conspicuous one) and in marinas and facilities. However, provided the probability of changes are recognized, this new edition should be of service for some years to come.

The alterations in recent editions, including datum and metric conversions, have been so extensive, with numerous amendments on almost every page and chart, that the work involved has proved almost as great as compiling a new book. Great care has been taken over the task, and everything has been double checked individually but in the absence of independent checking, such as is available in a hydrographic office, the reader should recognize that the risk of human error remains and that no responsibility can be accepted for mistakes or omissions.

Radio Beacons. Those most useful in the sea area covered in this book are listed on page 11, but are liable to alteration.

Charts Recommended. Up-to-date charts are, of course, essential for cruising on these coasts. The minimum outfit of Admiralty Charts comprises Chart 2615 Portland to Christchurch; Chart 1106 Approaches to Cherbourg; Chart 2669 the Channel Islands and adjacent coast of France which is the key to the whole area; and the following charts for the particular localities to be visited: Chart 60 Alderney and the Casquets; Chart 3654 Guernsey, Herm and Sark; Chart 3655 Jersey and Chart 2700 Port of St Malo and approaches. Navigation is easier and infinitely more interesting with the aid of the very large-scale charts. There are particularly good large-scale Admiralty charts for the whole of the Channel Islands, available from all chart agents, and large-scale French charts can be obtained by post from Le Service Hydrographique de la Marine at 29283 Brest Cedex, France. This takes a little time involving invoicing and payment made through any bank. A list of French charts is available on application. References to French charts have been given in the text and the following are particularly useful: 5631 Abords de Goury et abords de Omonville (exceedingly useful as it also covers Cap de la Hague); 827 de Port Bail à Diélétte (including Passage de la Déroute and Les Ecrehou on small scale); 824 de Cancale à Bricqueville (which covers the whole of the Baie de St Michel including Cancale, Iles Chausey and Granville); 829 Iles Chausey and 4233 River Rance. Messrs Imray, Laurie, Norie and Wilson publish an excellent coloured chart No C33 of the Channel Islands and St Malo and adjacent coasts. They also publish coloured charts of the English Channel.

International Buoyage Systems. Symbols of the IALA (International Association of Lighthouse Authorities) maritime buoyage system are shown on page 201. This system applies to the whole area covered by this book, in which all charts and harbour sketches have been corrected accordingly, using international abbreviations.

French Port Signals

The following signals are used on the signal stations in French harbours for regulating entry or departure:

Entrance prohibited. A cone point up between two balls, vertically, or a red flag. By night. A white light between two red lights, vertically, or a red light.

Entrance and departure prohibited. Two cones, points together, above a ball, vertically, or a red flag above a green flag. *By night.* A white light above a red light and below a green light, or a red light above a green light.

Departure prohibited. Two cones, points together above another cone point down, or a green flag. *By night.* A white light between two green lights, vertically, or a green light.

Customs

It is necessary to notify the Customs of intended departure for the Channel Isles or France. Customs form C1328 giving details of crew, including passport numbers, must be completed and the top copy lodged with H.M. Customs before sailing.

For cruising in French waters passports are required.

On arrival from a British port at Channel Island harbours the regulations are the same as at other British ports.

On returning from France to the Channel Isles the 'Q' flag must be worn and Customs cleared at a recognized port of entry (St Helier or Gorey for Jersey; St Peter Port, St Sampson or Beaucette for Guernsey, Herm and Sark; Braye for Alderney). The same procedure must be followed again when arriving at a British port. Anti-rabies regulations are strictly enforced at all British ports.

Radio Beacons

Radio beacons, which are useful in the sea areas described in this book, have been brought up to date and are listed below. Like buoys and lights they are liable to alteration and the latest Nautical Almanac should always be consulted.

Marine Radio Beacons

Station	Lat. North	Long. West	Range Miles	Freq. kHz	Signal	Mins. past each hour
Start Point LH	50° 13½′	3° 38½′	70	298.8	SP (· · · · — — ·)	01, 07, 13, etc.
Casquets LH	49° 43½′	2° 22½′	50	298.8	QS (— — · — · · ·)	02, 08, 14, etc.
Roches Douvres LH	49° 06½′	2° 49′	70	298.8	RD (· — · · ·)	03, 09, 15, etc.
Cap Frehel	48° 41′	2° 19′	20	305.7	FÉ (· · — · · · — · ·)	01, 03, 05
Corbière, Jersey	49° 11′	2° 14½′	20	305.7	CB (— · — · — · · ·)	02, 04, 06
St Peter Port	49° 27.4′	2° 31.4′	10	285	GY (— — · — · — —)	Continuous
St Helier, St Malo,	49° 10½′	2° 07½′	10	287.3	EC (· — · — ·)	Continuous
Le Grand Jardin	48° 40′	2° 05′	10	294.2	GJ (— — · · — — —)	Continuous

Charts, Tides and Navigation

Station	Lat. North	Long. West	Range Miles	Freq. kHz	Signal	Mins. past each hour
Nab Tower LH	50° 40′	0° 57′	20	312·6	NB (− · − · · ·)	00, 03, 09, etc.
Cherbourg (Fort de l'Ouest LH)	49° 40½′	1° 39′	20	312·6	RB (· − · − · · ·)	02, 05, 11, etc.
Portland Bill LH	50° 31′	2° 27½′	50	291·9	PB (· − − · − · · ·)	00, 06, 12, etc.
St Catherine's Pt	50° 34½′	1° 18′	50	291·9	CP (· − · − · · − − ·)	01, 07, 13, etc.
Pointe de Barfleur	49° 41½′	1° 16′	70	291·9	FG (· · − · − − ·)	05, 11, 17, etc.
Channel LV	49° 55′	2° 55′	10	287.3	CR (− · − · · − ·)	Continuous
Poole Harbour	50° 40.9′	1° 50.9′	10	303.4	PO (· − − · − − −)	
Chichester Bar Buoy	50° 45.9′	0° 56.3′	10	303.4	CH (− · − · · · ·)	

Aeronautical Radio Beacons

Station	Lat. North	Long. West	Range Miles	Freq. kHz	Signal
Hurn	50° 48′	1° 43½′	35	394	HRN (· · · · · − · − ·)
Alderney	49° 42½′	2° 12′	50	383	ALD (· − · · − · · − · ·)
Guernsey	49° 26′	2° 38½′	30	361	GUR (− − · · · · − − · ·)
Jersey East	49° 13′	2° 02′	75	367	JEY (· − − − − · · − −)
Jersey West	49° 12½′	2° 13½′	25	329	JW (· − − − · − −)

VHF Radio Lighthouses

Station	Lat. North	Long. West	Range Miles	Freq.	Signal
Anvil Point	50° 35.5′	1° 57.5′	14	Ch88	AL (· − · − · ·)
Scratchells' Bay	50° 39.7′	1° 34.6′	30	Ch88	HD (· · · · − · ·)

PART I
SOLENT TO WEYMOUTH

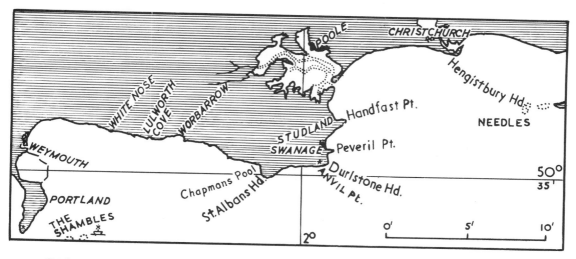

1 Christchurch

Double High Water: In entrance at springs 1st HW highest − 1 hr. 55 m. Dover; at neaps 2nd HW highest about + 1 h. 0 m. Dover. At the Town Quay times are about 25 min. later. Portsmouth HW times give a more accurate result and, if used, the corresponding times are − 2 h. 10 m. and + 0 h. 50 m. but note that at neaps the time of HW may be indefinite owing to the long stand of tide.

Heights above datum: MHWS 1m5. MLWS 0m1. MHWN 1m2. MLWN 0m6. The datum is referred to MLWS approximately as the water within the harbour is impounded at this level owing to drying sands on the bar.

Streams: In 'The Run' 4 to 5 knots on ebb, 3 to 4 knots on flood; comparatively weak outside.

Depths at Low Water: 0m4 at Bar (variable); 2m2 or so in 'The Run'; 0m4 to 2m7 between entrance and Town Quay; 0m4 to 1m8 above Town Quay in Rivers Avon and Stour. Apart from the channel and creeks the broad expanse of the harbour nearly dries out. The depths at bar and in harbour are influenced by prevailing meteorological conditions, prolonged N and NE winds tending to reduce the depth.

Yacht Clubs: Christchurch Sailing Club. Highcliffe Sailing Club.

Christchurch—at one time Twynham—lies at the junction of the Rivers Avon and Stour and about two miles from their mouth. Three-quarters of a mile below the junction, the easterly flowing rivers open out into a wide shallow expanse of water, sheltered on its southern side by Hengistbury Head and almost closed off from the sea on the east by Mudeford Sandspit. At the northern end of this spit is the harbour's outlet known as 'The Run'.

To owners of small craft the harbour's doleful reputation of a difficult entrance can be somewhat offset by its asset of a double high water and good protection. Any craft with a

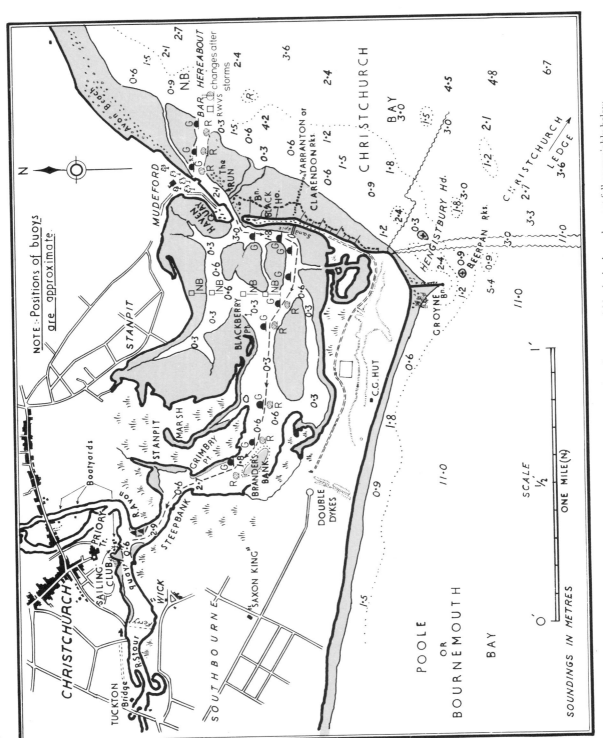

Christchurch Harbour: Datum approximately at MLWS as the water within the harbour does not fall appreciably below this level. (Based on British Admiralty Chart No. 2219 with the permission of the Controller of HM Stationery Office and of the Hydrographer of the Navy).

draft of 1m4 or less can, with local knowledge, enter the harbour at the top of a spring tide and find deep water berths near the town. For such craft there are winter moorings and slipways at local boat yards.

Buoyage in the harbour and entrance is undertaken privately by the Christchurch Harbour Association (for the convenience of yachtsmen). Buoys may be withdrawn during the winter months, certainly those in the entrance. Further, as the depth and position of the bar is far from stable—it varies from year to year and after storms—great care must be exercised when entering and leaving. Certainly the harbour should not be approached for the first time in foggy or bad weather on the ebb, or if the wind is Force 5 or more and is more south than south-west.

Tides

The most important factor governing entry and use of the harbour is the tides. The double high water, although quite apparent, is in effect a stand of the tide for a period of about 3 or 4 hours. At springs the 1st HW is the higher by about 0m15, whilst at neaps the 2nd HW is higher by the same amount (although under both conditions the actual height of 2nd HW is in theory much the same). However, states of flood (or drought) in the river and meteorological conditions can cause a variation from the predicted height by 0m3 or more.

Flood and Ebb in 'The Run'. Under certain conditions the full rate of the ebb in 'The Run' may be 6 knots or more, although the average is about 3 or 4 knots. Owing to this high rate and the narrowness of the channel it is obvious that auxiliary motor power is required to make the passage into the harbour against the stream. However, on the first ebb, entry under sail only is possible with favourable winds.

The full strength of the ebb—the second ebb—comes an hour or so after 2nd HW, and lasts with diminishing strength until after LW at the bar. (At springs it is not actually slack at LW until half an hour after the tide has begun to rise.)

The flood then commences and comes away more strongly about an hour later (i.e., $1\frac{1}{2}$ hours after LW) when it reaches perhaps 3 or 4 knots, with a strong cross inflow sweeping around close to the end of the Sandspit. This causes minor back eddies and a little turmoil. By 3 hours after LW it has eased considerably and presents little hazard.

At springs the most favourable conditions for entering the harbour are from 3 hours after LW until after the 2nd HW (a period of some 5 hours). At neaps the most suitable period is between the two high waters.

Between the two high waters there is an ebb and flow each with a rate of perhaps 1 to 2 knots.

Navigational Instructions

Off-lying Dangers. To the east there are no dangers except for general shallowness offshore, whilst to the west the groyne on the southern extreme of Hengistbury Head and its adjacent Beerpan Rocks (0m9 MLWS)* should be given a clear berth of about 3 cables, although there is a narrow passage between them.

Christchurch Ledge extends from the groyne for $2\frac{1}{2}$ miles to the Southeast. The depths vary from 3m to 8m and rise steeply on the west flank from 14m or more, falling away

*These have been known to dry out under exceptional conditions.

Christchurch

1.1 Looking SW across harbour to Bournemouth Bay at half-tide. The boat (*bottom left*) has just crossed the bar. The flattened 'c' towards the centre of the harbour is Blackberry Point.

1.2. Looking NNW across the harbour towards Stanpit at half-tide. Note the pleasure-boat landing-stage near the centre of the sandspit in the harbour, whilst on the seaward side the submerged Clarendon (or Yarranton) Rocks are faintly discernible.

16

1.3. Hengistbury Head from the east, with the low lying Mudeford Sandspit and beach huts. (The Black House is just off the right of the photo.) The groyne shuts behind the Head as the bar is crossed.

1.4. The seaward end of the entrance channel is marked by this RW vertical striped buoy. *D. L. Sylvester-Bradley.*

1.5. In 'The Run' channel running parallel to right (northern) shore—deep water 2ml at LW.

1.6. Entering harbour from 'The Run' Channel bears to port and close to Sandspit shore towards pleasure-boat landing stage.

1.7. Christchurch at the junction of the Rivers Avon and Stour looking NNW. At the bottom right is the Steep bank reach. The Sailing Club with flagstaff is below the centre of the Priory and just to the left of E. F. Elkins Ltd. boatyard.

more gently into an area of 9m or so in Christchurch Bay. Minor overfalls and general roughness of the sea here can be experienced because of this.

Fallen rocks from the headland and small groynes extend to the low-water mark from Mudeford Sandspit—one particular ledge, an old mouth of the river, known as the Clarendon (or Yarranton or Long) Rocks, is submerged at HW but extends some 2 cables to seaward from the centre of the spit.

The Approach. Hengistbury Head forms a conspicuous landfall from all directions. It is about 30 m high at its western end where it is crowned by a coastguard hut, whilst from its foot Mudeford Sandspit—dunes covered with beach huts—extends NE for about half a mile. At the extremity of this spit is the Black House acting as a sentinel on the seaward (southern) side of the harbour's outlet—the northern side being flanked by a seawall known as Mudeford Haven or Quay, upon which is a small group of charming old houses.

The Entrance and Run. About 4 cables ENE of Haven Quay is the bar (about 0m4 MLWS) marked in the summer months by a RW pillar buoy and pairs of buoys, red to port, green to starboard. In this area the conspicuous grey square tower of Christchurch Priory, 2 miles inland, may be seen over the top of the low tree plantation bearing about 287° true and open east of the Haven houses; farther to the east it is hidden. Also the distant higher land of Southbourne with its red square water tower may be seen through the harbour entrance between the Black House and Haven Quay.

However it cannot be too greatly emphasized that *owing to the changing nature of the bar, both in depth and in position, precise sailing directions cannot be given.* The entrance buoys are relaid at Easter, and their position is altered to conform with any alteration in the channel. This

18

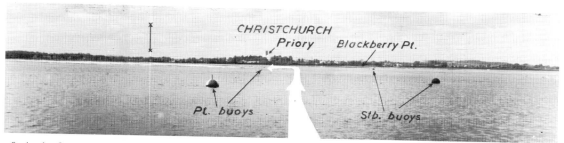

1.8. At the first porthand buoy in the harbour about ¼ mile from landing stage. Priory bearing about 308° over Stanpit Marshes. (The vertical crossed line indicates same position in view 9.)

1.9. Abreast of Blackberry Point. The long reach heading towards the 'Saxon King' (brg. about 274°) has only about 0m3 MLWS.

1.10. At Brander's Bank at the inner end of the long shallow reach. *C. Stewart.*

rarely occurs in the summer months except perhaps after an exceptional gale. Once over the bar, course is altered to port. The starboard or northern side is then flanked by the seawall, whilst the port side is confined by the submerged shingle and sand extremity of Mudeford Sandspit. This part of the channel is known as 'The Run' and as the quay is approached the fast tidal stream keeps it naturally dredged to some 2m1 or so—the greatest depth being near the quay.

On the quay are a café and public house with a bus service about ½ a mile away. However, craft cannot lie alongside for any length of time, although a landing can always be made at some point.

The Harbour. In contrast to the bar, the channels in the harbour are very stable both in direction and in depth.

From the inner end of the Haven, off which there is a deep pool of 3m0, the channel bears even more to the south and runs close to and parallel to the sandspit shore for about ¼ mile. *No attempt should be made to head up the harbour towards Southbourne from the Haven*—the starboard side of the channel is marked by small green buoys.

Halfway along the sandspit there is a concrete barge and scaffolding jetty for the use of local pleasure boats; here the channel turns up the harbour. Near the root of the jetty is a public telephone box, the office of the beach attendant and a small café.

The first port-hand buoy (R spherical) is about ¼ mile from the turn, and when it is reached the Priory should be seen ahead bearing about 308° true (NW mag) over the low-lying Stanpit Marsh.

Shortly before coming up on Blackberry Point the channel bears to port (marked by buoys) and the long shallow reach (0m3 MLWS) heads towards the 'Saxon King', a modern buff-coloured public house with blue tiles, bearing about 274° true. (It is below and to the left of the highest part of the Southbourne skyline.)

On reaching Brander's Bank, where the harbour narrows, the main channel is to starboard and there is a gradual deepening of the water. After passing its inner end do not come too close to Grimbry Point but keep the Priory just touching the edge of Steepbank.

This narrow and deep reach is flanked by tall reeds to starboard and low fields to port. It is known as Steepbank and is usually well lined with craft of every kind as it offers a safe but limited anchorage to deep-drafted boats. The stream is not hard but is appreciable.

It is now only a matter of a few metres before Christchurch Priory comes into full view, but the channel now lies to port of the centre line—it being shallow on the north side. After this head towards the sailing club flagstaff and the centre of the junction of the two rivers, but take care not to go too close to the Stour side of the channel as dinghy moorings cover a shallow patch. (See aerial photograph of Christchurch.)

The Rivers Avon and Stour

Around high water the River Stour can be navigated as far as Tuckton Bridge, a mile or so farther up. The least depth is about 0m5 (LW) between the Town Quay and Wick Ferry, above which the depths are generally deeper—about 1m8. Moorings can be had at Tuckton Bridge, where there is a boat-yard.

The Avon offers a much constricted but pleasant stretch for about half a mile, after which progress is stopped by bridges. As the chart and aerial photograph show, the river separates, forming an island, the sides of which are lined with boats. The right branch is shallow at low water.

The left branch of the river offers a very pleasant view of the old castle ruins and the Priory and has average depths of 1m with moorings on each bank.

Moorings and Anchorages

Moorings are usually laid privately on the river bed, whilst those off the boat-yards are available on application to the yard concerned. Christchurch Sailing Club keeps one or two moorings for visitors. Visiting yachts should secure alongside the club and report for directions. Boats can anchor anywhere that is convenient but should keep clear of the centre line of the channel, as many pleasure boats ply up and down the harbour at all states of the tide.

A stranger with a fixed-keel boat wishing to visit the town would do well to bring up in Steepbank and proceed ashore by dinghy.

Facilities

Facilities for yachtsmen are good. There are several yacht yards and shops of all kinds in the town. Early closing day is Wednesday. Good communications by rail or motor bus. Water at Haven Inn, café on Mudeford Spit (also stores) or at yacht yards.

2 Poole Harbour

Double High Water at springs: Entrance, −2 h. 21 m. and +1 h. 14 m. Dover. **Low Water:** +5 h. 4 m. Dover. Poole Entrance.

Heights above datum: MHWS 2m0. MLWS 0m3. MHWN 1m6. MLWN 1m1.

Notes on Tides: Although the above constants are given, the tides in Poole Harbour vary in character between springs and neaps, and for strict accuracy local tide tables should be used from a nautical almanac. The tides are also influenced by the wind and other factors. At *spring tides* the water normally holds up for nearly 3½ hours, falling about 0m6 after the first high water, rising 0m2 or more for the second and then falling for nearly 3 hours. The first high water is thus 0m4 or more higher than the second. At *neaps* the tides are weak and almost unpredictable. Normally the tide rises to first high water, stands easy and finally rises 0m3 or more to second high water, which is therefore higher than the first, instead of lower as at spring tides.

High Water is progressively later the greater the distance from the entrance. For example, compared with the entrance, it is 35 minutes later at Poole Quay, 75 minutes later at Russel Quay, 1 hour 35 minutes later at Wareham Quay. Tides at Bar Buoy are rotary and weaker. Rise at Poole Bridge is 0m2 higher at MHWS than at entrance.

Although the range of the tide is small, the rate is high in the channels, especially in and near the entrance.

Stream Sets outside near the bar to the east +5 h. Dover and to the west −1 h. Dover. The Channel Flood appears to divide off Anvil Point. The main stream flows towards the Isle of Wight, but inshore it follows the coast, setting NNE past Durlston Head, Peveril Point and Handfast Point towards Poole Bar. On the ebb, part of the water in Poole Bay sweeps along the east side of the Hook Sand, past Handfast Point down to Durlston and Anvil, where it joins the main Channel stream. There are patches of overfalls off this coast, and quite a tide race off Old Harry, off Handfast Point, especially on the ebb tide.

Depth at Low Water. There is normally about 3m7 on the bar at MLWS and as far as Poole Quay. The Main Channel is deep and most of the Channels are navigable by deep-keeled yachts for considerable distances even at low water.

Stakes. The port-hand stakes marking smaller channels are not painted their entire length, but only for 1 metre or so from the top. The tops of these port-hand stakes are painted red and carry a red-can topmark. These red cans are sometimes carried away, but the red paint on the stakes themselves affords some aid to navigation. When only one side of the channel is marked by stakes these are placed on the western side. At the intersection of channels some stakes have cardinal top marks and some carry boards showing the names and direction of channels. Yellow stakes indicate oyster beds.

Yacht Clubs. Royal Motor Yacht Club, Parkstone Yacht Club, Poole Yacht Club, Poole Harbour Yacht Club, Lilliput Sailing Club, Redclyffe Yacht Club, East Dorset Sailing Club.

Poole is one of the principal yacht centres on the south coast of England, and being a natural harbour of some 100 miles in circumference it is almost an inland sea. Within its area is the commercial port of Poole itself, several islands, numerous navigable channels and creeks and some anchorages, in lovely surroundings, especially in the southern part near the heath country which lies unspoilt between the harbour and the Purbeck Hills. There is plenty of deep water for large yachts, and for shallow-draft and centreboard yachts the harbour offers innumerable creeks for exploration. The accompanying chart shows the entrance and channels, but as the bottom is uneven it is recommended that the large-scale Admiralty Chart No. 2611 should be used if exploring the upper reaches in a deep-keeled yacht. As a rule, the best water is found on the outer side of bends in the channels. The facilities for yachts and boats are excellent, for on the south coast Poole Harbour ranks second only to the Solent in this respect.

The harbour has the advantage of a long high water, and although the streams run hard it is accessible at any time and in any weather, except in strong onshore winds, when the seas on the bar can be dangerous, especially on the ebb tide.

The Approach

Poole is one of the easiest harbours to find and to enter.

From the east steer for Handfast Point. This is the northerly end of a stretch of chalk cliffs which, viewed from the eastward, look like an island, standing out white against the grey and green hills which rise above them in the background. The chalk cliffs are high to the south and slope to the north, where the chalk pinnacle of rock named Old Harry lies off Handfast Point. On a clear day Durlston Head, 3 miles to the SW, and Anvil Point will also be seen from a considerable distance.

Poole Fairway Buoy, RWVS (*L Fl 10s*) is situated 6 cables NW of Handfast Point. Once identified, course may be altered towards it, leaving Handfast Point on the port bow, thus avoiding the tide race which lies off Old Harry.

Allowance should be made for the alteration in the direction of the stream which, on the west side of Poole Bay, sets into the Bay on the flood and out of it on the ebb.

Approaching from the westward follow the coast round from Anvil Point, giving a good berth to Peveril Ledges (near Swanage) which are marked by a buoy, and off which there is a race on the ebb, extending ¾ mile seaward from Peveril Point. There is a race, although a less violent one, off Ballard Point and, as mentioned, off Handfast Point. In bad weather the seas are steep all along this coast, but in westerly winds some protection is afforded by the land.

Bar and Entrance

There is reckoned to be at least 3m7 of water MLWS on Poole Bar, but the depth varies a little from year to year. The entrance is through the Swash Channel, which lies between shallow water and a training bank on the west side and the Hook sands on the east side. The bar can be very rough in strong onshore winds, but farther up the Swash Channel some protection is afforded either by the training bank or by the Hook Sands, unless the wind is blowing right up the channel.

Poole Bar green conical Buoy (*Q G Bell*) should be left close to starboard, though local yachtsmen often leave it to port as there is plenty of water for a quarter-mile northward of it.

The yacht should then be headed for the prominent Haven Hotel standing on the east side of the entrance at 324° true (say, NNW mag) when No 12 red Channel buoy (*Fl R 2s*) will be seen on the same bearing. This buoy is near the centre of the channel, but should be left to port and the Hook Sands No 11 green buoy (*Fl G 3s*) to starboard.

The Swashway is marked by conical green buoys (uneven numbers) on the starboard side and by red can buoys (even numbers) on the port side, beyond which lies the training bank. This is awash at HW Neaps and covered at HW Springs, but it is marked by 10 red stakes and at its southern end by a beacon (*Q R*).

When the Channel buoy is abeam, the entrance will clearly be seen between sand dunes on either side, with the conspicuous white building of the Haven Hotel and new block of flats on the east side. Beyond the entrance Brownsea Island will be seen with its castle. The next fairway buoy, Brownsea No 42 buoy East Cardinal (*Q 3 10s*), will be found almost in line

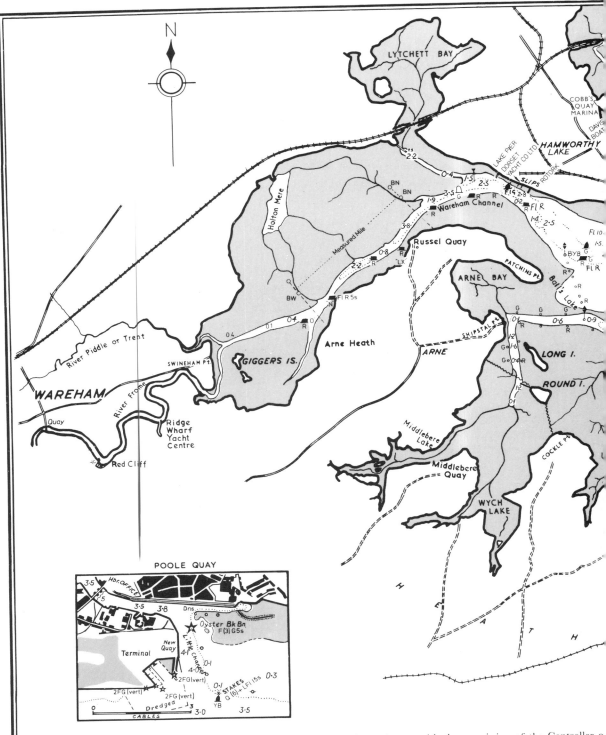

Poole Harbour: (Based on British Admiralty Chart Nos. 2611 and 2175 with the permission of the Controller o
Stationery Office and of the Hydrographer of the Navy).

2.1. Handfast Point and Old Harry from SW.

2.2. After passing the Bar buoy two red can buoys and the training bank beacon (shown here) are left to port. The training bank is $\frac{3}{4}$ mile long and covers at HW but it is marked by ten red stakes.

2.3. Brownsea Island. Brownsea Castle seen from the harbour entrance.

2.4. East Looe buoy to port leads to a short cut into Poole Harbour from the east, inshore off Sandbanks, when the tide allows enough water. *E. Bruce.*

Poole Harbour

with the Castle, just a little to the west of it. Hold on the course to the Haven Hotel, or to the ferry slipway (*2FG Hor*) west of it, until Brownsea buoy bears 310° true, when steer for the buoy.

This leads past the sand dunes to port, with the Haven Hotel to starboard, then between the Ferry slips on either side and into the harbour, leaving to starboard a west cardinal beacon (*Q (9) 15s*) off North Haven Point, which should not be approached too closely. The Ferry has to keep clear of ships, but it is usual where possible to pass under her stern if she is crossing. There is a tidal set through or out of the East Looe (see below) and in the narrows of the entrance the stream is often fierce. For courses from Brownsea buoy to Poole Quay see *North Channel*.

By Night. Entry into Poole Harbour by night is not difficult. At Anvil Point (*Fl 10s*) 4 miles to the south there is the powerful lighthouse, visible for 24 miles, and to the NE is the glare of the lights along the long front of Bournemouth.

Poole Fairway buoy (*L Fl 10s*) is thus easy to locate, and from there course is set between Poole Bar buoy (*QG*) and No. 2 (*Fl (2) R 10s*). The further course, leaving to port the Training Bank beacon (*QR*), is between No. 12 the Channel buoy (*Fl R 2s*) port and No. 11 the Hook Sands buoy (*Fl G 3s*) starboard. At night it is best to steer from the Channel buoy towards the two fixed green lights and the light (*FY*) to SW of the hotel on the east side of the entrance, with North Haven beacon (*Q (9) 15s*) beyond, and not to alter course for No. 42 Brownsea buoy (*Q (3) 10s*) until the yacht is approaching the entrance, when she will pass between the two lights (*QR*) to port and two (*FG Hor*) to starboard on the ferry slipways, and then leave to starboard the North Haven beacon (*Q (9) 15s*).

East Looe. This short cut from the eastward to join the Swash Channel at the entrance of Poole Harbour lies inshore off Sandbanks, with its entrance nearly ½ mile east of the Haven Hotel. It is much used by local yachts of shoal or moderate draft.

The approach is marked by No. 16A East Looe red can buoy (*QR*) but to seaward of this buoy there is something in the nature of a bar, with depths as low as 0m4. The best water will be found by steering for the buoy at approximately 300° true (NW by W). Leave the buoy close to port and alter course to port to pass close north of the north cardinal beacon, marking the northern extent of Hook Sand, to enter the Swash Channel near the Haven Hotel to starboard, distant about ½ cable.

The depths over the sands in the vicinity of the bar are liable to occasional changes, so when attempting this short cut a stranger should choose good weather and a rising tide and take frequent soundings. When using the East Looe for the first time it is easier to leave rather than to enter by it. The channel is not difficult but as the rise of tide is only 1m6 neaps, 2m0 springs, there is little margin for error, especially in fresh easterly winds or swell.

The East Looe can also be used at night. Approach in the white sector of the East Looe shore light (*Oc 6s 9M*) to the buoy (*Q R*). Then proceed as before at 250 degrees to join the Swash Channel, leaving the South Haven Point ferry lights (*Q R*) to port and the Haven Hotel lights and Sandbanks (*F Y*) to starboard.

The North Channel to Poole Quay

Of the three channels in the northern part of Poole Harbour the North Channel leading to Poole Quays is recommended for yachts. It can be summed up by saying 'keep to the right'. When the yacht has entered the habour, Brownsea buoy will lie ahead and North Haven beacon to starboard. Alter course to starboard to pass between these two marks, giving a

28

good berth to the beacon. After leaving to starboard No. 19A green conical buoy (*Fl G 5s*), the S Middle Ground No. 20 south cardinal buoy (*Q (6) + L Fl 15s*) will be seen. The North Channel is immediately east of this buoy and follows a semi-circular course along the mud flats on the east and north sides of the harbour. It is marked by R can buoys on the port side and green conical to starboard. On the starboard side off North Haven many yachts are moored, some in shallow water, and ½ mile up on the starboard side is Bullpit west cardinal beacon, (*Q (9) 15s*). Beyond this beacon the Main Channel continues to curve turning gradually through north to NW leaving the Poole Harbour YC Marina and Saltern's south cardinal beacon (*Q (6) + L F 15s*) to starboard. South of this beacon there is the port hand No. 36R light buoy (*Fl R 4s*). In this vicinity and SE of it the channel is very narrow. On no account sail direct from the No. 36 light buoy direct to the yachts on moorings seen about west magnetic of it as this would cross shoal water. The main channel bears towards NW here and three more port hand buoys must be passed before rounding Parkstone Shoal to reach them.

The course of the channel from Saltern's Beacon to the Little Channel leading to Poole Quays is best followed on the chart. There are five green conical buoys and Parkstone YC starting platform on the starboard hand to pass before reaching the Stakes south cardinal buoy (*Q (6) + L Fl 15s*) at the entrance to Little Channel. The west cardinal Diver light buoy No. 51 marks the junction with the Middle Ship Channel.

2.5. The Little Channel to Poole Quays.

Little Channel. This leads to Poole Quays at roughly N mag leaving on the port hand Hamworthy Jetty and quay. On the starboard hand there is Stakes buoy at the entrance, two posts and Oyster Bank Bn (*Fl G (3) 5s*), which mark the edge of the mud on the east side. At the entrance the tides set athwart the Channel, and when approaching the blind corner into the channel between Quays keep to starboard and a sharp look out should be kept for vessels which may be leaving the quays correctly on their starboard side but hidden behind buildings on the quays. The streams run hard and there is a bridge $\frac{1}{4}$ mile up the reach between the quays, so warps and fenders should be ready for berthing at the quay on the north side.

By night. The North Channel is easy to follow at night as it is well marked by the light-buoys green flashing to starboard, red flashing to port, referred to and shown on the chart, but a look-out should be kept for the unlit buoys.

If proceeding from the North Channel to Poole Quays enter the Little Channel midway between Stakes south cardinal buoy (*Q (6) + L Fl 15s*) and the lights at the southern end of the Hamworthy Jetty (*2 F.G. Vert*), leaving the jetty to port. Follow up the line of the quay leaving Oyster Bank Bn (*Fl(3)G 5s*) to starboard and bear to port. There are lights along the inner quays so that the channel is well illuminated.

2.6. Poole Quays as entered from Little Channel showing yachts berthed at the North Quay (shown left of the power station) as directed by the Harbour Master.

Parkstone Lake. This shallow creek is $\frac{1}{2}$ mile above Salterns Pier and leads up to Parkstone Yacht Club. It is occupied by permanent moorings, but is useful for dinghies and offers a good landing, if permission is obtained from the Club.

Holes Bay. This is reached from the channel between quays by passing through Poole bridge into the Back Water Channel. The bridge clearance is only 1m8 at very high springs or about 4 metres at LAT. Bridge opening times: Weekdays, 09.30, 11.30, 14.30, 16.30, 18.30, 21.30, 23.30; Saturdays, Sunday and Bank Holidays, 07.30, 09.30, 11.30, 13.30, 15.30, 17.30, 19.30, 21.30. The stream through the bridge may be strong at springs.

Above the bridge, the first reach, with 2m7 to 4m0 of water, leads NE, leaving the Quays to starboard and the Power Station and piled moorings to port. After passing the Sunseeker Marina on the eastern bank the channel gradually bends to NNW and is marked by stakes. Keep to the centre near the craft on moorings. At the end of this reach the channel divides into Creekmore Lake running about NNE, and Upton Lake leading to

Cobbs Quay Marina and then continuing NW. For Upton Lake bear sharply to port. The channel is well marked by stakes but keep to the centre in the best water, about 1m2 MLWS, 1m8 MLWN close to moored craft, and bear to NNW leaving Cobbs Quay Marina pontoons to port and a trot of moorings to starboard.

Middle Ship Channel to Poole

This channel lies to the SW of the North Channel, separated from it by the Middle Ground, and is the middle of the three channels on the north side of Brownsea Island.

The Middle Ship and Small Craft Channels to Poole

The Middle Ship Channel is used by the many commercial vessels sailing from Poole. It is dredged to 5 metres and is well lit, but only 60m wide. Yachts are advised that it should be left clear for shipping.

A Small Craft Channel for yachts of up to 1.5m draught runs parallel and alongside the port hand marks of the Ship Channel from No. 44 to No. 56 port hand buoys. It is marked by beacons to port and the Ship Channel port hand buoys are left to starboard when inward bound. Yachts with insufficient water to be able to utilize the Small Craft Channel should take the North Channel in case commercial shipping is encountered.

If using the Small Craft Channel make for No. 44 port hand buoy (*Fl R 4s*) leaving it close to port and leaving the moorings also to port, aim to pass to the east of two red beacons approx. 2 cables to the north and leave No. 46 port hand buoy (*Fl R 4s*) to starboard. The Channel starts its turn to the NE, so leaving No. 48 port hand buoy to starboard (*Fl R 4s*) aim to pass between the east cardinal beacon and No. 50, Aunt Betty, red can buoy (*Fl R 4s*). The turn is completed once the next red pole beacon is left close to port and the Channel runs in a line to No. 56 red can (*Fl R 4s*) where the main Channel can be entered. Care should be taken not to go south between the 4 red pillars along this last stretch, since there are drying banks close by. Both Nos. 52 red can and No. 54 red can (*Fl R 4s*) should be left to starboard.

Poole Harbour Quays

The port of Poole offers yachts good protection in all weathers, although it can be uncomfortable in S or SE gales and good fenders will be required.

It is a busy commercial harbour for coastal shipping, ferries, pleasure vessels, tugs, etc., so that its capacity is often taxed, especially during the summer months when the port is visited by many yachts. These yachts moor alongside the North or Town Quay but not at its eastern end; the South Quays are generally used by commercial concerns. Owing to the limited space available at the North Quay, yachts often have to lie alongside each other, and should not be berthed until the Berthing Master has given directions. Yachts are usually hailed as they enter, and the Harbour Authorities take considerable trouble to make them welcome, and to berth them in the most convenient place that is available. Warps should, of course, be carried out fore and aft, in addition to breast ropes and springs to quay or other vessel, and yachts berthing temporarily must be ready to move to a more permanent berth. Arrivals and date of departure must be reported to the Harbour Master or to the Berthing Master at his office on the quay.

Water can be obtained by hose from two points on the quay free of charge. A public telephone call box is handy and it is only a short distance from the Town Quay to the shops. As Poole is a regular yachting centre, facilities are excellent, and in the district there are some ten yacht yards, and engineers, designers, brokers, ships' chandlers, sailmakers, etc. Early closing day Wednesday. There are frequent buses to Bournemouth and neighbouring towns, and a main line station.

Marinas

Poole Harbour Yacht Club Marina. Situated in the North Channel just E of Salterns Beacon adjacent to the Yacht Club at Lilliput, this marina has 217 berths, with dredged depths from 1m0 to 2m5 MLWS, maximum length 20m O.A. and chain moorings outside in the harbour. The marina is open to visiting yachts depending on berth vacancies, usually around 10 pontoon berths and/or chain moorings. Tel: 0202 707321. Temporary membership of the Club available to visiting yachtsmen and excellent restaurant. All facilities, water, fuel, chandlery, repairs etc. and yacht yard adjacent.

Cobb's Quay, Hamworthy. Situated in Holes Bay. Depths about 1m2 MLWS, 1m8 MLWN, very soft mud bottom accommodating deeper draft. All facilities, licenced club and restaurant. Car parks, chandlery, water and fuel. The boat yard slips up to 2m4 draft and provides comprehensive services, including laying-up and repairs. Tel: 0202 674299.

Sunseeker International Marina. On the starboard side just above Poole Bridge. 52 pontoon berths. All facilities, bar/restaurant, showers, washing/drying machines and engineering. No fuel. Tel: 02013 685335.

Ridge Wharf Yacht Centre. Tel: 09295 2650. See under Wareham Channel.

Dorset Yacht Co. Ltd. Also at Lake Drive. Limited dry storage and some swinging moorings. Launching facilities. Visitors are asked to come to the pier head and report to the office. Fuel at pier head. Gas, water and usual facilities. Tel: 0202 674531.

Other Anchorages

The best positions in Poole Harbour are occupied by moorings, but there are places in the deep channels of Poole Harbour where large and medium-sized yachts can anchor, and many anchorages available to shallow-draft yachts. When choosing a berth a stranger should remember it is a big harbour and at high water it is like a large lake, with a considerable fetch for the seas which can render an exposed anchorage uncomfortable. Furthermore, although the range of the tide is small, the stream runs hard and when opposed to a fresh or strong wind makes many anchorages rough, with too much sea for a dinghy. Therefore, in considering an anchorage a yachtsman should select one in the lee of the land in unsettled weather, and in gales should allow for the probable shift of wind when the depression passes. For example, in the Wych Channel there are sheltered positions in a southerly gale on the north side of Brownsea Island, but when the wind veers towards the NW weigh anchor and find shelter on the east side of the island. Do not anchor in the fairways.

The following are a few of the principal anchorages or mooring positions:

1. Brownsea Road, north of Brownsea buoy and E of Brownsea Island, which is sheltered in the winds off the island. With strong winds from north and south this anchorage can be very rough, and the water is deep. The best positions are occupied by permanent moorings owned by members of the Royal Motor Yacht Club at Sandbanks, and they should not be

picked up without first applying to the club launchman or at the club for permission. The RMYC welcomes visiting yachtsmen.

2. Off Sandbanks. The fairway must be left clear for ships, and there is little room for anchoring outside the fairway, owing to permanent moorings.

3. Clear of the fairway between Poole Harbour YC Marina and Parkstone Yacht Club starting platform, or SE of the Marina. All the best positions are occupied by moorings, so care must be taken not to foul the anchor. In strong winds, especially southerly, the anchorage is exposed.

4. Off Lake. This is a good centre a couple of miles up the channel off the Dorset Yacht Co., but it is uncomfortable in strong SW or SE winds. There may be room to anchor above or below the moorings.

5. See also Wych Channel and South Deep.

Wych Channel

This is a broad channel along the north and west sides of Brownsea Island, which then pursues a wandering course between mud flats to Shipstal Point on the Arne Peninsula, thence in a southerly direction west of Long Island and Round Island. It affords several pleasant anchorages.

The approach to the Wych Channel from the harbour entrance is easy to follow, as it curves round Brownsea Island. There is deep water fairly close to Brownsea Pier, but on the NE of the island is a mud flat, marked by stakes with red can tops, which must be given a wide berth. The entrance to Wych Channel lies between these port hand stakes, and the green starboard hand stakes marking the southern extent of the Middle Mud. Bear round to port and follow the line of yacht moorings on the north side of Brownsea Island (where the depths in the centre range from 2m8 to 4m0 and more in parts for the first mile). The channel is well marked by piles on either hand, but do not approach these closely as some stand in shallow water.

When west of Brownsea, care is needed in pilotage, as the piles are less frequent and the bottom is uneven, depths varying from 0m4 to 4m0. There is an extensive mud flat off the NW of Brownsea, and the channel turns rather sharply round this, from west almost to south. The next pronounced turn is just over a cable south of the pottery pier situated on the western point of Brownsea. This is a 'V' bend through west to NW. Whiteground Lake and Ramshorn Lake (see *South Deep*), joins the Wych Channel here. There are many shallow patches. After passing these creeks the channel becomes deeper nearly as far as Ball's Lake, where it shallows again to about 0m5 and turns towards Shipstal Point off which there is another 'V' bend towards the SSE. Just short of this bend the channel is only about 12 metres wide and 0m1 deep, and is marked by a stake on either side. It deepens again in the reach between Shipstal Point and Long Island where a pool with 1m2 to 1m6 LAT can be found by taking soundings. There are moorings here so, if room can be found to anchor, use a trip line in case of fouling one. Shallow draft craft can anchor south of the moorings in about 0m5, which gives 1m6 at neaps. There is also a narrow creek running northwards from Shipstal Point into Arne Bay with 1m8 in parts, but here again there are many moorings.

There is a hard (rough and muddy at low water) at Shipstal Point from which a private road leads to Arne. This affords a delightful walk through woods and heathland to the old village and church, but there are no facilities. Long Island, where there is a bird sanctuary, and Round Island are private property. The channel is staked as far as Round Island pier and a ¼ mile south of this it forks into two drying creeks; the western one winds up past the disused Middlebere Quay and wanders deep into the heathland.

Middle Mud Channel (Wills Cut). Provides a useful short cut between the Wych Channel and Poole Quays across the Middle Mud. It is nearly awash at LAT but carries about 2m0 HW springs, 1m6 HW neaps. The channel is marked on the west side by five red stakes, besides northerly and the most southerly BYB stakes carrying east cardinal top marks.

Ball's Lake. The most westerly of the creeks beween the Wych and the Main Channel. Like the others it is about awash at LAT; it has six red stakes on the western side, besides BYB stakes at each end carrying east cardinal top marks.

Anchorages. The anchorage in the Wych Channel on the north-east and north sides of Brownsea Island provides one of the most sheltered in bad weather, except in strong west and NW winds when Brownsea Road is better. Brownsea Island is owned by the National

2.7. The anchorage in the pool off Shipstal Point in the Wych Channel. Be sure to use a trip line if bringing up close to local moorings.

Trust. Landing from yachts is permitted at the Pottery Pier on the west side, 1st April to 30th September, on payment of a small landing fee. There is a sheltered anchorage in easterly winds off the pier clear of the oyster beds marked by yellow stakes. The most westerly anchorage is in the pool between Shipstal Point and Long Island. The best positions near landing places are now occupied by moorings.

Wareham Channel

West of Hamworthy Jetty the Main Channel continues to be wide and well marked. Note from the chart the sharp bend at No. 72 red can light buoy (*Fl R 5s*), which is moored 3 cables north-east of Patchins Point. The port hand red can buoys from Lake Pier onwards are seasonal, being in position from March to October. They are placed on the edge of the channel which may vary from year to year.

From the yards at Lake to Lake Pier the best water lies on the north side and a wide area of mud on the south side dries out at low water. The green conical buoy No. 75 (*Fl G 5s*) west of Lake Pier is the last of the starboard hand marks until the staked channel about 1½ miles on. This reach includes a measured mile marked by BW beacons on the north-west side. Here the best water is to be found close to the port hand buoys.

The final port hand buoy is No. 84 and from here the channel is clearly indicated by stakes.

The depth of water progressively decreases and nearly dries at LAT where it leaves the Arne Peninsula, but it is staked on both sides. It then forks close to the land NW of Giggers Island, the northern arm being the River Piddle or Trent, which is hardly navigable, and the southern one being the River Frome, which pursues a winding course of about 3 miles to Wareham.

In the River Frome there is little water at Wareham itself, but below there are depths up to 1m5, and off Ridge Wharf there are over 2 metres. Local advice can be obtained at the Ridge Wharf Yacht Centre.

2.8. Wareham wharf looking down the river. *D. L. Sylvester-Bradley.*

By night. There are no lights in the Wareham Channel above the red can buoy No. 82 (*Fl R 5s*).

Anchorages. There are moorings and all facilities at Lake, which has already been referred to, and there are positions further up the channel offering anchorages which are secluded (such as off the demolished Russel Quay), but far from facilities.

Rocklea River. This is the largest of the several creeks on the starboard hand of the Wareham Channel above the Dorset Yacht Yard. It carries 0m5 to 1m5 and leads under the low railway bridge to Lytchett Bay. Except at slack water the tide, which runs diagonally under the bridge, is dangerously fast for passage by dinghy.

River Frome and Ridge. The Ridge Wharf Yacht Centre can accommodate some visiting yachts, but at holiday time it would be wise to check by telephone. There are nearly 2 metres alongside the quay. Pontoon berths and river moorings may be available. Yacht yard, fuel, chandlery, water, showers etc. and a pay telephone. Tel: 09295 2650. There is a nice walk of about $\frac{1}{2}$ hour along the river bank to Wareham.

Wareham. Stores of all kinds and petrol. Early closing Wednesday. Frequent buses and main line station. Yacht Club: Redcliff Yacht Club.

South Deep

The entrance to South Deep lies on the west side of the entrance channel south of Brownsea Lightbuoy and almost opposite North Haven beacon. The entrance is marked on the port hand by No. 18 red can buoy, close to the shingle bank known as Stoney Island, and on the starboard side by a green post No. 1 (*Fl G 5s*).

When in the entrance of Poole Harbour do not alter course for South Deep too rapidly when No. 18 buoy comes abeam, as this is situated very close to the spit of shingle which projects somewhat into the channel. It is better to enter midway between the two buoys, and then steer SW until the lines of stakes have been identified. These are the usual green to starboard, red to port, and the port hand stakes have a can at their tops. Frequently yachts are at anchor or on moorings in the centre of the channel near the entrance.

The channel is clearly marked, but the stakes are on the edge of the mud, and should be given a liberal berth and, as may be expected, the best water is found on the outer sides of the bends in the channel. A possible source of confusion to a stranger lies in the red poles placed at the entrances of the two creeks which run into South Deep on the north side. These are placed on the port side of the entrances to the creeks, and will lie on the starboard hand when sailing up South Deep, so must not be confused with the larger red stakes to the south of them which mark the port side of South Deep itself. The paint on the stakes sometimes becomes faded and weatherworn.

On the south side of South Deep there is a wide creek named Redhorn Lake, and $\frac{1}{4}$ mile beyond this South Deep takes a sharp bend to the NW towards Goathorn Point. Care should be taken when rounding this bend, as the best water lies on the port hand.

There are a few private moorings SE of Goathorn Point, but plenty of water remains for anchoring. A cable beyond Goathorn the best water (2 to 7 metres) lies on the starboard hand near the green stakes on the outside of the 90° bend from NW to SW. Two cables cross the bed of the channel NW of Goathorn to Furzey Island. At the second one the depth is only about 1m0 and course should be altered diagonally across to the other side of the channel close to the red port hand stakes. This leaves to starboard a small drying middle ground and the water is deep. The channel then continues south of Green Island (where there are remains of an old causeway) and then northward into the narrow but well staked Ramshorn Lake to join the Wych Channel. The least water is about 0m4 so with the help of the large-scale Admiralty Chart No. 2611 a keel-yacht drawing 1m8 can be navigated through the channel near high water on a rising tide. Certainly the effort would be rewarded, for the surroundings are really beautiful and there are deep pools in which to anchor.

Anchorages. It is possible to anchor almost anywhere in South Deep except in the parts where permanent moorings are laid. In fresh or strong winds the reaches where the wind and tide are opposed should be avoided. The first reach in South Deep is convenient for obtaining facilities at Sandbanks, but the crossing from South Deep can be rough in a dinghy and the streams strong.

Redhorn Lake is suitable for shallow-draft yachts drawing less than 1m2. Larger yachts can anchor off its entrance, and go up in the dinghy to Redhorn Quay. A short walk leads to the main road, thence by bus to Studland (see Chapter 3 for facilities) or to Sandbanks by bus and ferry.

The author's favourite anchorage is near Goathorn Point, although some of the best berths are now occupied by permanent moorings. It is protected even in gales, though if the wind is blowing hard up or down the channel it is uncomfortable at high water especially at Spring tides. To the south of the point the holding ground does not seem quite so good and anchors have been dragged in bad weather. Goathorn Point is private and no facilities are available nearer than Studland. A sheltered and peaceful anchorage in from 2 to 4 metres can be found round the bend in the channel. It lies between Goathorn and the SE corner of Green Island beyond the drying middle ground.

Blood Alley Lake. This creek and its continuation in White Ground Lake lies to the south of Brownsea Island and links South Deep and Wych Channel. It carries a minimum of 0m3 MLWS and is marked by stakes, but there is a drying area west of Furzey Island pier and another one before the creek joins the Wych Channel.

3 Studland Bay

High Water (approx.): −2 h. 30 m. and +1 h. 5 m. Dover.
Heights above datum. Chart 2175, MHWS 2m0. MLWS 0m3. MHWN 1m6. MLWN 1m1.
Stream Sets outside to the west −1¼ h. Dover and to the east +5 h. Dover, but sets approximately NE and SW inshore between Old Harry and Anvil Point.

3.1. The line of chalk cliffs from Handfast Point westward into Studland Bay. The three prominent projections are known as "The Yards" off which there is foul ground.

Studland provides a delightful anchorage in offshore winds from south, through west to NW. The bay (see Chart of Poole) affords plenty of room to anchor, with a sandy bottom and good holding ground. In fresh northerly winds it is uncomfortable, and it is entirely open to easterly winds. However, Poole is near at hand as a port of refuge, if the wind comes in from the wrong quarter.

Studland Bay is easy to enter anywhere between Poole Bar buoy and Old Harry Rocks. The best water between 2½ and 1½ fathoms lies in the southern part, as to the west of the Bar buoy there are the Bar Sand and the Milkmaid Bank, which have depths of under a fathom.

On the chalk cliffs west of Old Harry there are conspicuous projections, known locally as the 'yards'. The remains of old wrecks make a foul bottom between the first and the second 'yard', about 1½ cables offshore, which should be left to port.

At night Poole Bar buoy (QG) is left to starboard, and the bay is so wide that there is little difficulty in entering, provided it is not too dark to see the cliffs against the sky.

The recommended anchorage is about 3 cables off the 'yards', but in practice it is usual to enter the Bay and to take soundings in order to anchor as far inshore as is prudent in relation to the draft of the yacht. A yacht drawing 1m5 will be able to bring up less than ¼ mile off-shore, while deeper yachts will anchor progressively farther offshore. There are boathouses and bathing huts on the shore, but little of the village itself can be seen from the sea. Redend

38

3.2. The pretty anchorage in the SW corner of the bay off the bathing beach.

Point will be noted, and there are rocks off the point extending over a cable seaward. The anchorage is over $\frac{1}{4}$ mile from the shore, where landing is effected on the open beach. A path leads up to the village, where there are small shops, a hotel or two and a post office. There are frequent buses to Swanage and Sandbanks. The surroundings are beautiful, and there are many pleasant walks. The church of St Nicholas dates from Saxon times.

4 Swanage

High Water: −2 h. 51 m. and +1 h. 09 m. Dover, at neap tides the time of HW may be indefinite.
Heights above datum: MHWS 1m9. MLWS 0m3. MHWN 1m6. MLWN 1m1.
Stream sets in the offing to the SW about 1 h. before HW Dover or earlier, and to the NE about 5 h. after HW Dover. The tides are strong outside the Bay, but weak within it.
Yacht Club: Swanage Sailing Club.

Swanage Bay offers a useful anchorage in offshore winds from south to west. As with Studland Bay, it is exposed if the wind backs east of south and in bad weather the anchorage is uncomfortable if the wind goes north of NW. The author has sheltered there in SW gales when, except for a swell, it is safe, but in the event of a shift of wind Poole as a port of refuge is not so handy as it is from Studland Bay.

The Approach

Swanage Bay is deep and clear of dangers, except for the Tanville ledges, which a yacht rarely approaches as the rocks are in the bight of the Bay, lying over ½ mile from the anchorage.

Approaching from Poole give Handfast Point a good berth. If there is a strong wind contrary to the ebb stream the race off the point can be rough. Then shape a course towards Swanage pier. The stream runs hard and the only danger for a yacht without an engine is that of becoming becalmed and carried on to Peveril Ledges; so in light weather keep inshore where the tide is weak.

Peveril Ledges extend off Peveril Point due east towards Peveril Ledge red can buoy (*no light*) which is nearly ½ mile off the Point. There is a tide race, especially on the ebb, between the Point and the buoy and for ½ mile to seaward of it. The tide sets straight across the ledges, and the outermost dangerous rock lies under 2 cables off the Point, so that in moderate weather a short cut can be made a cable inside Peveril buoy. The race is a lively one when the wind is over the tide, but in westerly winds there is some shelter from the land.

Approaching from the west, allow for the tide which inshore follows the general direction of the coast. The east and NE inshore stream begins at +4 h Dover and the SW and W stream at −2 h Dover. In light weather give Peveril Ledge a wide berth as the tide sets across it. With a fair tide running NE alter course quickly to enter the Bay once Peveril buoy is abeam, to avoid being set too far north. In a SW gale there are particularly bad seas S and

4.1. Approaching Swanage from northward showing Durlston Head, Peveril Point and Swanage to the right.

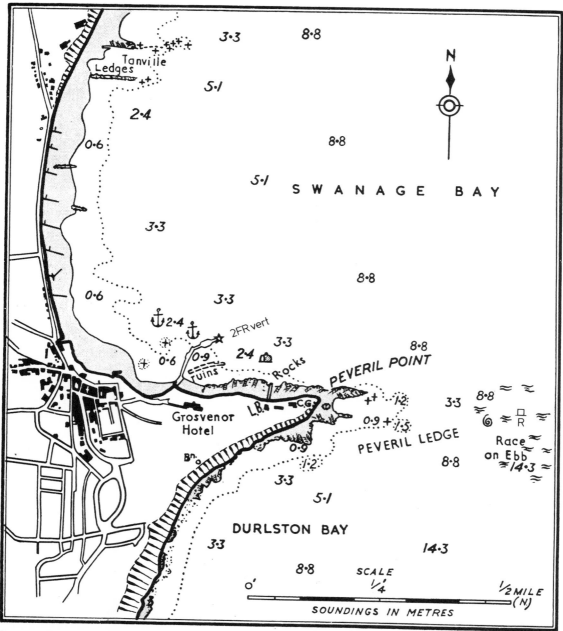

Swanage Bay: (Based on British Admiralty Chart No. 2172 with the permission of the Controller of HM Stationery Office and of the Hydrographer of the Navy.)

Swanage

4.2. Anvil Point and Durlston Head are passed when coming from the westward, and course is altered to leave Peveril Ledge buoy to port.

4.3. When the buoy is rounded from the south steer to leave Swanage Pier about a cable to the south. Allow for a possibly strong tidal stream which, if running SW, sets strongly on Peveril Ledges. *D. L. Sylvester-Bradley*.

4.4. Swanage Bay showing the pier and the anchorage west of it, seaward of the local moorings.

E of Anvil Point when wind and stream are opposed. Some shelter may be gained close in under the cliffs in Durlston Bay, but a yacht has to come out again to avoid Peveril Ledges and may pass a cable W inside the buoy in about 4m5 where the race is fairly narrow in extent.

By night. There are two lights (*F R vert*) on the pier and stronger shore lights in the town.

Anchorage. The usual anchorage is about a cable NW of Swanage Pier in 2m0 to 3m3 of water. A number of moorings for local boats of modest draft will be seen inshore and yachts anchor outside these, taking soundings to find a suitable depth. The holding ground varies. In some places it is good; in others there is weed on the bottom and it is indifferent. Buoy the anchor unless well clear of inshore moorings, as it was reported that a yacht fouled her anchor here. On the eastern side of the pier there are the ruins of an old pier, a lifeboat house and a few local moorings.

Facilities. Swanage is a small town and seaside resort with hotels and shops of every kind (early closing Thursday) and bus services. Landing from the dinghy is on the shore, where a boatman will keep an eye on it, or to the west nearer the centre of the town. There is an active sailing club which races dinghies and other classes, and on a summer's day the bay is dotted with pedal-boats which are let out on hire. Petrol and water are easily obtained. Although crowded by visitors in the summer the town is a pleasant one and there are good walks along the cliffs either towards Studland or to Durlston and Anvil Head.

5 Chapmans Pool

5.1. Rounding St Albans Head from the eastward by the inner passage.

5.2. View from Hounstout Cliff facing east over the anchorage in Chapmans Pool. Shading of the water indicates the best anchorage. Note the rocks off the small buildings opposite. *C. Sergel*.

44

This little cove lies a mile NNW of St Albans Head, at the foot of the Purbeck hills. It provides a strange anchorage dwarfed by its surroundings and at night, when the few day visitors have left, it seems to be in another world remote from civilization.

The anchorage is only a fair weather one which is sheltered in winds between N to E, but gusts come down in strong winds from the heights above. There are sands, good bathing and lovely coastal walks to the west up the cliff path to the summit of Hounstout (150 metres high and once called 'Adlard's Peak' by his disrespectful crews in memory of a great ascent). From here, where the photograph was taken, one looks down on the gently shelving shore and along the coast southwards to St Albans, which provides another rewarding walk. No facilities are available but visitors arrive in daytime down a rough road to the shore. The nearest village appears to be Worth Maltravers, 2 miles distant.

Approach and Entrance. The approach from the east is easy with the aid of the Admiralty chart 2615. It will be made inside St Albans Race, leaving the head about 50 to 100 metres to starboard. The inshore E running stream starts about +4 h Dover and the W running about −2 h Dover. After rounding St Albans and passing through only a few overfalls if the wind is offshore steer WNW for 3 cables and then alter course to N by W for Hounstout Cliff on the west side of the cove, gradually closing with the shore to starboard. This can be followed up at distance of a cable off the shore. As the entrance of the cove is approached there are rocks projecting westward, as shown in the photograph, near some small buildings on the hillside. There are usually lobster pots on the outer fringe of these rocks. Keep seaward of these and enter in the middle of the pool. Approaching from westward keep seaward of Kimmeridge ledges and shoals extending 6 cables SW of Hounstout Cliff. The stream on the east going tide will be setting strongly towards St Albans Head. Make good a position about ¾ mile NW of the Head and then steer for the middle of the cove; the stream weakens as it is approached.

Anchorage is on sand in the centre of the cove in about 2m5, but with the aid of soundings it is possible to get enough water a little nearer the shore at the NE corner. The holding ground is good and there is little stream inside the cove but it may be unwise to remain at night if there is any prospect of a shift of wind or break in the weather.

6 Lulworth Cove

High Water: −4 h. 38 m. Dover. **Tidal Data:** approximately as Swanage, page 40.
Tidal Streams: See tide chartlets Swanage to Portland, and note stream turns early inshore. Within the cove itself there are no tidal currents of significance.

Lulworth Cove is part of the Lulworth Castle Estate. It is a famous and popular beauty spot and in summer time is visited by thousands of tourists by road, foot and boat. The Cove and the cliffs around it offer a fascinating study in geology. The cove was formed when the seaward strata of Portland and Purbeck stone were breached by the sea. Behind them the soft layer of Wealdon and Upper Green Sands was worn away by the sea, air and rain; but this erosion was held up farther back by the harder consistency of the chalk of Bindon Hill. To the east, low down on the cliffs, where the Purbeck stone joins the soft and hard cap of Portland stone, is the Fossil Forest.

For the yachtsman it offers a beautiful and unusual anchorage. But it must only be used in fair weather, as it is exposed to all winds with south in them. When it blows hard from one

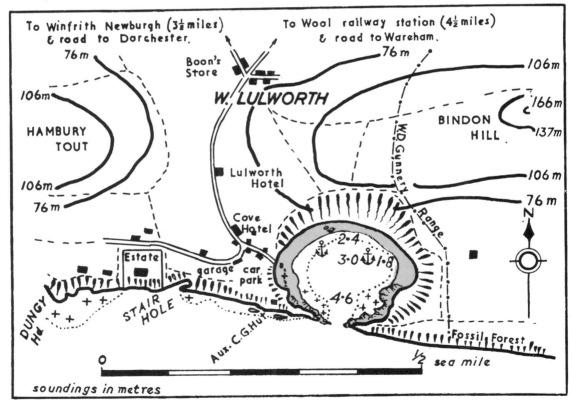

Lulworth Cove: Drawing approximate.

6.1. White Nothe, the prominent headland, 3 miles west of Lulworth Cove.

6.2. Worbarrow Bay, with Worbarrow Tout shown on the right, some 2 miles east of the entrance to Lulworth Cove.

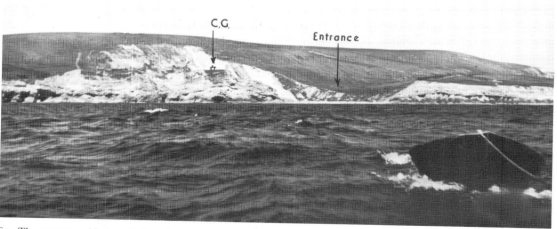

6.3. The entrance of Lulworth Cove is not conspicuous. It lies between two relatively low headlands.

47

Lulworth Cove

6.4. Taken from the cliffs during a gale, this picture clearly shows the rocks on each side of the entrance. A yacht should enter just east of the midway between the headlands on either side. *R. Coles.*

6.5. View facing eastwards across Lulworth Cove. The yacht is in the middle of the cove, but there is also sufficient depth of water to anchor further to the NE.

of these directions a heavy swell comes in, and in addition the winds funnel down and around the cliffs and through the narrow entrance, causing a yacht at anchor to sheer about in all directions. Because of this and the narrowness of the entrance it is essential that yachts should leave the cove before bad weather arrives.

Approach and Entrance

The entrance of Lulworth Cove is through a gap in the limestone cliffs, which is about 3 miles east of the prominent White Nothe headland, and 2 miles west of Worbarrow Tout which is at the east end of Worbarrow Bay—see photographs. The coast to the west of the entrance comprises a series of high turf-topped chalk cliffs, bitten into by the sea. On the cliffs to the west of the entrance are two huts, and beyond and behind it is a large rounded hill, Hambury Tout, 133m high. When approaching from the east a conspicuous white chalk road will be seen running diagonally down from the Tout. The entrance lies close at the lower end of this road. To the east of the entrance the cliffs are of less height and are fairly steep-to, except for a few rocks lying up to $1\frac{1}{2}$ cables off Dungy Head. A red can buoy marks the eastern end of these rocks (summer only).

The navigable width of entrance is about half of that which is apparent; its centre being just to the east of the mid-point between the cliffs. There are ledges of rocks running out from the edges of the cliffs on both sides, those to port on entering extend rather farther than those to starboard, leaving a channel is about 70 metres wide, 4m5 deep. Ahead, as the yacht enters, is a 90 metre high chalk cliff where the western end of Bindon Hill has been eroded by the sea. On the port bow there are rocks and a few small mooring buoys and a portable landing stage. To starboard there is clear water.

Anchorage, Facilities and Surroundings

The best anchorage is in the NE corner of the cove. Here the anchor drops into a good holding ground of clay, sand and seaweed in about 3m0. It is found from experience that it is a good plan to put a kedge astern towards the shore to hold the bows of any yacht anchored in the cove towards the entrance, thereby reducing the effect of swell which often enters even in good weather. The anchorage is sometimes crowded and one has to anchor as best one can. There is no anchorage outside the cove owing to telegraph cables.

There is no regular coastguard at Lulworth; auxiliaries (fishermen, local residents and the like) keep a bad weather watch only. No special rescue facilities are available from them. There is a boatman who will give advice and help to visiting yachtsmen.

Fresh water may be obtained from a tap beside the attendant's hut in the car park; or nearer at hand at the café where they will oblige if not too busy. Petrol can be obtained from the garage behind the car park. There is a post office in the village, also several restaurants, cafés and hotels. Near the Cove there are a few small shops and stores, and also up the road at West Lulworth. Buses run to Wool in the summer time. Trains run from Wool to Weymouth and to London.

Lulworth Gunnery Ranges

The War Department Gunnery Ranges create danger areas which at sea extend some 5 miles southwards of Lulworth Cove and eastwards almost to St Albans Head. Ashore red flags give warning of the land danger area.

The sea danger area is divided into parts and the times of firing and areas to be used are notified in a weekly firing programme sent to all yacht clubs within the area. Information is also available on application to the Range Safety Officer, telephone: Bindon Abbey 462721 Ext. 819 or from the guard room: Ext. 824. When firing is in progress Red flags and International Flag U are flown by day from a flagstaff or at night red flashing lights are exhibited on the summit of Bindon Hill, about 2 cables E by N of the Cove entrance, and at St Albans Head. In addition the sea danger area is patrolled, except in inclement weather, by two Range Safety vessels who will advise on the extent of the area.

Firing times are broadcast on Radio Solent during the shipping and weather news at about 0745 on weekdays. Range Control listens out on channel 8 when firing is taking place.

Yachts are allowed to pass through the sea danger area provided they do not stop, but the passage should be made as quickly as possible; anchoring or fishing will not be permitted. The range areas and regulations are always liable to alteration.

7 Weymouth

High Water: −4 h. 38 m. Dover. **Heights above datum:** MHWS 2m1. MLWS 0m2. MHWN 1m4. MLWN 0m7.
Yacht Clubs: Royal Dorset Yacht Club, Weymouth Sailing Club.

Weymouth Harbour offers good yachting facilities and is a busy commercial port. The town itself is a popular holiday resort, with bathing and boating sands, hotels and all the usual amenities.

St Albans Race, the Approach and Entrance

Approaching Weymouth from Poole and the Solent, the race off St Albans Head provides the principal navigational consideration. The race is not so severe as Portland Race and in moderate weather extends little over $1\frac{1}{2}$ miles. Its position varies according to wind and tide, being rather to the east on the flood stream and to the west on the ebb. Except with strong onshore winds a passage of relatively smooth water is found close inshore, though this is never entirely free from overfalls. Close inshore the tide turns to the west about −2 h Dover and to the east +4 h Dover. In moderate weather the inshore passage is a useful one, and the only disadvantage is that it takes a yacht across the gunnery range, referred to in the previous chapter. At $1\frac{1}{4}$ miles south of St Albans the W stream starts $-\frac{1}{4}$ h Dover; E stream $+5\frac{3}{4}$ h Dover. For Portland Race and approach from the westward see the following chapter.

The entrance to Weymouth Harbour is rather inconspicuous. It lies behind a breakwater which runs out from a low green hill called The Nothe. This hill is easily recognized by the fortifications at its base, and its isolated situation. It separates Weymouth Harbour from Newton's Cove, and is the only headland between Portland Harbour and Redcliff Point, the latter being at the northern end of Weymouth Bay.

The mouth of the Harbour faces NE and if it is approached from east a sharp alteration of course to port is required before the harbour is actually entered. Approx. 400m WSW of the S. Pier is the Mixen red can buoy (*Fl R 5s*). This marks two sewer outfalls and the edge of the deep water.

In approaching Weymouth Harbour leave this to port and open out the breakwater

7.1. The south side of the entrance to Weymouth Harbour showing the Nothe. Visitors' fore and aft moorings are no longer available here as the space is required to facilitate movement of car ferries to and from their berth.

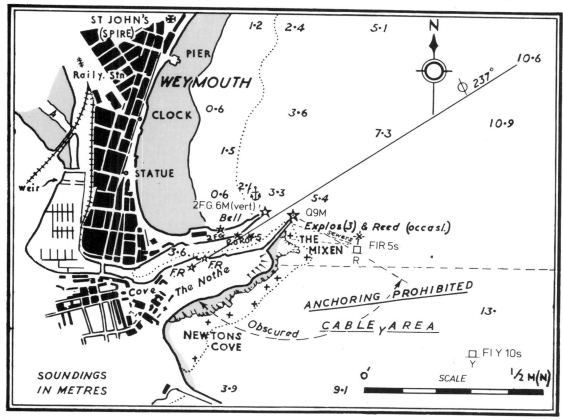

Weymouth Harbour: (Based on British Admiralty Chart No. 2255 with the permission of the Controller of HM Stationery Office and of the Hydrographer of the Navy.)

(south) pier to bring the yacht off the entrance to the harbour. Course is then altered to the SW and the yacht enters between the two piers. Keep clear of motor boats etc. rounding the south pier head, which should not be approached too closely.

About 3 cables inside the entrance on the southern side of the harbour are two white triangular boards placed one above and behind the other. At night they carry *fixed red lights*, they are the *leading marks*. When in transit they lead up the centre of the channel in 4m5 MLWS at 237°.

On the two piers at the entrance of the harbour are lights and fog signals. The South breakwater pier has a light (*Q*) at an elevation of 9m. Its fog signal is either explosion 3 ev. 5 min or a reed (*15s*). The Northern 'Pleasure' pier has lights (*2 F G vert*) and in thick weather a bell. Fog signals are only used in exceptional circumstances when a large ship is expected.

The harbour is long and narrow. It extends some 6 cables from the entrance to end at the Town Bridge. Above this the water is shallower and is seldom used by vessels of any size, for which the bridge has to be swung open. The upper harbour is used almost exclusively by local boat-owners, and by the town's by-laws people are not allowed to live aboard craft moored here.

51

Weymouth

7.2. The entrance to Weymouth Harbour. On the right is the north (Pleasure) pier. Water is obtained at the steps, where also notices about weather and Lulworth Ranges are sometimes displayed.

7.3. Further up the channel showing the leading marks. The Cove where most yachts of average size bring up lies on the south side beyond the yachts in the middle of the picture.

Moorings and Anchorages

Yachts entering should close the North pier where they will be hailed by the Pier Master or his deputy at any time between 8 a.m. and 10 p.m. He will direct them to a suitable berth, alongside the quay farther up, most probably the Cove which is on the south side just above the lifeboat station where the harbour widens out a little. Note that the harbour regulations provide that boats must not impede the passage of vessels entering or leaving the harbour—see Regulating Signals below. At night it is not so easy to find a mooring and there is considerable traffic in the harbour, principally cross-Channel ferries and hydrofoils. If arriving in darkness some yachtsmen prefer to anchor outside, or in Portland.

Owners are requested to give the Harbour Master (Tel: Weymouth 206421) notice of arrival. Harbour dues are payable. The Harbour Master is pleased to give local information and assistance to visiting yachtsmen.

Owners must not leave their yachts unattended for longer than an hour or two, and when the crew is going ashore the hatches and doors should be firmly locked. If the boat is to be left for longer periods, then it is best to seek the advice of the Harbour Master.

In Weymouth Bay the most convenient anchorage is 1 cable to the NNW of the Northern pier end of the main harbour. The bottom here consists of fine sand and weed, and is covered by about 2m0 of water at MLWS.

Regulating Signals

Signals are displayed on a mast at South Pier.

3 Flashing Red Lights	– Port closed. Serious emergency.
2 Red and 1 Green Lights	– Entrance foul, entry or departure forbidden.
3 Red Lights	– Indicates a vessel is leaving the harbour and no vessel is to approach so as to obstruct the entrance when this signal is shown.
3 Green Lights	– Indicate that a vessel is approaching the entrance from seaward and no vessel is to leave the harbour.
Green White Green	– Vessel is to move only when instructed.

Vessels must obey the signals and remain clear of the channel while they are displayed.

When no signals are displayed on the mast, it denotes the entrance is clear both inwards and outwards, but a look-out must be kept when a vessel is approaching in case the signal is put against her. Within the harbour and harbour limits, boats, whether under oars, sails or power, are to keep clear of the main channel and are not to obstruct or otherwise impede the passage of vessels entering or leaving the harbour.

Facilities

H. M. Customs office is situated at Ferry Terminal Building. All enquiries and documents to Long Room. There is a lifeboat station on the South Quay. The Royal Dorset Yacht Club welcomes visiting yachtsmen.

Fuel and calor gas can be obtained ashore. Diesel oil can be had from a tank at Custom House Quay between 9.0 a.m. and 10.0 a.m. Water can be obtained from a tap at the Cove or, for a small charge, from the steps at the north pier. In Weymouth itself and on the South Quay there are many shops and stores of all types. Early closing day is Wednesday. Also banks, hotels and all the amenities of a fairly large town. There is an A.A. office on the Commercial Pier.

Train services run direct to London and Southampton. Buses run to Portland and the rest of Dorset. Ferries run to Cherbourg and hydrofoils to the Channel Islands.

PART II
CARENTAN TO ANSE DE ST MARTIN

Introduction

This Part covers the French coast on the east and north sides of the Cherbourg Peninsula from Carentan to Cap de la Hague, which is the nearest stretch of French coast to the Solent, Poole and Weymouth, with Cherbourg as the natural port of entry, being the only one which offers every kind of facility for the yachtsman. Port Lévi to the east is very small, but Barfleur, which is round the Pointe de Barfleur, is an excellent harbour in westerly winds for yachts which can dry out alongside the quays, or which have legs. Barfleur is a pretty village, and well worth a visit. The harbours to the south of Barfleur provide further interesting cruising grounds, calling at St Vaast and paying a visit to the St Marcouf Islands.

Eight miles west of Cherbourg breakwater is Omonville, a charming little place with a harbour in which yachts can lie afloat protected from westerly and southerly winds. Still farther west the drying harbour of Port Racine (the smallest in France) in the Anse de St Martin has a good anchorage a cable outside it in settled weather.

The rise and fall of tide on this coast is greater than on the corresponding English side, Although not so considerable as in the Channel Islands and the Gulf of St Malo. A feature in the navigation in these waters which is frequently referred to in the following pages is the early inshore stream, as the tide along the coast turns earlier than the main Channel stream farther seaward. The rate of the streams along the north of the Cherbourg Peninsula is fast, attaining its maximum at the two ends of the Peninsula, in the Race of Barfleur and the Race of Alderney respectively. (See table page 60.)

Approaching this piece of coast the navigation is aided by the powerful lighthouses of Barfleur on the east and Cap de la Hague and Alderney on the west, and by other lighthouses and numerous lightbuoys on nearer approach. Cherbourg is easier of approach by night than by day and Barfleur Harbour has good leading lights. There are also Radio Beacons at Pte de Barfleur, Cherbourg and to the west on the Casquets. See page 12.

54

8 Cherbourg

High Water: −3 h 17 m Dover. **Heights above datum:** French Chart No 5628. MHWS 6m4. MLWS 1ml. MHWN 5m0. MLWN 2m6.
Streams in the Offing: 5 miles of Cherbourg Breakwater, the tides conform approximately with the main English Channel streams, but attain a rate up to 4 knots and have a set into the bay between Cap de la Hague and Pointe de Barfleur. **3 miles N of Cherbourg Breakwater,** the westerly stream starts −1¼ h Dover and the easterly +5½ h Dover, both 3 knots, springs.
Inshore Tides: The tides turn earlier inshore, especially to the west and east of Cherbourg. In the west entrance the west stream starts −3½ h Dover attaining 1¼ knots and the east stream +4 h Dover, streams attaining 2 knots at spring tides. In the Grande Rade the tides turn about half-hour earlier with a rate up to 1½ knots. In the Petite Rade there is a counter-current, which sets westward along the south side towards the naval dockyard, and then turns northward and eastward along the western inner breakwater (Digue du Homet) during the SE stream in Grande Rade. (See also page 60.)

Cherbourg is the natural port of entry in France for yachts stationed in the vicinity of the Solent and Poole. It is a large port with an excellent yacht club and all facilities. It is accessible in all weathers, though in northerly gales it can be exceedingly rough in the offing.

The Approach

In clear weather the approach to Cherbourg from England is easy, as it lies almost in the centre of the indentation between Cap de la Hague to the westward, and the Pointe de Barfleur (photograph 11.1) to the eastward, and one or other of these headlands will be seen. In bad weather with poor visibility, or in fine but hazy weather, it is not so easy, and yachts quite often make a landfall either east or west of the entrance. The allowance for a 12-hour passage with the effect of the tides cancelling out is not sufficient. The yacht's position should be estimated hourly, to allow for the strong streams near the English coast and the still stronger ones in the approach to Cherbourg, particularly on a spring tide, when it is usual to plan a landfall up stream of the Cherbourg entrances. Radio beacons assist in an accurate landfall. In fog it is possible for the last 20 miles to home on the radio beacon at Fort de l'Ouest lighthouse.

Cherbourg itself will be recognized by the long high breakwaters and the breakwater forts. The high cliff behind Cherbourge, which is shown in photograph 8.2, is sometimes considered a help in identifying the position of the harbour. In the offing, 3 miles NW of the western entrance, is a pillar whistle buoy 'CH 1', red and white stripes, (Oc 4s).

To the west of Cherbourg breakwater there are: 3 miles W, the Raz de Bannes beacon tower; 8 miles W, the headland at Omonville (photograph 14.1); 9 miles W, Jardeheu Point (a low promontory, with a white washed building and semaphore station, and conspicuous rocks off the end) and the whistle buoy (VQ) 1 mile seaward; 12 miles W is Cap de la Hague Lighthouse, (Fl 5s 22M Horn 30s), La Plate light tower (Fl (2 + 1) WR 12s) is a weaker light situated 1¼ miles ENE of La Hague lighthouse.

At the eastern end of Cherbourg Harbour is Ile Pelée with its fort and beacon towers on the rocks extending 4 cables off it; 5 miles east is the low headland of Cap Lévi with lighthouse (photograph 10.1) (Fl R 5s) and the YBY buoy (Q(9) 15s) of Cap Lévi Race. There are two buoys (VQ) and (Q) off shore farther east, and 15 miles east is Pointe de Barfleur lighthouse (Fl (2) 10s 27M Read (2) 60s), see photograph 11.1.

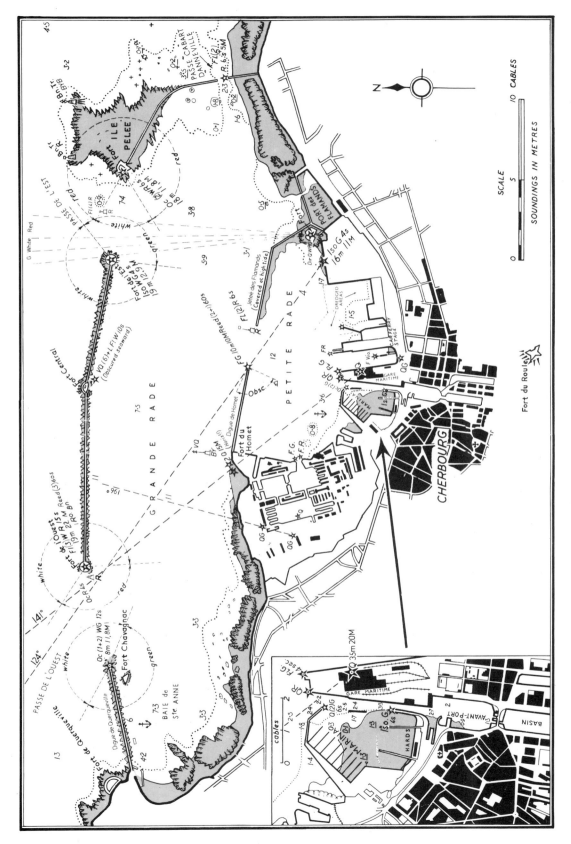

Cherbourg Harbour: (Based on French Chart No. 5628 by permission of the Service Hydrographique de la Marine.) Depths in marina, add 1m at MLWS, 2m 6 at MLWN.

Approaching from east or west keep well to seaward to avoid the numerous outlying dangers, and refer to tide charts, for, as previously stated, there are reverse eddies near the coast at certain states of the tide. Sometimes the division between the eddy and the main stream is clearly marked, with the main English Channel stream one way and the inshore stream (which varies in width) running in the opposite direction. There will be overfalls in whichever stream is running against the wind. With large-scale charts and experience there is plenty of scope for rock-dodging inshore, but it is dangerous for those unfamiliar with the coast, as the tides are very strong. There is a considerable tide race off Cap Lévi, and it is rough off *all* headlands to the east and west in fresh winds and a weather-going tide.

By night. The approach to Cherbourg is usually easier at night. There are the powerful lights of Anvil Point and St Catherines on the English coast, and not long after these have been lost the loom of the French lights at Cap de la Hague (*Fl 5s 22M*), and probably Alderney to the west (*Fl (4) 15s 28M*) or Barfleur (*Fl (2) 10s 27M*) may be seen. The principal light on Cherbourg Breakwater at Fort de l'Ouest (*Fl (3) WR 15s 19m W22M/R18M Reed (3) 60s*). The buoy CH I is (*Oc 4s*) and there are many other lights which are best seen on the chart.

8.1. Fort de L'Ouest and the red buoy left to port when entering the Grande Rade de Cherbourg.

The Entrances

The principal entrance to the Grande Rade (roadstead between outer and inner break-waters) at Cherbourg is the western one, and is wide and deep. It is immediately west of the Fort de L'Ouest (*Fl (3) 15s*) but the fort should not be approached too closely as there is an obstruction on the SW side marked by a buoy (*Oc R*), photograph 8.1. On the west side of the western entrance there is another fort at the end of the breakwater (*Oc (1 + 2) WG 12s*) which should not be approached closely. There are also leading lights as shown on the chart, but the entrance is so easy these are not usually followed.

The eastern entrance lies between Fort de l'Est (*Iso WG 4s*) and the fort on Ile Pelée (*Oc (2) WR 6s*), and has been swept to a depth of 6 metres. There are shoals on the east side of this entrance near Ile Pelée, so a yacht should keep to the west side near Fort de l'Est.

When in the Grande Rade shape a course for the entrance to the Petite Rade, between the inner

Cherbourg

GARE MARITIME

8.2. After entering the Petite Rade steer for entrance of the Avant Port and marina which are just to the right of the Gare Maritime shown in this picture. In the background on the left is the high cliff behind the town.

8.3. Entry to Cherbourg marina and the waiting pontoon.

8.4. Cherbourg Marina. The visitors' berths.

breakwater (*light FG*) and the red buoy (*Fl (2) R*) to the NW of the eastern breakwater which may be covered at HW.

As the yacht enters the Petite Rade, the Gare Maritime (with prominent cranes and large buildings—see photograph 8.2) will be seen to the south. The Transatlantique ocean dock lies on its east side but the Avant Port and the yacht marina is on its west. Shape a course to leave the Gare Maritime to port, with a light (*Q R*) at its NW corner. On arrival the wall of the northern breakwater of the marina with light (*Oc (2) G 6s*) at its east end will immediately be seen to starboard. The marina is entered just beyond the light structure by turning to starboard.

Yacht Marina and Facilities

The layout of the marina, which covers a wide area, consists of a series of pontoons extending from the sea wall promenade and road with short finger berths at right angles which provide individual berths against which yachts can lie. There is a waiting pontoon with an illuminated sign 'Attente' south of the entrance where yachts may wait for a berth. These range in depth from 2.3m at the NE end to 1.3m at the inner end. The visitors' pontoons are close to the NE and are clearly marked. If no visitors' berths are free it may be possible to obtain a residents' berth on application to the Capitainerie. If none are available anchor north of the entrance in the south of the Petite Rade, well clear of the fairway. A better anchorage is off Querqueville at the W end of the Grande Rade.

The administrative centre includes offices of the Capitaine du Port and Customs and the hospitable yacht club and bar. Nearby bonded stores can be obtained. The showers and lavatories block is situated about half way along the sea wall. Fuel can be had alongside when the tide allows. Other facilities include sailmakers and chandlers.

About ¼ mile distant there is an interesting quarter of Cherbourg with small shops and restaurants. The centre of Cherbourg is about ½ mile distant where there is a casino, the Café du Théâtre and a wide variety of restaurants. French charts from Nicollet, 40 Rue de Commerce. Frequent car ferries to Southampton and Poole. Air services include Southampton, Alderney, Guernsey and Jersey.

The Wet Basin

If no berths are available at the peak of the season or an alongside berth is wanted close to the town, it is still possible to proceed up the Avant Port to the commercial basin. The dock gate opens about 1h before to 1h after high water. The signal to request opening of the swing bridge is one long and two short blasts. Tide gauges indicate depth over the sill and the depth within the basin is usually maintained at about 3 metres when the dock gate is closed. The basin is mainly commercial and sometimes dusty but it is convenient and completely sheltered from all weather.

Passe Cabart Danneville. This is a boat passage at the eastern end of the Grande Rade. It lies in a gap between the outer and inner eastern breakwaters, and there is a light (*Fl (2) R 9s 5M*) at the end of the breakwater on its southern side. It can be navigated, with great care, with the aid of the large scale French Chart No. 5628, but the channel leading from the Grande Rade to the pass and to the east of it is not easy as it lies between shoals and close to a rock drying 1m8 on its north side. It is better to treat the channel as drying 1m8 at LAT and wait, if necessary, for sufficient rise of tide before attempting it. A course can then be steered from Grande Rade by keeping the middle of the pass

Cherbourg

bearing east magnetic, and when through it hold on keeping the middle of the pass on a stern bearing of west magnetic. Do not go north of the west–east course, until $\frac{1}{2}$ mile eastward of the pass in 2 metres LAT clear of the shoals. Tidal streams in the pass are strong and eastward of it. It should not be used in rough easterly weather owing to the seas over uneven bottom.

Inshore Tidal Streams along the Cherbourg Peninsula

The following table is prepared by reference to information in the Channel Pilot and charts, the approximate times being in relation to HW Dover and the rates at Spring tides average unless otherwise stated.

	East Going Stream			West Going Stream		
	Approx. Direction	Rate	Begins	Approx. Direction	Rate	Begins
West end of Peninsula between C de la Hague and Raz de Bannes 4 miles W of Cherbourg	ESE	3	+0500	WNW	3	−0530
Off Pte Jardeheu	ESE	5	+0500	WNW	4	−0330
West entrance of Cherbourg Harbour	SE	2	+0400	NW	$1\frac{1}{4}$	−0315
Close Inshore, 1 mile E of Cherbourg	E	$1\frac{1}{2}$	+0345	WNW	$1\frac{1}{2}$	−6000
1 mile W of Port de Lévi	ENE	$1\frac{1}{2}$	+0145	WSW	$1\frac{1}{2}$	−0130
Close northward of buoy off C. Lévi	E	$4\frac{3}{4}$	+0500	W	$4\frac{3}{4}$	−0100
In Chenal Hédouin, inshore between the shoals W of Pte de Barfleur	E	$2\frac{3}{4}$	+0330	W	$2\frac{3}{4}$	−0300
Offshore, 3 miles N of Pte de Barfleur	SE	5.3 max	+0530	NW	5 max	−0030
Inshore, $\frac{1}{2}$ mile NE of Pte de Barfleur	ESE	4	+0430	NNW	4	−0130

9 Port du Becquet

Tidal Data: See Cherbourg.

9.1. The white leading towers at Port du Becquet. To the left is La Tounette port hand red beacon tower and below the house on the right lies the entrance to the harbour, just behind the end of the breakwater.

9.2. The harbour is opened up immediately after rounding the breakwater end. The yachts in the centre of the harbour dry out on legs.

This small drying fishing harbour lies 1 mile east of Cherbourg. It is sheltered by land or the breakwater from all winds other than NNE and E, but it is stated that there is a violent surge in the harbour during fresh winds from north as well as NE.

Approach and Entrance. The approach is easy by day or night, even with a small scale chart. There are two conspicuous white 8-sided light towers (*Oc (2 + 1) W (front) R (rear) synchronized 12s*) in line 187°. On close approach a red beacon tower marking rocks will be left to port and a breakwater to starboard. Ahead will lie a rocky shore but the moment the end of the breakwater is passed the harbour opens up and course is altered 90° to the W into its shelter. If coming from Cherbourg use the Passe Cabart Danneville and steer E until on the leading transit of the light towers.

Berths and facilities. The south quay is unsuitable for berthing but vessels can dry out alongside the inner side of the north breakwater, drying 1m4 to 3m0 on sand and mud. Bilge keels or legs allow a yacht to lie in the middle about half way up the harbour. Some provisions can be had. Water from tap in SW corner of port. Petrol at top of main street. Trains or buses to Cherbourg. The harbour is off the beaten track, hence it is worth a visit.

10 Port de Lévi

High Water: See Cherbourg. **Streams:** See p. 60.

10.1. Cape Lévi lighthouse and headland from the westward. The harbour is out of the picture to the right.

10.2. The entrance to Port de Lévi, showing the white patches on the ends of the breakwaters and the white leading mark open between them.

Port de Lévi is situated just over half a mile south of Cap Lévi and close to the south of Fort Lévi. The approach from westward past Cherbourg is easy, but care should be taken when approaching Port de Lévi to keep well into the bay to avoid being set into Cap Lévi race. Approaching from the eastward keep a good two miles seawards to pass outside the buoy off Cap Lévi to avoid the rocks and shoals and the worst of the race, except in light weather, when it may be safe to take a short cut inside at the right state of the tide. In Port de Lévi anchorage the N stream runs from +01 h Dover to −03 h Dover 2 knots springs; the S stream −03 h Dover to +01 h Dover, 2¾ knots. Eddies occur inshore between Cherbourg and Cap Lévi, west of Lévi the W stream runs 3 hours only. (See p. 60.)

The harbour, which dries 1m2 at the entrance, is formed by two jetties, having a narrow entrance. As shown on the sketch chart there are rocky ledges outside the jetties and widely fringing the cliffs north and south. The ends of the jetties are painted white and the entrance should be made with the end of the southern jetty bearing approximately east, with the end of the north jetty just open. A white rectangle on the inner wall is then open between the piers. There is a rock alongside the outer side of the south jetty, nearly at its end, to the right

62

of the white mark in the photograph. Leave the south jetty about 9 metres to starboard when abreast of it and then steer to leave the north jetty about 9 metres to port. There are rocks at the foot of its SE corner of the latter and on its east side and the southern part of the harbour has a rocky bottom. Elsewhere it is hard sand which dries about 1m8 at the quay and more at the northern end.

The harbour is sometimes occupied by fishing boats as shown in the sketch. There are mooring chains on the bottom, but a yacht equipped with legs could lie with stem to a mooring or buoyed anchor and stern to the quay. A yacht without legs would have to lie and dry out alongside the quay near the light on top of the wall on the east side of the harbour. The co-operation of the fishermen is required, as fishing boats may have to be moved from their regular moorings in order to leave a quayside berth. The harbour can be used in east and southerly winds, but there is a surge with even moderate onshore winds and heavy surf if it blows. It dries from 1m2 to 3m6.

The anchorage outside the harbour in 2m5 to 7m0 is sheltered in easterly winds, but exposed from S through W to NNE. The bottom outside the harbour is rock, except for a comparatively narrow patch of sand off the entrance. The tide attains a rate of $2\frac{3}{4}$ knots at Springs. The nearest harbour of refuge is Cherbourg only 5 miles to the west, but to the eastward the nearest is Barfleur, which involves rounding Lévi and Barfleur Races. A mobile restaurant sometimes parks on the harbour. There is a pleasant walk along the coast road to the fort and Cap. Provisions at Fermanville distant one mile.

Light. There is a fixed light with WRG sectors, visible 11, 7 and 6 miles.

10.3. Give the inner breakwater end a berth of 8 or 10 metres and bring up alongside the quay opposite.

Port de Lévi

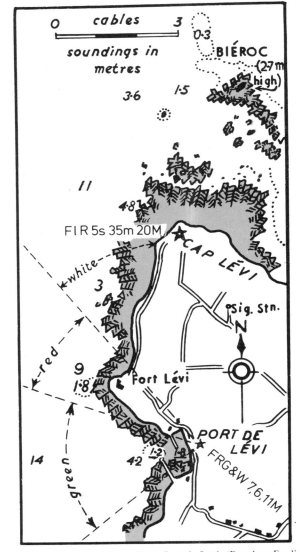

Above: Coast from Cap Lévi to Port de Lévi. (Based on English Channel Pilot Misc. 715 with the permission of the Controller of HM Stationery Office and the Hydrographer of the Navy.)

Below: sketch of the harbour

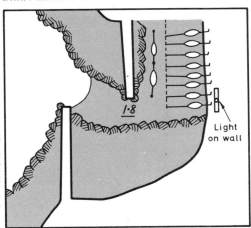

11 Barfleur

High Water: −2 h 33 m Dover; (+0 h 44 m Cherbourg).
Heights above datum: Chart No. 2073. MHWS 6m4. MLWS 1m0. MHWN 5m1. MLWN 2m3.
Stream sets to the northward between Pointe de Barfleur and the harbour 4¾ h before HW Dover and to the south 4½ h after HW Dover, attaining 2 knots.

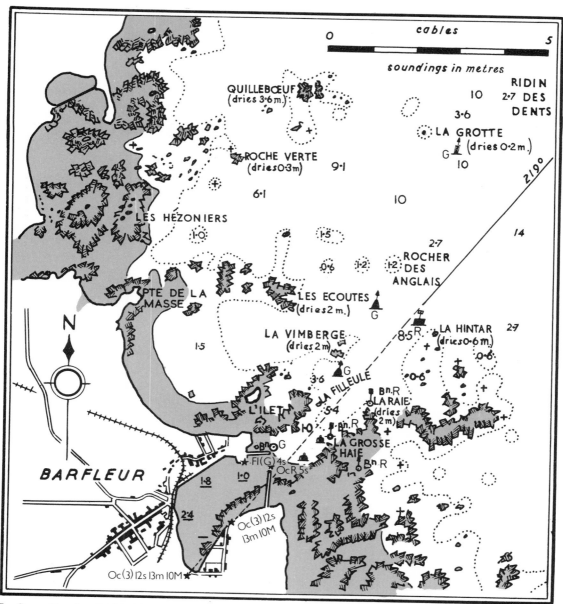

Barfleur: (Based on British Admiralty Chart No. 2073 with the permission of the Controller of HM Stationery Office and of the Hydrographer of the Navy.)

Barfleur

11.1. Pointe de Barfleur lighthouse and beacon from the eastward.

Barfleur is situated 1½ miles south of the Pointe de Barfleur. The small town is attractive and although the harbour dries out there are excellent berths against the quay, and an anchorage outside which is protected from the prevailing winds. For some reason its convenience and advantages have been overlooked by the majority of yachtsmen. Proposals for a marina with access through the harbour are under consideration.

The Approach and Entrance

Approaching from west or north the race of Barfleur (which extends 3 or 4 miles to the E and NE of the point on the flood stream) should be avoided in rough weather. The tides here require attention. Three miles N of Barfleur Point Lighthouse (*Fl (2) 10s 72m 27M Reed (2) 60s*) the main streams turn to the NW about $-\frac{1}{2}$ h Dover, and to the SE about $+5\frac{1}{2}$ h Dover, but S of Barfleur Point there is an eddy where the tide runs parallel with the shore north or south, the latter for only about $3\frac{1}{4}$ hours, starting at $+4\frac{1}{2}$ Dover. This eddy is strong in the vicinity of the Pointe de Barfleur and there are overfalls where the eddy meets the main east or west running stream. It is weaker about $\frac{3}{4}$ mile S of the Pointe de Barfleur, attaining a speed of about 2 knots only. When approaching from the eastward keep well south of Barfleur Point to avoid the race. Note that the streams in the Hédouin Channel (the inshore passage W of Pointe de Barfleur) are over two hours earlier than the main streams offshore. (See page 60.)

There are shoals and numerous rocks off the coast between the Pointe de Barfleur and Barfleur Harbour; so yachts should keep a mile to the east of the beacon east of Barfleur Point and ½ mile east of La Grotte, the outer green starboard hand buoy of the channel leading to the entrance, which can be identified by the conspicuous church on its NW side. In moderate offshore winds and in the absence of swell the shoals can be crossed in 2mo least water a cable east of the line from the beacon to La Grotte but nothing to the west.

The leading marks are rather inconspicuous in daylight. They consist of two light structures *within* the harbour, the front one being a square white light tower and the rear a white tower with a black top built over the dark roof a a white dwelling–see photograph 11.1. These must not be confused with the low hexagonal white light tower at the outer end of the eastern jetty which is very conspicuous. The leading marks should be brought into line at 219° true and when in transit will be seen over the top of the eastern breakwater, about a third of its length from its outer end. The channel is sheltered by the land in winds from S through W almost to NW.

If the leading marks cannot be identified it does not greatly matter as the entrance channel is clearly marked. After passing La Grotte outer buoy it is marked by two more

11.2. The leading lights giving the line of approach must not be confused with the light structure at the end of the breakwater. On near approach leave the transit and head for the entrance.

11.3. Close up view of the leading lights from inside the harbour. The rear one is often difficult to see as only the top peeps over the breakwater.

11.4. Starboard side of entrance showing two beacons and the top of an isolated rock which covers near HW.

Barfleur

11.5. Yachts dried out at LW.

starboard hand green buoys and on the port hand by one red buoy and two R beacons with can tops. See chart and, although the channel is wide, take no liberties, especially with La Filleule and associated rocks. When about a cable off the eastern breakwater (with sufficient rise of tide) alter course to leave it to port, with two G beacons and the northern breakwater to starboard, then enter the harbour. Note the drying rock on the edge of the channel close to the beacon shown in the photograph. At night the approach is clear as the leading lights (*Oc (3) 12s 10M*) are synchronized. There is a light (*Fl G 4s*) at the root of the northern breakwater, and a light (*Oc R 4s*) at the end of the eastern which is just to the north of the transit of the leading lights. The transit leads close to the unlit La Hintar buoy.

Moorings, Anchorage and Facilities

There is a convenient anchorage in offshore winds outside the harbour NW of La Grosse Haie beacon, close to the leading line (riding light necessary) in 4 to 5 metres LAT clear of La Filleule drying rock, but the holding ground is said to be poor. At neaps with the aid of soundings it is possible to get nearer the entrance with 2 or 3m, where it is better sheltered. It is usual however to enter the harbour and bring up alongside the long NW quay, which dries about 1m8 to 2m4. The best end is near the church but the obliging Harbour Master usually directs to a berth and takes warps. Ladders are provided to the quay. The bottom along the eastern breakwater on the opposite side of the harbour is rough except at the outer end and far from facilities. There is a strong surge in the harbour during fresh onshore winds.

The harbour master lives in the house carrying the rear leading light. Customs Office between church and lifeboat house. Water tap at quay, hose by arrangement with harbour master. Water tap also at public lavatory (not five star) behind the hedge across the road, also laundering troughs and dustbins. Petrol from garages. Hotel Moderne and the PO are in Place de Gaulle a short distance at the back of Hotel Phare. Good restaurants at hotels.

Barfleur is a charming old town extending from the church along the harbour front to the main streeet where there are plenty of small shops for supplies. There is a good bathing beach northward of the town and frequent buses to Cherbourg and elsewhere.

68

12 St Vaast-la-Hougue

High Water: Approx. HW Cherbourg + 1.

St Vaast-la-Hougue lies 8 miles south of Barfleur. A wide breakwater has been constructed to enclose the old fishing quay, providing a basin which contains a marina with 655 berths, including 150 for visitors, with a minimum depth of 2.3 metres. The entrance gate opens $2\frac{1}{2}$ hrs before HW St Vaast and closes 3 hours after, but with neap tides and high pressure it may close $1\frac{1}{4}$ hours earlier.

The Approach and Entrance

From the north attention should be paid to the tides off Barfleur (see p. 67) and a course parallel to the shore should be maintained to take advantage of the early tide change, keeping well outside the beacons along the shore. Distinctive features are Réville church spire and the fort on Ile Tatihou. La Gavendest Buoy (cardinal S unlit) clears the rocky patches SW of Ile Tatihou and course should then be altered to leave the La Dent buoy (cardinal S unlit) to starboard. From there the light structure at the end of St Vaast jetty should be approached on a bearing of 040°. If the gate is not open, proceed towards the jetty and anchor clear of the fairway on the St Vaast side. This anchorage can be uncomfortable in easterly winds.

After rounding the jetty the gate will be seen, with the Capitainerie on the north side. There are no signals and traffic leaving has priority, so approach needs care, especially when the gate has just opened and the fishing boats are leaving. There can also be a strong stream through the gate.

During the periods that the gate is open, contact can be made with the Capitainerie on

12.1. St Vaast Harbour entrance.

12.2. Fort de la Hougue.

St Vaast-la-Hougue

Channel 9. The attendant displays a board as the yacht enters, indicating on which pier the yacht is to berth. The visitors' berths are usually on piers B, C, D & E and are so marked.

By night. After passing the Pte de Saire (*Oc (1 + 2) 12 sec*) keep just east of the alignment of that light and Barfleur light (*Fl (2) 10 sec*) until the La Hougue light (*Oc 2 6 sec*) is in line with Morsalines (*Oc 3 + 1 12s*) on a bearing of 267.5°. Follow these leading lights until you are in the white sector of St Vaast jetty light (*Oc 2 R W & G 6 sec*) on a bearing between 310° and 350°. Take care not to confuse the jetty light with La Hougue, as both have the same characteristics. Watch for the numerous lobster pot buoys and beware of unlit anchored vessels in the approach.

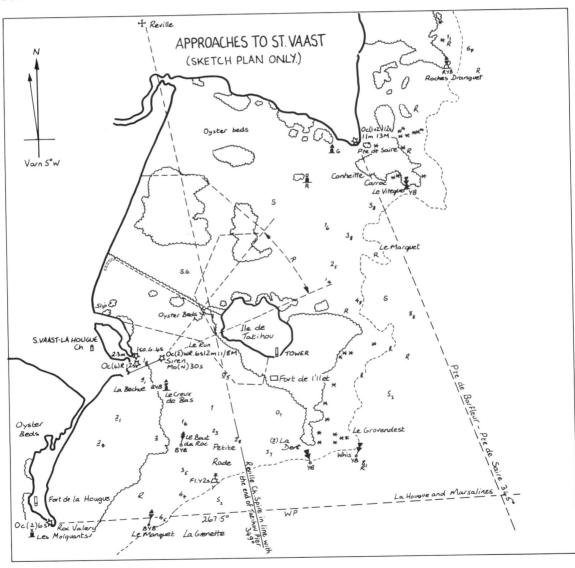

Facilities

Water and electricity are available on the pontoons and fuel at the Capitainerie. There are toilets and showers at the Capitainerie and at the Club house of the Cercle Nautique de la Hougue where visiting yachtsmen are welcome.

St Vaast is an attractive old town. There are several cafés and restaurants along Quai Vauban, and also in the Hotel Fuschia in the Rue Marechal Foch. The Gosselin super-market will supply duty free stores by arrangement, and fresh oysters can be purchased from a shop on the Quai Vauban near the beginning of the breakwater.

Ile de Tatihou may be visited by dinghy or on foot at low water via the track through the oyster beds in Le Run. There are interesting walks along the shore and a handy bathing beach just north of the beginning of the breakwater. The repair and chandlery facilities in St Vaast are mainly geared to the fishing fleet, but can also help with yacht matters. There are buses to Cherbourg from the Café du Commerce on the front.

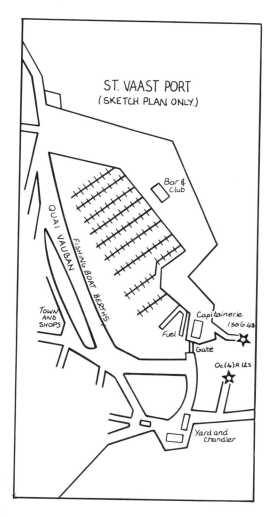

Sketch plan of St Vaast port.

13 Carentan

A marina has been constructed in the existing dock, just north of the town, some 8 miles up the Chenal de Carentan. There are moorings for 550 yachts including 55 for visitors.

Approach and Entrance

From the North or East, close the CI buoy and identify the Chenal de Carentan which is about 2 miles to the SSW. The buoys marking the channel where it crosses the Banc de la Madeleine are not readily visible at this distance, as they are rather small.

Port and starboard beacons mark the entrance to the river, after which continue straight to the lock which normally operates during the period 2 hours before to 3 hours after HW, (approximately HW Cherbourg + 1).

The Harbour office listens on Channel 9 between 0800 and 1800, and during the operating hours of the lock. It is advisable to plan to arrive at the lock at HW or soon after, as the ebb can be quite strong. At the lock, the lock keeper will allocate a berth. Pamphlets are available at the Capitainerie giving more precise details of depths and access time in relation to the tidal coefficients.

The characteristics of the lights on the buoys, beacons and leading marks are indicated on the diagram.

Moorings and facilities

There are pontoons with finger berths on the east side of the dock and the Capitainerie, fuel berth and chandlers are towards the southern end. Toilets, and hot and cold showers (free) are nearby. There are good shops and restaurants in the town about $\frac{1}{4}$ mile south of the dock. It is about 50 km by road from Cherbourg and the railway line from Cherbourg to Paris passes through the town.

Iles de St Marcouf

These islands lie $6\frac{1}{2}$ miles SW of St Vaast.

There are anchorages SW of the Ile du Large, which can be rather exposed. This island has interesting fortifications and is a popular picnic spot, with a convenient landing at the small dinghy harbour on the west. There is also an anchorage SE of the Ile de Terre, which is a bird sanctuary and landing is prohibited.

It is possible to visit the Islands and return during the 5 hours that the gate at St Vaast is open.

13.1. View from W bank of marina.

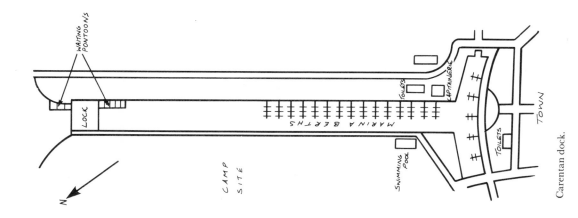

Carentan dock.

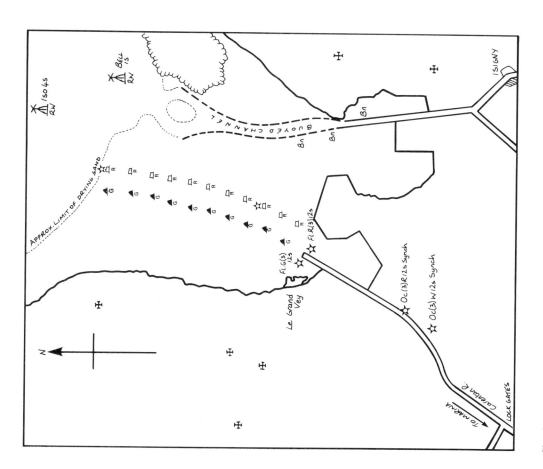

Sketch map of approach to Carentan.

14 Omonville

High Water: −3 h 41 m Dover (−o h 24 m Cherbourg).
Heights above Datum: MHWS 6m3. MLWS 1m0. MHWN 4m9. MLWN 2m4.
Inshore Stream, see page 60. The local inshore eddy runs from about −5 h 30 m to +5 h Dover, setting WNW 3 knots from Le Tunard beacon tower across the rocks south of Basse Bréfort buoy off which the WNW stream begins 2 hours later.

Although Cherbourg is one of the best ports in the whole of France for yachtsmen, many prefer the charm of a small harbour. Omonville la Rogue, which lies less than 8 miles west of Cherbourg, has the advantage of being quiet and unsophisticated, but of course it lacks all the facilities of a large port.

The Approach

Approaching from northward the first landmarks which will be sighted are Cap de la Hague and the tall chimney and buildings on the skyline 3 miles SE of it. The chimney lies to the south of the Anse de St Martin, and stands 2 miles SW of Omonville harbour. The next landmark to identify is the Pointe de Jardeheu, 3½ miles east of Cap de la Hague. It is a low promontory with a white-washed building and semaphore station at the end. Half a mile off the Pointe is the Y whistle buoy, Basse Bréfort (*VQ*) situated in a very strong stream usually setting WNW, with rocks between it and the shore. Take care not to be set too far west as Omonville lies about a mile to the eastward, and on the headland at the entrance sprawl the remains of an old fort, looking more like a wishbone of green-covered walls than

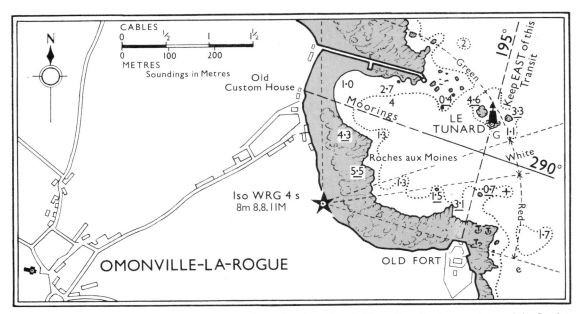

Omonville: Dotted contours indicate the 3 metre lines. (Based on French Chart No. 5631 by permission of the Service Hydrographique de la Marine.)

74

14.1. The conspicuous high chimney and buildings which stand on the skyline 2½ miles SW of Omonville, and the **Basse Bréfort Y lightbuoy** 1½ miles NW of Omonville. The stream is very strong running W for over 8½ hours. On the left of the picture is the white semaphore building identifying the low Pointe de Jardeheu.

14.2. The old fort on the hill east of Omonville harbour, Le Tunard green beacon tower and on right the end of the breakwater. Keep the fort open to the eastward of the beacon tower when approaching from a northerly direction.

14.3. The new light structure (Iso WRG) on the SW of the harbour.

the broken pile of masonry one might expect. On nearer approach a green beacon tower (not conspicuous) named Le Tunard will be sighted, and the harbour breakwater over which will be seen the new RW light structure. When approaching keep well to the east of the transit of the beacon tower and the old fort at 195°, to clear the rocky shoals of Les Tataquets, and in particular to allow for the strong cross tide, usually running WNW towards the rocks.

Approaching from the westward keep at least a mile off shore until well east of the transit of the beacon tower and the fort, then steer to leave the tower well to starboard.

From the eastward the approach is much easier, as the coast is less rock-strewn. The beacon tower of Raz de Bannes will be passed three miles west of Cherbourg and soon Le Tunard and the fort will be seen. Allow for the tide, and avoid being set north of Le Tunard.

Omonville

14.4. Composite photograph facing northward over Omonville harbour. When entering from E, the beacon tower is left about 50 metres to starboard, after which the yacht is headed parallel with the breakwater. There are rocks between the beacon and the end of the breakwater and the stream is usually setting hard towards them.

Entrance. The entrance lies between the beacon tower of Le Tunard and the fort. Le Tunard stands on a reef, and there are rocks between the tower and end of the breakwater, and also for about ¼ cable E and ESE of the tower, which should, therefore, not be approached too closely. A cable NE of the fort there is a rock which just dries at LAT, and the proper channel is under a cable wide at low water.

When entering from the eastward steer for the former custom house (a tiny building with a high roof and a chimney at each end) at about 290°, or simply leave Le Tunard beacon tower about 60 metres to starboard and make good a course leading south of the breakwater towards the bigger fishing boats or moorings in the harbour. Be prepared for the strong stream usually setting NW off Le Tunard beacon tower and across the rocks between it and the breakwater. When within the harbour keep north of the Roches aux Moines (see chart) which are steep-to and covered near high water.

If coming from the northward leave Le Tunard beacon tower at least ½ cable to the westward before coming on the line for the entrance from the east, when proceed on it.

By night. Omonville light (*Iso WRG 4s 11/8/8M*) is shown on the accompanying chart. Enter in white sector with the light bearing between 252° and 262°, but alter course to starboard into the harbour when south of Le Tunard Beacon.

Anchorage. The best positions in the harbour are occupied by moorings. Visiting yachts may lie to the big white mooring buoys, if necessary several abreast, as the moorings are very heavy. It is sometimes possible to find room to anchor in good holding ground between the moorings and the rocks south of them, but take care as these are steep-to and often covered. Except near spring tides there is room to anchor nearer to the beach but soundings must be taken. If the harbour is full anchorage can be found to the east of the moorings, but the water is deep, the stream strong and the position less sheltered. Yachts can dry out on sand bottom alongside the breakwater for ¼ cable west of the short offshoot or spur, but rocks border the breakwater east of it. There are a few small fishing dories moored south of the jetty on the edge of the shallow water.

The anchorage is sheltered except from winds in any direction from the east, but in a gale from the south it was on one occasion too rough to row a dinghy to the yacht even from the breakwater.

Facilities. Land at steps west of the breakwater offshoot, or in calm weather on the shingle shore. A restaurant facing the harbour has been closed and re-opened at various times. Water at tap nearby. Petrol at garage 600 metres up road bearing right. Shops in village and milk at farm before 8 a.m. or reserved if ordered the night before. Infrequent bus service to Cherbourg. Twelfth/thirteenth century church with attractive gallery.

14.5. The inner harbour. At neaps a vessel can find anchorage as close inshore as soundings permit. The former office of the Douane is the small two chimneyed building to the right of the white house on the extreme left.

15 Anse de St Martin and Racine

High Water: Approx. $-3\frac{3}{4}$ h Dover, $-\frac{1}{2}$ h Cherbourg.
Heights above Datum: Approx. MHWS 6m4. MLWS 1m1. MHWN 5m0. MLWN 2m5.
Stream sets within the Bay SE at $+5$ h Dover and to NNW at -5 h 30 m Dover.

As the chart shows, the Anse de St Martin, half way between Cap de la Hague and Omonville, provides a natural anchorage sheltered from winds between SE through S to W. It has a shelving shore and provides good holding ground. It is however only suitable in settled weather, as in a southerly gale there is the probability of a veer to the NW. As there are no lights in the bay it would be difficult to leave at night in the event of the wind coming onshore. The harbour of Racine though protected from north is small and dries out, but in offshore winds and settled weather the Anse de St Martin affords a pleasant and secluded anchorage with plenty of room.

The Approach
The NW and NE corners of the entrance of the bay are encumbered by rocks but near the centre the three rocks La Parmentière (awash at LAT), and La Francaise and Erte (with less

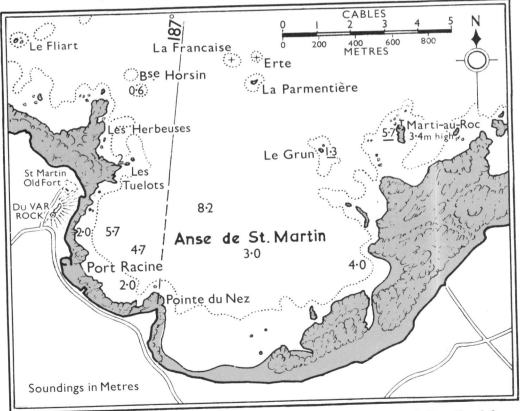

Anse de St Martin and Racine: Dotted contours indicate the 3 metre lines. (Based on French Chart No. 5636 by permission of the Service Hydrographique de la Marine.)

15.1. The line of approach is with the Pointe du Nez bearing 187°. The Pointe is at the W end of a sandy beach on the south of the bay. The conspicuous chimney will be open to the east of the Pointe but the picture was taken when leaving the anchorage and not exactly on the correct bearing.

15.2. Les Herbeuses from the SE near LW. The rocks appear much the same when approached from seaward and are left about two cables to starboard.

than 1m8 over them) are well covered above half tide, although there might be breakers on them during fresh winds.

The simplest approach to the bay is made with the Pointe du Nez bearing 187°. This is the low promontory on the SW side of the bay with a rock off it which never covers. It is not conspicuous from seaward but its position can be identified as it lies at the W end of a long sandy shore to the east of it. When on the correct line the high chimney referred to in the last chapter will be fine on the port bow. Allow for the very strong streams in the offing, which may at times require an alteration as much as 45° to crab across the tide on the correct bearing on the headland. This leaves La Francaise, Erte and La Parmentière over a cable to port and Basse Horsin with 0m6 over it to starboard. When these have been passed the prominent Les Herbeuses rocks (some of which never dry) will lie about 2 cables to the west. Les Tuélots, drying 2m0, will be left over a cable to starboard and the stream will have

15.3. Port Racine, looking north. It is one of the smallest harbours in France.

weakened to a maximum 2 knots at springs. Alter course to steer into the SW corner of the bay to the west of Pte du Nez and take soundings to bring up in the depth required, probably just to seaward of a number of fishermen's moorings with plastic buoys east of Port Racine. Holding ground good in sand or mud.

Port Racine. The harbour is difficult to find, as it is hidden behind a reef of rocks until the yacht is to the SE of the entrance and in shallow water. The entrance faces south, and the harbour is formed by breakwaters on the south and east, and protected by land to the west and north. There is a reef of rocks extending over 100 metres to the ENE of the east jetty.

The harbour is very small and dries out completely. Yachts could, however, lie alongside the jetties, but moored as near the outer ends as possible to get the best water, as the bottom is steeply shelving. In practice, however, it would now be difficult to lay alongside the jetties as there are many local craft moored with long ropes aft and by chains forward across the harbour to the east jetty. A deep keeled yacht could only enter with local co-operation. In bad weather a chain is put across the entrance. The harbour provides the best landing place from a dinghy. There is an hotel with bar and restaurant close by. A cheaper restaurant will be found $\frac{1}{2}$ mile on the road uphill to the right on the outskirts of Danneville where provisions can be obtained. Good coastal walks. Occasional bus to Cherbourg.

PART III
THE CHANNEL ISLANDS

Introduction

Chart Datum: The charted depths and drying heights given in this part of the book have been altered to conform with LAT datums. Tidal data are shown at the head of each chapter.
Admiralty Chart 2669.

The principal attraction of the Channel Islands lies in the varied coastlines, the strange rock formations, the sandy bays, the clear water and the constantly changing scene which results from a tremendous rise and fall of the tides. The number and variety of the anchorages under suitable conditions is remarkable. A month could happily be spent with the yacht based on St Peter Port making short cruises exploring the waters round Guernsey, Herm and Sark. Likewise Jersey has a marina and many excellent and beautiful anchorages which are available in offshore winds and settled weather. There is no great difficulty in entering the main ports, except in thick weather. Alderney with its deep harbour is only 60 miles from the Solent, and even less from Poole or Weymouth. The Little Russel leading to St Peter Port is rough with a fresh SW wind blowing against a spring tide, but a stranger can avoid this by going round Guernsey and entering from the south. Navigation in the approaches to St Helier is a little more complicated. But if, on the occasion of his first visit, the yachtsman will wait for settled clear weather and a neap tide he need have no anxiety. The Channel Islands form a compact cruising ground with harbours never far apart, and are also convenient for visiting many ports on the neighbouring French coast.

As so much of the enjoyment of sailing in the Channel Islands lies in the coastal cruising and and the whole area may appear difficult to those who have not sailed there before, Part III, which follows in this book, has been expanded to include sailing directions in addition to descriptions of the harbours and anchorages themselves. Navigation on the coasts of Herm, Sark and SE Jersey calls for greater experience and caution than elsewhere, and it is due to Channel Island yachtsmen that information is given on the local transits and clearing marks, which are coupled with sketches and photographs to assist in their identification.

The principal requirement when cruising in the Channel Islands is an understanding of the tides. The reader should consult the Admiralty *Tidal Stream Atlas* for the Channel Islands and Adjacent Coasts of France, and there are many references in the text to emphasize the importance of inshore eddies. Eddies, such as those found on the north coast of Alderney and off Herm, sometimes run contrary to the main stream, and then two opposing currents may be separated by only a narrow band of water. Rock dodgers must be prepared to find inshore eddies which are too local to show on any tidal map, and of course the rates, direction and position vary between springs and neaps, and are also influenced by weather conditions.

In general the direction of tidal streams round the islands constantly progresses in an anti-clockwise direction, being north-easterly at high water (St Helier) (-4 h 47 m Dover), north-westerly at half tide down, south-westerly at low water, swinging round rapidly to south-easterly at the first of the flood, and gradually to easterly about $1\frac{1}{2}$ hours before HW.

Introduction

In the Russels between Guernsey and Sark the NE to N stream begins −2 h 50 m St Helier (+4 h 40 m Dover) and the SW at approximately +3 h 30 m St Helier (−1 h 25 m Dover) both streams attaining over 5 knots springs, $2\frac{1}{4}$ neaps.

Visiting yachtsmen may find it convenient to work their tides in relation to Dover as the standard port for the whole of the English Channel, but it is more accurate to work on local tide constants. Accordingly constants are given for both Dover and St Helier. The times of HW for St Peter Port and St Helier will be found in the appropriate nautical Almanac.

Pilotage in the Channel Islands is based on transits, land marks, beacons and rocks. The compass is necessary to assist in finding these marks, but in narrow waters with perhaps unpredictable (to the stranger) currents it is far easier to keep known marks in line, rather than depend on a compass bearing. Photographs and sketches are reproduced to assist identification of the principal marks, which once recognized will make it easier to find the position of the less conspicuous ones. (If a newcomer can kidnap a local yachtsman or pilot as navigator for the first cruise to Herm or Sark so much the better, or failing that, he could do worse than take passage in one of the many excursion boats from St Peter Port in order to familiarize himself with the features of the coast, before piloting his own yacht there.)

Finally, for those who are unfamiliar with cruising in restricted waters, with a great rise and fall of tide, the following notes may be of service.

The scene in the Channel Islands at high water is one of islands with a few outlying rocks, towers and tops of beacons standing out of the water; but at low water the rocks will have grown to islets, the beacons may be on top of rocks as big as houses, and vast areas of islets, rocks, ledges and sands will be uncovered. A small isolated rock is known locally as a 'boue', and much can be done to avoid dangerous boues by keeping a watch for them, as was done before the era of aids to navigation. In a smooth sea rocks below the surface can sometimes be seen, and if there is a strong tide they will be revealed by ripples and circles of oily looking water. If it is a little rough there will be overfalls over the rocks, and if a swell is running the waves will break, spurting white columns of spray. It will be seen on the chart that some of the larger rocks which are always above water are steep-to. Such rocks can be treated like beacons as by passing close to them the yacht's position can be fixed.

Overfalls occur in the Little Russel, and are unavoidable on certain passages. But many overfalls such as the Schôle Bank are local, occurring over shoal banks. The navigator should lay his courses to avoid these shoals, but if overfalls are sighted they can be avoided by altering course to go round them, as the patches are usually quite distinct.

Fog and thick weather in the Channel Islands provide the principal hazards, although a flat calm can also be awkward to a yacht without auxiliary power, if the stream is setting on to dangers. If a fog comes down when approaching the Channel Islands it is safer to retreat. It is best to treat a forecast of poor visibility in much the same way as one would treat a forecast of a gale, because gales are preferable to fogs when sailing in restricted waters. Attention is drawn to these risks because if they are recognized they are robbed of half their danger. Nevertheless, navigation in Channel Island waters requires a special degree of caution and vigilance. Further, it is recommended that the charts in this book should be supplemented by large scale Admiralty charts when piloting in strong streams and rocks such as are found off Herm and Sark.

16 Casquets, the Swinge and Alderney Race

Tidal Stream

The SW stream at the Casquets begins westerly about −o h 30 m HW Dover (+4 h 30 m St Helier) and soon turns SW. The NE stream begins about +5 h 30 m Dover (−2 h St Helier). The streams attain 4½ to 5 knots at springs. It is stated that eddies exist SW from the Casquets during the SW stream and NE during the NE stream. In the channels between the Casquets and Alderney the streams are stronger and there are severe overfalls over banks, shoals or irregularities on the bottom.

Admiralty Chart 3653.

Yachtsmen sailing to Guernsey and the Gulf of St Malo will either leave the Casquets well to port, clearing the tide races in the vicinity, or will take one of the inshore passages, either through Alderney Race or the Swinge, or more rarely the Ortac Channel. Thus Alderney (see Chapter 17) and the reefs to the west of it may be said to lie in the gateway of the passage to the Channel Isles and Gulf of St Malo. Such being the case they merit special attention.

For navigation in these waters the Admiralty Chart No. 60 of Alderney and the Casquets is particularly recommended. It also contains large-scale local tidal insets.

The Casquets

This prominent group of rocks has been a landmark for shipping throughout the ages, and is situated 7 miles west of Alderney Breakwater. Between the Casquets and the island are several islets, detached rocks and shoals, with wide passages between them. These passages can be navigated but, owing to the strength of the tide, the overfalls and detached dangers, local knowledge is needed, other than for those points described below.

The Casquets have accounted for many wrecks, but the hazards have been reduced by navigational aids. The group of rocks is prominent, and the white lighthouse (*Fl (5) 30s 37m 28M*) and buildings can be seen for a considerable distance on a clear day. In fog or thick conditions the whole area is a disagreeable one, but there is a powerful fog signal (*Dia (2) 60s*) on the E tower, and as most yachts are equipped with DF the *radio beacon* is invaluable in these waters.

The Casquets group of islets and rocks extends nearly ¾ mile east to west. They may be approached within ¼ mile on the north side as sunken outliers extend less than a cable off the principal rocks which are always above the water. There is little to be gained by approaching closely, as the tide runs very hard, at times setting somewhat towards the rocks, and there are overfalls over the uneven bottom. In particular there are overfalls N of L'Auquière, on 'The Ledge' (covered 2m4), 1 cable NW of Noire Roque (the rock SW of the group), and over the 'Eight Fathom Ledge' just under a mile west of the lighthouse. It may be said that overfalls may be expected anywhere in the area where banks or shoals exist, even if well covered. For this reason the SW Casquet Bank 2 to 6 miles off, and the Pommier Banks, 2 miles to the NE should be avoided in rough weather or at spring tides.

There are several landing places on the principal Casquet rock which are used for relief of the lighthouse, but landing by the public on the Trinity House property is forbidden, and also risky.

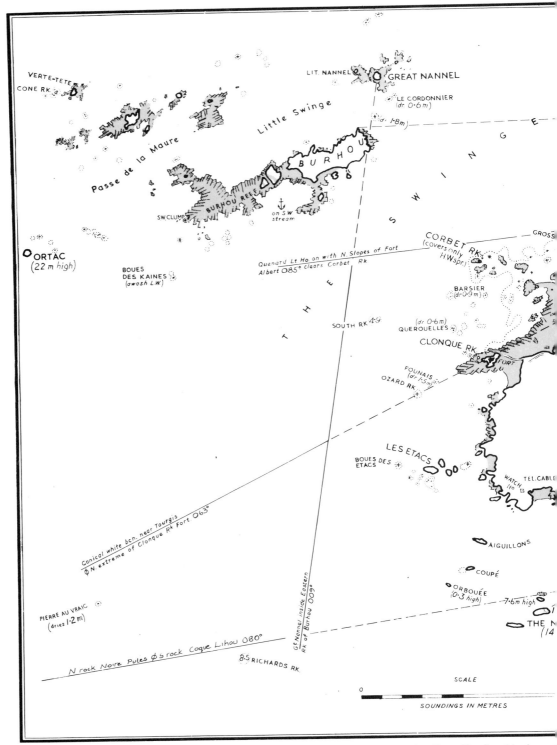

VERTE-TETE
CONE RK.

LIT. NANNEL   GREAT NANNEL

LE CORDONNIER
(dr. 0.6m)

(dr. 1.8m)

Little Swinge

Passe de la Maure

BURHOU

S

W

I

N

G

E

BURHOU REEF

SW.CLUMP

⚓ on S.W
stream

ORTAC
(22 m high)

CORBET RK.
(covers only
H.W.spr.)

GROSS

BOUES
DES KAINES
(awash L.W.)

Quenard Lt Ho on with N Slopes of Fort
Albert O85° clears Corbet Rk

BARSIER
(dr 0.9 m)

T

H

E

SOUTH RK 4.9

(dr. 0.6 m)
QUEROUELLES

CLONQUE RK.

FORT

FOUNAIS
(dr 1.5m)
OZARD RK.

S

LES ETACS

BOUES DES
ETACS

Conical white bcn. near Tourgis
⌀ N. extreme of Clonque Rk Fort O63°

WATCH
Ho   TEL.CABLE

AIGUILLONS

COUPÉ

ORBOUÉE
(0.3 high)

7.6m high

PIERRE AU VRAIC
(dries 1.2 m)

Gt.Nannel inside Eastern
Rk of Burhou O09°

THE N
(14

N rock Noire Putes ⌀ s rock Coque Lihou O80°

8.5 RICHARDS RK.

SCALE

0

SOUNDINGS IN METRES

Alderney and the Swinge: (Based on British Admiralty Chart No. 60 with the pe

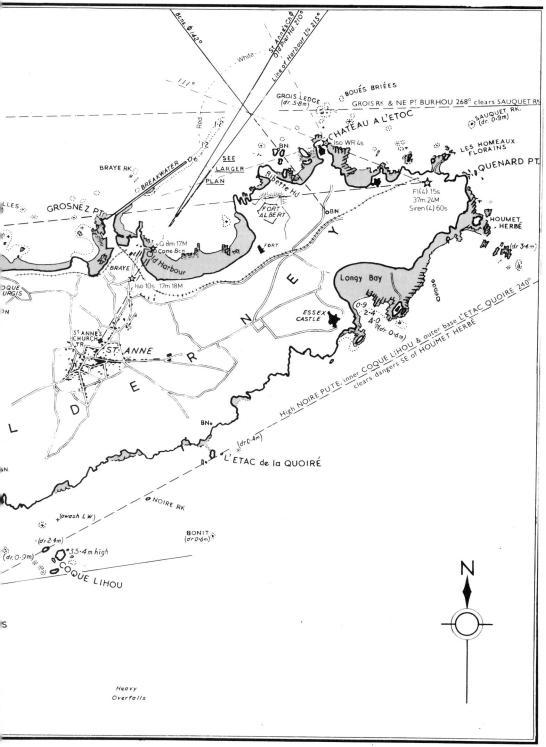

16.1. The Casquets lighthouse from the northward.

16.2. The Ortac Rock is a nesting place for gannets. It is at the SE end of the Ortac Channel and a useful mark on which to take a bearing.

16.3. Corbet Rock looking E towards the breakwater.

Ortac Channel

This channel is rarely used by strangers, but it is a wide one which may be navigated with the aid of the large-scale Admiralty chart. It is entered at the north end, to the west of the Verte-Tête group of rocks. This consists principally of Verte-Tête itself, a two-headed rock 8m high, and westward of it the Cone Rock, which is conical and 3m0 high. Just westward of Cone Rock is a boue which dries 2m4. The Ortac Rock marks the southern end of the channel, and the yacht will pass westward of this. The rock, which is a nesting place of gannets, is 24 m high and can be seen and identified (see photograph) from a considerable distance. It is most useful for taking bearings.

Simple directions are steer to approach with Ortac bearing 155° true until Verte Tête (8m) and Cone Rock, ½ mile farther north, come in line with Great Nannel. Then make good a course of 189° leaving Ortac about ½ mile to eastward. Ortac itself is fairly steep-to on its west and south sides, but there are shoals within 2 cables WNW of it, on which there are overfalls, although they are covered 1m2 and 3m4 even at LAT.

The principal consideration in the Ortac Channel is the tide, which attains 7 knots. This causes overfalls, severe when contrary to the wind. NE stream starts +5 h Dover (−2½ h St Helier) and SW at −1 h Dover (+4 h St Helier), but the streams vary in direction, setting at High Water Dover towards the Casquets, and there are eddies, so the tidal charts should be consulted. It should not be attempted without auxiliary power unless there is enough wind to ensure command over tidal eddies. Plan the passage preferably near slack water at neap tides.

The Swinge

The Swinge is the channel on the west side of Alderney, between it and the group of islets and reefs which lie on the other side. This group is about 2 miles long from the Nannels at the NE to Ortac at the SW and the largest islet is Burhou which, if one includes the reef on its SW (which dries at low water), is about 1 mile long.

The Swinge affords the quickest passage between Alderney and Guernsey, and is the one most often used by local vessels and yachts. The streams attain rates up to 8 knots at springs and the bottom is rocky, so there are violent overfalls in bad weather and when wind and tide are opposed. Navigation in the Swinge therefore depends on choosing the right time, and one of the roughest area of tide rips lies about 1 mile ENE of Burhou; less disturbed water may be found nearer Alderney.

When bound southward via the Swinge, local yachtsmen usually plan to enter the Swinge off Alderney Breakwater at −2 to −1 h Dover (+2½ to 4 h St Helier). (See page 90 for times of westerly eddy.)

The yacht should be sailed into a position north of the submerged end of Alderney Breakwater (½ mile N of breakwater end) on the line of the beacons—see next chapter. Then steer west towards the southern side of Burhou Island.

The stream running to SW should set the yacht to the south. Until the Corbet Rock has been cleared do not allow her to be set south of the line of Alderney (Quenard) Lighthouse (photograph 17.1) on with the northern slopes of Fort Albert at 085°. This is the fort on the hill, SE of the breakwater end, on the opposite side of the harbour entrance, and will be seen to the eastward over the breakwater.

The Corbet Rock is the principal consideration in the Swinge, as it lies ½ mile from the shore off Roque Tourgis, and reduces the navigable width of the Swinge to little over ½ mile between Burhou and the Corbet. This rock is covered only at HW springs, and will probably be about 3m3 above water at the state of tide when the yacht passes it but should be given a berth of at least half a cable to avoid outlyers. Beware also of the Barsier Boulder, 2 cables to the SW. The Corbet is cleared when Fort Clonque (almost an island joined to Alderney by a causeway) is well shut in by the high land of SW Alderney. It is better to hold on the course with the north slope of Fort Albert and the lighthouse astern until Great Nannel (a 15m high rock, 3 cables N or Burhou) is just shut inside the extreme eastern side of Burhou at 008°. Then steer on this stern bearing, leaving Les Etacs rocks, of which the highest is 37m, about ½ mile to the eastward.

Keep on this course (or rather to the east of it after passing Les Etacs) until the Noires Putes (a group of four rocks ½ mile S of Alderney, highest 19m) come abeam, whence steer for Guernsey or as desired, but note the presence of Pierre au Vraic, 1 mile to the west.

Pierre au Vraic is a dangerous isolated rock situated in deep water 1¾ miles W by S of Les Etacs, right in the SW approach of the Swinge, almost on the transit of Coupé and

16.4. Looking WNW across Clonque Fort and Causeway to the Swinge. The isolated Ortac Rock will be seen on the left and Burhou across the Swinge on the right.

Coque Lihou inner (northerly rock), best seen on the chart. Pierre au Vraic dries 1m2 at LAT, and if there is a swell running the seas break on it, even if well covered by the tide. It is cleared on its east side by the transit of Great Nannel just shut in by the E side of Burhou, and on its south side by keeping S of the line from the inner (northern) rock of the four Noires Putes to the southern rock (17m7) of the Coque Lihou group (which is unmistakable as its northern neighbour is a rock 35m4 high) at o8oT. This transit also clears just S of Bonit; dries out, E of Coque Lihou. On its western side it is avoided by keeping on or west of the transit, conical white beacon just S of Fort Tourgis in line with N extreme of Clonque Rock Fort (063° T). Pierre au Vraic has greater nuisance value when approaching the Swinge from the south from Guernsey as if the weather is thick the yacht will be in the vicinity before the transits can be picked up, and allowance for tidal streams must be made as accurately as possible.

In the Swinge the NE stream commences at +5h Dover ($-2\frac{1}{2}$ h St Helier) and continues to $-1\frac{1}{2}$ h Dover ($+3\frac{1}{2}$ h St Helier), when the SW stream begins, but north of the Corbet Rock along the north of Alderney, the inshore eddy runs easterly only for three hours approximately +5 h Dover ($-2\frac{1}{2}$ h St Helier) to -4 h Dover ($+\frac{1}{2}$ h St Helier). Thus a yacht coming up with a fair tide from Guernsey may meet a foul stream beyond the Corbet Rock, though the eddy is modest compared with the reputed 8 knots springs in the southern part of the Swinge. Other eddies exist which can be used only with local knowledge. A good temporary anchorage on the SW stream is shown on the chart SW of Burhou but a yacht could get closer in under suitable conditions. Another anchorage is in Hannaine Bay, S of Fort Clonque.

Alderney Race

The race of Alderney provides the usual passage for ships and yachts rounding the NW corner of the Cherbourg Peninsula. It is over 7 miles wide and has Quenard Point (Alderney) lighthouse (*Fl (4) 15s 37m 24M Siren (4) 60s*) on the NW side and Cap de la Hague lighthouse (*Fl 5s 48m 22M Horn 30s*) on the French coast opposite. Strangers may be deterred from using this passage as the rate of $9\frac{1}{2}$ knots attained by the stream in Alderney Race sounds alarming, but it will only be encountered at the peak of an exceptionally big spring tide on the NE side of the race. The yachtsman is not likely to meet with more than 6 knots, and probably less, particularly if he can plan to pass through the northern end of the race near slack water.

There are overfalls in Alderney Race whenever the stream is running fast over shoals or unevenness on the bottom, such as Blanchard, Inner Race Rock, Race Rock, and Alderney South Banks. The positions of the shoal patches are shown on large scale chart No. 60 and courses should if necessary be planned or altered to avoid them. In very calm weather they will be no more than ripples and oily whirlpools, but if the wind is against the stream, or obliquely against the stream, they will be lively and in strong winds possibly dangerous, though in such circumstances much can be done by easing the yacht through them, letting the tide carry her past.

Although the Alderney streams attain higher rates than in the Portland Race, the wave formations are less irregular and are not considered so dangerous. As the tides play such an important part in the navigation of the Alderney Race, varying both in speed and direction, they require special consideration, preferably consulting Admiralty Chart No. 60 or the Tidal Stream Atlas.

The only navigational hazard on the Alderney side is the Brinchetais Ledge, a reef which extends over $\frac{1}{2}$ mile into the race. It is cleared by the transit, Noires Putes high rock, inner rock Coque Lihou and S shoulder L'Etac de la Quoiré, 240° T.

Tidal Streams. In the centre of the race and its approaches well clear of the land on each side the streams are straightforward. The SW stream starts at $-\frac{3}{4}$ h Dover ($+4$ h St Helier); the NE stream starts $+5\frac{1}{4}$ h Dover ($-2\frac{1}{4}$ h St Helier). Both streams attain $5\frac{1}{2}$ knots at springs. Slack water does not last long, but affords an interval when the tides are weaker and the Race less unruly.

The strongest streams are found on the French side of the Race. Off Gros du Raz lighthouse the NE stream begins at $+5$h 10 m Dover and at top springs is 9.7 knots 2 or 3 hours later. The SW stream begins at -1 h 35 m Dover and later attains the high spring rate of 6.8 knots. A mile W of La Foraine beacon tower the streams begin about at the same time, the NNE stream attaining $9\frac{1}{2}$ knots and the SSW $6\frac{1}{2}$ knots at springs.

If approaching from Cherbourg and the east, use can be made of the early inshore reverse eddy. Off Anse de St Martin the WNW eddy starts about -5 h Dover and will take a yacht fast along the coast when the offshore stream is foul, but careful chart work is needed to keep north of the outlying rocks. The inshore stream does not bend round towards the rocks off Gros du Raz (which must be given a good offing) to La Foraine beacon until nearly $1\frac{1}{2}$ hours before HW Dover, so there is no point in being too early. If sailing from Cherbourg, Omonville or Anse de St Martin this eddy is useful in good weather, as by this means a yacht can get through the Alderney Race on the east side before the tide attains its maximum. The early eddy which is fair when approaching Alderney Race from the east is of course contrary for a yacht approaching from the south, late on the tide.

Casquets, the Swinge and Alderney Race

On the Alderney side of the race there are notable and most useful eddies. Round the north-east of Alderney the NE stream turns to follow the coast westward towards the Swinge for the last three hours from about $-4\frac{1}{2}$ h Dover ($+\frac{1}{2}$ h St Helier) and continues W until about $+5$ h Dover (-2 h St Helier). This stream at springs attains over 3 knots. The main W going stream divides east and west of Alderney on a transit, Quenard Pt LH and the SE corner Essex Castle, 210° T, which passes close to the Sauquet Rock, on which the stream sets strongly. One arm of the stream runs west along Alderney while the other sweeps into Alderney Race. The main E going stream divides just east of Les Etacs.

Inshore on the south and east sides of Alderney there is little detailed information but it is stated in the *Channel Pilot* that in an area between the coast and a line from Orbouée to about 1 mile SE of the Noires Putes and thence NE to Brinchetais Ledge off Houmet Herbé Fort the east-going stream begins $+3$ h 0 m Dover and continues until -2 h 0 m Dover. Maximum rates springs E and NE 2 knots, W and SW 3 knots.

17 Alderney (Braye Harbour)

High Water: −4 h 19 m Dover (+0 h 28 m St Helier).
Heights above Datum: Chart No. 2845. MHWS 6m3, MLWS 0m8, MHWN 4m7, MLWN 2m6.
Tidal Stream: Well offshore the stream sets SW from −½ h Dover to +5½ h Dover, and NE +5½ h Dover to −½ h Dover. Inshore along the north coast and the west coast as far as the Corbet Rock there is a strong eddy (referred to in the previous chapter) setting westward and towards the Swinge at about 2 to 3 knots for 9 out of 12 hours.
Depths: Deep in the approach and harbour, except off the inner harbour.
Admiralty Charts: 60, 2845.

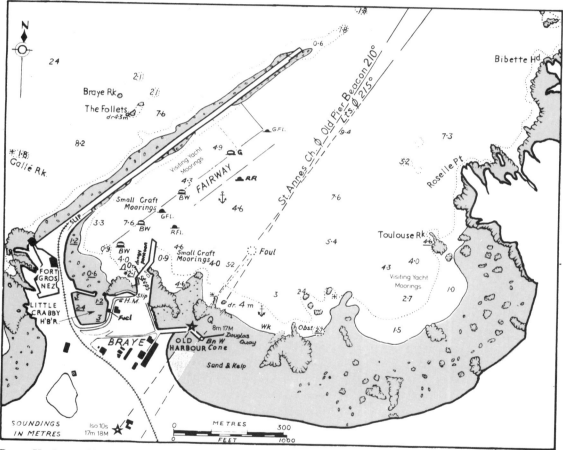

Braye Harbour, Alderney: (Based on British Admiralty Chart No. 2845 with the permission of the Controller of HM Stationery Office and of the Hydrographer of the Navy.)

Alderney Harbour used to be regarded as somewhat difficult of approach and entrance, but in clear weather it is easy enough, except for the strong tidal streams. It is only 60 miles from the Needles, and after Cherbourg it is the most popular harbour in the vicinity of Cherbourg Peninsula. The harbour is deep, the holding ground varies, but it is protected except from

Alderney (Braye Harbour)

N and NE winds. Facilities are good, but the best positions in the harbour are often crowded in holiday months.

The Approach and Entrance

The best approach to Alderney Harbour is from a general direction N to NE, and the island will be seen from a considerable distance in clear weather. When it is sighted fix or estimate the ship's position, and work out the tides over the remaining distance in order to make allowance for them. Close inshore on the N coast of Alderney the stream runs west except between +5 h Dover and −4½ h Dover, so it is usually best to lay a course for the NE part of the island. On nearer approach the lighthouse will be seen, situated about ¼ mile west of Quenard Point. There are detached rocks all along this north coast, from the Sauquet Rock over ¼ mile N of Quenard Pt to Grois Rock ¼ mile N of Château à L'Etoc. 1¼ miles west of the lighthouse is the harbour breakwater, composed of high masonry, nearly ½ mile long, which will be seen from a considerable distance, and the church at St Anne will be seen in the centre of the island. The stream will probably be setting strongly off the lighthouse along the coast towards the breakwater, which will bring the yacht nicely to the entrance, but take care not to be set too far to the west towards the Swinge and dangers in the direction of the Casquets. See chart, pages 86–87. Keep a good lookout for lobster pot buoys which are often half-submerged in the tide.

If coming from the south approach by the Swinge or Alderney Race as described in the previous chapter.

The entrance to Alderney Harbour lies between the submerged remains of the breakwater (which extend over ¼ mile from the end of the breakwater proper) and the rocks off the coast between Château à L'Etoc Fort (prominent on a headland) and Bibette Head. The navigable width of the entrance is only 2 cables, and for a stranger less.

In the immediate approach to the entrance the tidal stream has again to be considered, for the end of the Swinge causes quite a race off the submerged part of the breakwater, and overfalls in westerly winds. As stated the inshore stream varies in width, and towards the end of the easterly inshore stream the westerly eddy has already started within about ½ cable of the breakwater. There will then be a clear demarcation between east and west setting streams, and the sudden change may cause the yacht to sheer as she crosses it. The streams off the submerged breakwater are particularly strong at local high water springs and at 6 hours after, when caution is necessary owing to the strong eddies; they can be dangerous in rough weather.

The remains of the breakwater consist of blocks of masonry which can be imagined as forming its underwater continuation for 3 cables, first bulging a little into the entrance then curving slightly outwards to the north. Accordingly, if the inner side of the breakwater is kept slightly open (allowing for an athwartship tide) its submerged continuation will be left to starboard. However, the leading marks will be seen, which consist of a white conical beacon on Douglas Quay in transit at 210° true with St Anne's Church spire—see photograph 17.3. These lead close inside east of the submerged masonry. If tacking, keep the white beacon on Douglas Quay between the church spire and the water tower.

If the yacht is approaching from the W or NW, the end of the submerged breakwater will be cleared by keeping on a transit with the beacon on the prominent above water group of rocks NE of Bibette Head and a beacon on the hill behind at 142° true—see photograph.

17.1. Approaching the north side of Alderney, near Quenard Lighthouse.

17.2. Alderney coastline from Château à L'Etoc to Fort Albert, showing the leading beacons, which have opened out as the yacht has altered course towards the harbour.

17.3. The leading marks for the outer approach are the Douglas Quay white triangular beacon in line with the church at 210°. The principal anchorage lies between the jetty and the breakwater. *E. Bruce.*

17.4. The inside of the breakwater photographed from the Author's *Cohoe I* at anchor during a gale. Within the harbour there was nothing more than an uncomfortable swell. The breakwater has since been repaired.

Alderney (Braye Harbour)

Course may be altered to starboard to enter the harbour when the transit on Douglas Quay beacon is opened up.

In fair weather the submerged breakwater may be crossed safely until half tide down. The deepest water being found about 70 metres off the end of the breakwater by keeping the Pepper Pot Tower on the north side of Fort Essex (on the E side of the island see Chart, p. 85) on the southern slope of Fort Albert at 138° true. This gives 4m8 at half tide and is easy to find after the first trial.

Once inside the breakwater, shelter is found and the harbour widens out. Course may be altered to the anchorage N or E of Braye jetty, which lies between Douglas Quay and the breakwater. There is deep water all along the inside of the breakwater except for some boulders and blocks of stone immediately below it. Douglas Quay on which the beacon stands and rocks north and west of it dry out.

It may be added that the approach and entrance to Alderney Harbour have the advantage that if there is a headwind, so that the yacht has to beat in, the sea will not be unduly rough, blowing directly offshore.

By night. There are two powerful lights which assist in the approach to Alderney at night— Alderney (Quenard) lighthouse (*Fl (4) 15s 24M Siren (4) 60s*) and the Casquets (*Fl (5) 30s 28M Dia (2) 60s*) situated 8 miles to the west.

17.5. The Old Harbour and Douglas Quay showing the light structure and the beacon. It is a good harbour for yachts and other craft which can dry out, with prior permission from the harbour master.

94

Alderney (Braye Harbour)

Alderney Harbour leading lights consist of the front low light on the elbow of Douglas Quay (*Q 17M*) and the rear light on a column 17 m elevation (*Iso 10s 18M*). The leading lights come into transit at 215° true, but as the entrance is narrow a yacht must not depart far from the transit and should make short tacks if the wind heads in the approach. Château a l'Etoc beacon (*Iso W R 4s W10M R 7M*) shows a red sector over the submerged breakwater and white from 111° to 151°. When the yacht is inside the breakwater, course may be altered to the anchorage or as required. The two outer fairway buoys are lit.

Harbour and Anchorage. There are some 48 visitors' yellow mooring buoys N of the fairway, sheltered by the breakwater, a farther 15 S of it and 14 more near Toulouse in the SE corner. The moorings are strong and can accommodate up to four rafted yachts, but in bad weather it is best to secure to them by chain rather than light warps. If all the moorings are occupied there is room to anchor to seaward of them or NE of Douglas Quay. Orange buoys are for local craft only.

There is often an uneasy swell in the harbour, especially in NW gales, and small yachts like to go as close to the inner harbour as their draft allows in order to get less of it. When anchoring be sure to keep clear of the fairway marked by red and green buoys. The holding ground in the harbour varies, consisting of sand or mud or rock and weed in places.

The anchorages are well protected in all directions except from North and East, to which they are exposed, but SW and westerly gales cause a surge. During W to NW gales

17.6. The Inner Harbour, Braye Jetty and the moorings in the shelter of the breakwater. *E. Bruce.*

Alderney (Braye Harbour)

the seas sometimes break in a spectacular manner over the breakwater, as is shown by the photograph taken from the author's yacht on one such occasion many years ago. In bad weather from the NE yachts may find the most sheltered position in the harbour to be in Braye Bay under the lee of the land between Fort Albert and Roselle Point, S or SW of Toulouse Rock in 2m0 to 4m0 or even SSE at neaps but the cross swell will cause heavy rolling.

The Inner Harbour (Little Crabby Harbour). This is small and dries out 0m6 to 3m7. It is reserved for local craft, except for refuelling and water or by special permission of the Harbour Master. The narrow entrance should be approached from north and nothing E of 200° true to avoid the rocks drying 3m5 to 4m3 off the NE side of the entrance.

The Old Harbour is situated about 2 cables south of the outer end of Braye Jetty. It is protected by a short pier with rocks on its north side. The harbour dries out 2m4 to 4m6 on sand. Yachts can dry out (with harbour master's permission) along the south side of the pier and multi-hullers or twin keelers or yachts fitted with legs can dry out on the sand. It is pretty and convenient for going ashore but the beach is kept as clear as possible for bathers.

Facilities. In Braye Harbour land from the anchorage at the dinghy pontoon inside Bray jetty. Return completed Customs forms to the Harbour Master, who is also the Customs Officer or post in the box provided. His office is the square white building near the dinghy slip as also is the Alderney Sailing Club which welcomes visitors and provides a bar and teas during the summer. Yachtsmens' showers and toilets are provided on the eastern side of the jetty, near the RNLI boathouse. Mainbrayce Ltd., nearby at the entrance of the inner harbour, are yacht chandlers and marine engineers where from half tide up yachts can go alongside the quay for diesel, petrol and fresh water. Charts, books and sailing clothes as well as gas and chandlery are available. A ferry launch provides yacht to shore service (call Mainbrayce on VHF 37 or 80). Provisions and drinks and their

17.7. Braye Jetty to left, visitors' moorings are on the righthand side in lines parallel to the breakwater.

delivery can be arranged. Yacht care and maintenance is undertaken and there is a crane capable of lifting 12 tons.

Water for filling cans is available at the tap near the Harbour Master's office. Petrol and oil at warehouse opposite the Diver's Inn just beyond the Old Harbour and groceries at local shops. There are several restaurants.

At St Anne's there are doctors, a cottage hospital, pubs, hotels, banks, garages, shops, PO together with all the facilities of a small town. Early closing day is Wednesday and during the season hotels (as also at Braye) often require reservation in advance for dinner.

Small cargo vessels run weekly to Guernsey, Torquay and France, and there are air services to Southampton, Bournemouth, Cherbourg, Guernsey, Jersey and thence to Dinard. Alderney is a free and easy little place and there are interesting walks along the coast.

Harbour Office and VHF Radio

Call sign—'Alderney Radio'—VHF Channels 16 and 74.
Listening watch at the following times:
Summer: Mar/Apr/May/Sep/Oct—0800 to 1800
        Jun/Jul/Aug—0800 to 2215
Winter: Nov/Dec/Jan/Feb—0800 to 1700 Mon to Fri only.
RDF facility available at the above times.
An aero beacon is established near the Alderney Airport (383 K Hz symbol ALD. Range 50M.
Weather forecasts from the Harbour Master's Office on VHF 74.

Alternative Anchorage

Longy Bay. In westerly and northerly winds anchorage may be found in Longy Bay on the NE side of Alderney in 2m0 to 4m0. Allow for the strong stream across the approach and avoid the rock (dries 0m6) in the middle of the entrance. Longy is not a port of entry but is a pleasant anchorage, with a good restaurant ashore. It is a $1\frac{3}{4}$ mile walk to St Anne's or Braye, but may be useful if late on the tide. If sailing on to Braye a good time to leave is -1 h Dover ($+4$ h St Helier).

18 Guernsey

High Water at St Peter Port: −4 h 31 m Dover (+0 h 16 m St Helier). **Heights above Datum:** MHWS 9m0. MLWS 1m0. MHWN 6m7. MLWN 3m5.
Tidal Stream to SW in Little Russel begins −1 h 30 m Dover (+3 h 25 m St Helier), and to NE +4 h 40 m Dover (−2 h 50 m St Helier); in the Great Russel 5 minutes later. See Tidal Maps for other streams.
Yacht Clubs: Royal Channel Islands YC and Guernsey YC.
Admiralty Charts: 3654, 807, 808 and 3140.

St Peter Port is deservedly popular as it offers good shore facilities for yachtsmen and provides a most convenient port of call, especially for those bound for Brittany. It is also the commercial port which handles the passenger service and cargo produce for the island. There is a marina for visiting yachts in the old harbour and moorings on yellow buoys/pontoons outside the marina entrance, but in mid season St Peter Port becomes very crowded. There is also a marina close at Beaucette Quarry south of Fort Doyle in the NE corner of Guernsey, and the principally commercial harbour of St Sampson where yachts can dry out alongside the quay. Guernsey provides an interesting centre for local cruising as there are numbers of anchorages available in settled weather and offshore winds on the south coast of the island and nearby at Herm and Sark.

The usual approach to St Peter Port is by the Little Russel channel which is not difficult in clear weather, but can be rough if there is a fresh wind against the tide, which is very fast at springs. Alternatively the Great Russel (Chapter 19) may be used for approach, although here also streams are strong and there are overfalls.

When coming from England to visit Guernsey for the first time there is much to be said for leaving the island to the east, and approaching St Peter Port from the south. When approaching from the west, the southabout entrance is not only easier but probably quicker, especially if, on approaching the west of the island, it should be between low water and half tide up (local tide Guernsey), as at this time the tide will serve right up to the harbour after passing St Martin's Point. In case of very poor visibility it is quite essential to take the southern route as the west and north west coast from the Hanois light to the Platte Fougère light is a maze of rocks to a distance of two miles from the coast with strong tides running through them, which makes this landfall unwise without special local knowledge.

Approach from the North
The island of Guernsey is about 90 metres high all along the south coast, and slopes down practically to sea level (with a few exceptions) all along the north coast. As a result, seen from the northern approach, the land is frequently not picked up as soon as the higher contours of Sark (114 m) and Herm (70 m).

The Herm group of islands, islets and rocks extends from the Grande Amfroque at the northerly end, to the Lower Heads buoy at the southerly end, a distance of about 5½ miles, and divides the Great Russel from the Little Russel, which latter is the direct entrance to St Peter Port harbour. This whole group will appear as more or less one island when first picked up from the north.

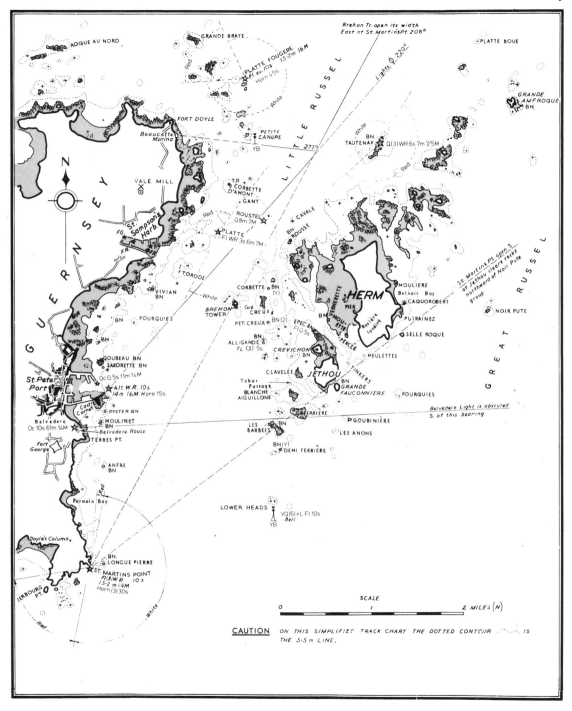

Guernsey, Little Russel and Herm: (Based on British Admiralty Chart No. 808 with the permission of the Controller of HM Stationery Office and of the Hydrographer of the Navy.)

Guernsey

18.1. The Grande Amfroque is the first port-hand mark approaching the Little Russel and is left well to port. Note the resemblance to the Casquets. *A. J. Barber*.

18.2. Platte Fougère Lighthouse (starboard).

18.3. Tautenay Light Tower (port).

18.4. Rousse (far to port).

18.5. Roustel Light Tower (to port).

18.6. Brehon Tower (Lit) (far to port).

18.7. Petite Canupe S Cardinal Light.

18.8. Corbette D'Amont (starboard). Yellow.

18.9. Platte Rock Light Tower (starboard). Green top.

18.10. Vivian Beacon (starboard).

18.11. Belvedere House (Light is 40 m to NW).

The Little Russel

On approaching the north of the Little Russel the first starboard-hand mark is Platte Fougère Lighthouse, white with a black waistband, 15m high. This stands in the sea 1 mile NE of the most north-easterly point of Guernsey. *Note.* Do not let the Platte Fougère bear anything east of south (mag), or come on with the island of Jethou (which is about the same thing).

The first port-hand mark is the most northerly island of the Herm group called Grande Amfroque, with two stone towers (lower white, higher BW HS. Both unlit.).

The second port-hand mark is the Tautenay Tower, BWVS harbour leading marks clear to the west of this about ½ mile and rather more from Amfroque, but as these are not always easily seen take as a leading mark Bréhon Tower open its width east of the extremity of St Martin's Point (the SE corner of Guernsey). If you are approaching from due north as from the Casquets you will not be so far east as this and will come on with the leading marks lower down the Russel, but if approaching from the NE, as from the Race of Alderney, Grande Amfroque should be left 1 mile to port. Platte Boue (dries 1m8 LAT), 8 cables NNW of Grande Amfroque, is the most northerly rock of the Herm group and the two Grande Amfroque towers in line lead on to it. It is cleared by ½ mile by the harbour leading lights and by 1 mile with St Martin's Point bearing 208°, and Bréhon Tower open its own width to the eastward. This is very important in approaching with light breeze, as the ebb tide sets very strongly towards Amfroque, especially immediately after local LW.

The next port-hand marks are: Roustel Tower, BW chequered and, farther south, Bréhon Tower, 17m high, with a small light beacon on top, roundish in shape and so fat as to have a silhouette practically square. Roustel has plenty of water quite close up, but beware drying rocks to the NE. Bréhon Tower has a half-tide ridge of rocks from W to NW of it and about 1½ cables away.

When coming up with Roustel you will see away to port a large conical rock with a small yellow tower surmounted by crossed anchor flukes, the Rousse, and more importantly to starboard two towers, both having outlying low-tide rocks on their E sides. First the Corbette d'Amont Tower, yellow, unlit and farther south the Platte Rock Tower, Green, lit. It should be noted that there are three outlying dangers to the eastward of the line joining these two towers. From N to S they are—Tasse, 2 cables east of Corbette d'Amont, drying 0m9; Le Gant, 2 cables south-east of Corbette d'Amont, drying 0m6, and an unnamed boue, 1½ cables east of Platte Rock 0m3 below chart datum.

Before this you will have come on with the leading harbour marks which pass less than a cable NW of Roustel. The lower one is the South Breakwater Lighthouse. The upper one is the square white light structure 40m NW of Belvedere House, not easily seen in the afternoon sun; but this does not matter as, having passed Roustel, you are all clear to port with the exception of Bréhon Tower with its already mentioned half-tide off lying rocks and after that open water, while for the starboard-hand the Platte Rock Tower on with Corbette d'Amont or Platte Fougère will lead well clear of all the small rocks off St Sampson's harbour (the entrance to which is south of the Platte Rock). When Bréhon Tower has come on to the south of Herm all the small rocks to the SE of St Sampson's (the Torode patch) will have been passed, Vivian Tower BWHS being to starboard at this point.

When entering St Peter Port keep a sharp look out for ferries and other vessels entering or leaving.

Guernsey

By night

Platte Fougère	*Fl WR 10s 15m 16M Horn 45s*
Hanois	*Fl (2) 5s 30m 23M Horn (2) 50s*
Pointe Robert	*Fl 15s 65m 28M Horn(2) 30s*
Bec du Nez	*Fl (4) WR 15s 14m 8M*
Tautenay	*Q (3) WR 6s 7/6M*
Roustel	*Q 7M*
Bréhon Tower	*Iso 4s 19m 9M*

Bearings on the first three of these lights will give an accurate fix till Hanois and Pointe Robert are lost at about 2 miles north of Platte Fougère when Tautenay and Roustel should be visible. When approaching from the NW, keep Pointe Robert light visible to clear north of the Grandes Brayes.

Roustel should then be brought on with Bréhon Tower 198°. This line will cross from the red to the white of the Platte Rock tower (starboard-hand mark) (*Fl WR 3s 6m 7M/5M*) at a point about 1 mile N of Roustel, having left Platte Fougère ¾ mile to starboard. This line (Roustel on Bréhon) leads down west of the leading lights of St Peter Port Harbour, which are Upper, Belvedere Light, (*Oc 10s 14M*) 40m NW of Belvedere House, Lower, South Breakwater Light (*Alt WR 10s 16M Horn 15s*). These lines will converge at about 2 cables N of Roustel (port-hand mark) the line of the leading lights at 220° passing less than a cable west of it.

When approaching from the NE the leading lights will naturally be brought on before the Roustel–Bréhon line. It is important to keep in the white sector of the Tautenay and to bring the harbour leading lights on while the Platte Fougère bears less than 245° true in order to be well clear of the Platte boue, off the NW of Grande Amfroque. *Note.* The red sector of the Platte Rock Tower covers all the rocks on the west side of the Little Russel, both north and south of itself *with the exception of* two boues already mentioned, one of them 2 cables NE, the other 1½ cables due E of the light itself. Bréhon Tower will be left ½ mile to port.

West of the Island

The Hanois Lighthouse 33m high, standing on rocks about a mile west of Pleinmont Point at the SW of the island, is cleared on its SE, S, and SW sides by a distance of a ¼ mile. To the NNW of it stand the Mauve Rocks (6m7 high) and to the W and NW of these are numerous low patches and ¾ mile north of it the notorious Banc des Hanois.

When approaching to round this lighthouse anywhere from the north keep the lighthouse open to the westward of Les Trois Pères (three large black rocks) 1 mile to the NE of it. (These will be seen between Lihou Island and the lighthouse.) This clearing mark coincides with bearing 201° true as marked on the chart and *just* clears W of all the rocks N and NW of Lihou Island, which forms the NW corner of Guernsey, but does *not* clear the Banc des Hanois, to clear which the lighthouse will have to be bearing 146° true. On this bearing the Mauve Rocks come on with the lighthouse. Give the Mauve Rocks a berth of half a mile till due west of the lighthouse; then all is clear.

Of course all this interesting part can be avoided by just keeping an offing of 4 miles all the way round. It is not advisable to try cutting inside the lighthouse without local knowledge aboard!

18.13. St Martin's lighthouse from the NE. Longue Pierre beacon and rocks lie about 1½ cables east (mag) of the lighthouse and are out of this picture.

18.12. Les Hanois Lighthouse on the SW of Guernsey.

Approach from the Southward

The south coast of the island is about 6 miles long running east and west and about 90 metres high all the way along, extending from Pleinmont Point at the SW to St Martin's Point at the SE. The whole of this coast between Les Hanois and St Martin's is clear of rocks at ½ mile from the cliffs.

Just to the south of Pleinmont Point and 1.6 miles from the Hanois stands the Gull Rock, or Tas de Pois d'Aval, 13m0 high and ¾ cable from the cliff. The Hanois light open south of this rock clears south of all rocks along the south coast (but passes close to Molière 3 cables E of it). When the German Watch Tower bears 360° the unmarked drying reef of Les Lieuses will be abeam and course may be altered to port to 090°. *Note.* Hanois lighthouse visible between Gull Rock and the land leads very close to Les Kaines d'Amont and Les Lieuses.

St Martin's Lighthouse is a small square white house on the rocky point at the bottom of the cliff. Longue Pierre Rock, marked with a yellow beacon, letters LP, is 1½ cables East of the lighthouse. This is the port-hand mark of entry to the Little Russel and when kept open W of Bréhon Tower leads clear to the east of all the rocks to the S of St Martin's and

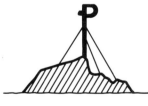

18.14. Longue Pierre 1½ cables E of St Martin's Point.

18.15. Goubeau 1 cable NW of Sardrette.

18.16. Sardrette just N of the entrance to St Peter Port.

Guernsey

Jerbourg Points. A straight line from Longue Pierre beacon to the harbour breakwater lighthouse (2 miles) which passes through Anfré (yellow beacon letter A) clears east of everything up this coast to the harbour with the exception of half-tide rocks a cable or less just to the SE and south of Castle Cornet. To clear these keep 2 cables from Castle Cornet by having N pier light open N of Castle Breakwater. Get this mark on when abreast of Terres Point and the Bathing Pool.

The starboard-hand mark of entry is the Lower Heads S cardinal buoy (*Q (6) + LFl 15s Bell*), 2¼ miles E of St Martin's Point. This buoy is 2 cables SE of the Têtes d'Aval or Lower Heads Rocks (dry at MLWS) and marks the southernmost point of the rocks and shoals S of Jethou. *Note.* The flood sets very strongly to the NE over these rocks and there can be nasty overfalls here in strong wind against tide.

From the Lower Heads, the Ferrières run about due north up to Jethou, well marked by the Demi Ferrière (yellow beacon letter M) which has 1 cable to its west side a boue called Musé (dries 1m2), Les Barbées (yellow beacon barrel topmark), and Blanche Aiguillon (4m), unmarked (close up to Jethou).

From a cable or two westward of this line all is clear up to the harbour.

By night. There are no lights on the south coast of Guernsey, except on the west Les Hanois (*Fl (2) 5s 33m 23M Horn (2) 60s*) and to the east St Martin's (*Fl (3) WR 10s 14M Horn (3) 30s*). The latter has red sectors covering the landward side north and south of itself and a white sector extending from about SSW round to about NNE.

Approaching from the westward a stranger will prefer to keep well away from the coast by cross bearings on these lights. By keeping Hanois Light open of (unobscured by) Pleinmont Pt, Les Lieuses and all dangers east of them will be avoided, and the yacht will enter the white sector of St Martin's Light about 2 miles to the south, and may then alter course towards the light. The Hanois Light will be occluded by the Gull Rock when the yacht crosses the transit and will reappear again between the rock and the land.

When finally approaching St Martin's Point in the white sector the lighthouse must be given a berth of 1½ cables to the eastward to clear Longue Pierre Rock. Open White Rock (North Pier) lighthouse (*Oc G5s 14M*) east of Castle Cornet to clear Longue Pierre and all dangers up to and including Anfré. North of this the eastern edge of the northerly red sector of St Martin's Light covers all rocks up the coast to the harbour.

Approaching from the SE direction, if the NE tide is running (commences 3 hrs before local HW), especially at Springs, keep right on to St Martin's Light until the Lower Heads buoy bears about NE.

Approach the St Peter Port harbour with Victoria Marina South Pierhead Lt (*Oc R 5s 7M*) showing between White Rock Lt to starboard and Castle Breakwater Lt *Al WR 10s 10M Horn 15s*) to port. Once into the entrance flashing red and green buoys show the fairway to the visitors' (Victoria) marina.

St Peter Port Harbour

A red light by day or by night at the signal station on the north pier-head prohibits entry of vessels except boats of 15m or less under power which may proceed keeping clear of the main fairway. Yachts will be received by a Port Control dory, which will indicate a berth and also hand over Customs and Immigration forms for completion. Yachts may be directed to moorings in the Pool, or, with sufficient rise of tide, into the Victoria marina in the old harbour. Anchoring requires the permission of the Harbour Master.

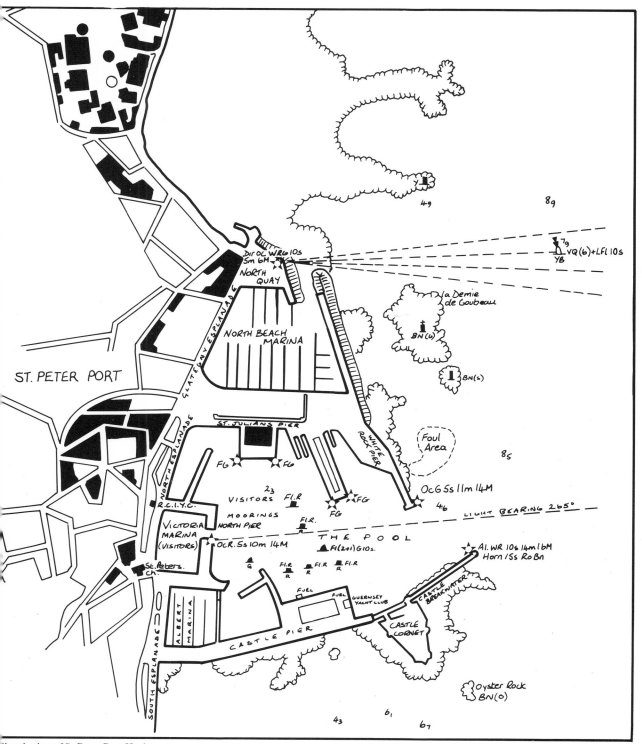

St. Peter Port

DIR OL WRG 10s
5m 6M

NORTH QUAY

NORTH BEACH MARINA

GLATEGNY ESPLANADE

NORTH ESPLANADE

St. JULIANS PIER

R.C.I.Y.C.

VICTORIA MARINA (VISITORS)

St. PETERS CH.

SOUTH ESPLANADE

ALBERT MARINA

FG

FG

VISITORS MOORINGS
2₃

Fl.R

Fl.R

NORTH PIER

OcR.5s 10m 14M

G

Fl.R

Fl.R

FG

FG

Fl.(2+1)G 10s

Fl.R

Fl.R

THE POOL

FUEL

FUEL

GUERNSEY YACHT CLUB

CASTLE CORNET

CASTLE PIER

CASTLE BREAKWATER

Al. WR 10s 14m 16M
Horn 15s Ro Bn

WHITE ROCK PIER

OcG 5s 11m 14M

4₆

LIGHT BEARING 265°

8₅

Foul Area

la Demie de Goubeau

BN(W)

BN(S)

4₉

8₉

VQ(6)+LFl 10s
7₉
YB

Oyster Rock
BN(O)

4₃

6₁

6₇

Sketch plan of St Peter Port Harbour

Guernsey

18.17. Entrance to St Peter Port showing fuelling berth on the left and entrance channel to Victoria Marina.

The visitors' moorings in the Pool consist of several large yellow buoys, pontoons east of the marina entrance and a larger waiting pontoon to lie alongside prior to entry into the marina. The pontoon and the inner buoys have at least 1.5m and the outer ones lie in 2m least water. Fuel (but not p.m. on Sundays) and fresh water is available with sufficient rise of tide at Castle Emplacement on the south side of the harbour, where there is a marine engineer and yacht repairs can be arranged. There are pontoons for tenders at the foot of steps on N and S sides of the entrance to the marina.

In the marina there are pontoon berths for boats up to 12.8m l.o.a. and 1.8m draft. The sill at the entrance dries 4.2m LAT and there is about 0.85m at half-tide. Movements in and out are normally restricted to 2½ hours either side of HW. The depth over the sill is clearly shown by the tide gauges on either side. Control lights are positioned on the S pierhead of the marina entrance where the Marina Office is also situated. A 24 hour watch is maintained on Channel 12. Telephone number is 0481 25987. Water is available on the pontoons and there are good toilet, washing and laundry facilities nearby.

Immediately south is the Albert Marina for local yachts. To the north of the harbour is the Queen Elizabeth II Marina, also mainly for local yachts although some berths may be allocated to visitors at the discretion of the Harbour Master.

The entrance fairway is marked by two orange (rear) and yellow (front) rectangular daymarks, 270° true, which lead S of Refee S cardinal buoy (*VQ (6) + LFl 10s*) about 4 cables to seaward. Port and starboard hand buoys (lit) are situated off the northern end of the E mole. At night, the white sector of a directional light (*Oc WRG 10s 6M*) gives safe passage. An auto tide gauge shows actual depth above the gate in either open or closed positions. Enter or leave by the starboard gate.

The only outside anchorage for yachts at St Peter Port lies in Havelet Bay immediately south of the harbour. It is entered from east between the beacons on Oyster Rocks (yellow beacon letter O) on the north and Moulinet (yellow beacon letter M) on the south. There are private yacht moorings at the north of the bay but plenty of room to anchor in the centre in from 2ml to 1ml LAT. The anchorage is a fair weather one, sheltered from WSW through W to N, but even so swell sometimes creeps in towards high water.

18.18. St Peter Port Harbour.

Customs and Immigration forms, handed out by Port Control Authority on arrival, must be completed and posted in one of the yellow Customs post boxes provided.

Facilities are excellent. There are many hotels and restaurants and very good shops of all kinds. Yacht chandlers and repair facilities for hulls, rigging, engines, electrics and sails are conveniently available.

The Royal Channel Islands Yacht Club is hospitable and faces the Victoria Pier on the N side of the marina, and the clubhouse of the Guernsey YC lies just east of the model yacht pond on Castle Pier. Communications by ferry to Poole or St Helier. Hydrofoil to St Helier, Weymouth and St Malo. Local services to Alderney, Herm and Sark. From Guernsey Airport there are frequent and extensive air connections.

Beaucette Marina

The Beaucette Marina was created by blasting a channel from the sea to a quarry about 2 cables south of Fort Doyle at the NE tip of Guernsey. The marina is deep and very well sheltered. The approach presents no particular problems in normal weather with a free wind or under power and is said to be less rough than the Little Russel, but it should not

Guernsey

be attempted for the first time in strong winds between N and E, and in NE winds of no more than force 5 the entrance may be difficult as the swell sets across the narrow entrance on to the south head.

The approach from the Little Russel is made from a point approximately half-way between Platte Fougère lighthouse and the Roustel light tower. The line between them should not be crossed until Petite Canupe S cardinal beacon and the leading marks have been identified. The rock faces of the marina entrance are conspicuous from seaward as they are painted white on both sides over a large area. The front leading mark is a wide vertical red line superimposed on white on the North Head of the entrance, and the rear mark is a pole erected on the roof of the Main Building which carries horizontal cross pieces painted red with a vertical white stripe but is difficult to see when the sun is behind it. The pole has a wind sock, and immediately to the left of the Main Building two large greenhouses are visible. Bring the marina leading marks in line at 277° and keep closely to their transit. This leaves to the northward: Petite Canupe S cardinal beacon (Q6 + LFl 15s), Grune Pierre, dries 2m, and four green conical buoys. To the southward: Grune La

18.19.   Entrance   to   Beaucette Marina.

18.20. Beaucette Marina looking South.

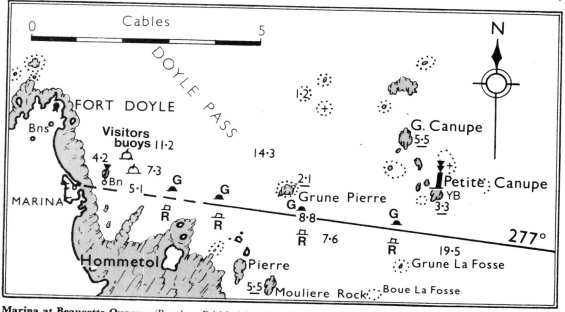

Marina at Beaucette Quarry: (Based on British Admiralty Chart No. 808 with the permission of the Controller of HM Stationary Office and of the Hydrographer of the Navy and approximate local information.) The entrance channel is marked by 4 port (red) and 4 starboard (green) buoys.

Fosse, Pierre and four red can buoys. The approach channel, until close to the entrance, is deep except where it passes close to the rocks shown on the accompanying chart, so keep strictly to the leading marks. The tidal streams run fast across the approach, but soon weaken towards the land and there is no current within a cable of the entrance.

When 70 metres from the entrance the leading line may be left as a slight southerly deviation will be necessary to clear the North Head, NNE of which there is a rock marked by a black beacon. Immediately after passing through the entrance channel (18 metres wide) a fairly sharp turn to the southward should be made to clear the white painted breakwater to starboard.

The sill at the entrance dries 2m3 LAT. There is about 2m7 at half tide. Tide gauges are placed inside and outside the entrance channel. While awaiting rise of tide, craft can moor to the yellow buoys placed about 100 metres off the marina entrance, a little north of the leading line. At night red leading lights are illuminated.

Within the marina, berths are provided for yachts moored bows to buoys and sterns to pontoons, where water is laid on. Customs clearance and comprehensive facilities including fuelling point, chandlery and grocers shop, good licenced restaurant, telephones, car park etc. Bus or hire cars to St Peter Port. Berths are available for visitors but it is best to reserve in advance. Tel STD 9481 45000, or VHF Marina Channel 37.

St Sampson's Harbour

The harbour dries out and is not generally used. There is about 3m0 in the entrance at half tide.

The approach is about ½ mile SW of the Platte Rock beacon, between the SW Platte rocks on the north side and the Torode rocks on the south. Off the south side of the

Guernsey

entrance is a red beacon on Grunette rocks. Approach with the Harbourmaster's office (clock tower) in line with the south pierhead (not outer breakwater). This leads up to the pierheads. Be prepared for a strong tide setting athwart the course.

By Night the approach is on the transit of the leading lights (*FR front 11m FG rear 14m*) at 295° but close to the transit there are the Torode and Grunette rocks. Do not confuse the leading lights with the lower 3m lights *R* and *G* on the outer piers ends.

Other Anchorages

Anchorages on the N and W of Guernsey require local knowledge, owing to the dangers in the approaches and the strong streams.

On the S coast of Guernsey there are beautiful anchorages which, in northerly winds and settled weather, are preferable to the crowded St Peter Port, except that they provide only beach landings (except on the rough slipway at Saints Bay). These are easy of access, as although there are rocks in the bays, they are few in number and clearly marked on the chart. The first bay is Petit Port, ½ mile W of St Martin's Point. Guernseymen regard the eastern corner of the bay as the Petit Port, which has some 200 precipitous steps at the landing. The western end of Moulin Huet Bay (the bay proper) offers a relatively easy ascent with few steps. Both bays need care when landing in a dinghy, as there is often an awkward swell, even in offshore winds. There is landing on sand except at high water.

Saints Bay is W of Moulin Huet Bay, but is included on the Admiralty chart under the general heading of Petit Port. It provides a summer fishing-boat anchorage with summer moorings and a rough slipway on its western side. The bay is open to the SE.

Icart Bay lies W of Icart Point and the bays just mentioned. It consists, from E to W, of La Bette Bay, Jaonnet Bay and Petit Bot Bay. The first two have extremely precipitous clambers up cliff paths and are not recommended. Petit Bot, which is stony above half tide, has a tea-room, road and a bus service. The bay is guarded by a group of rocks and should be approached with caution at low water. Clearance must be obtained at St Peter Port before landing at these anchorages if coming from 'foreign', and all are subject to swell, occasionally even in offshore winds.

Radio Facilities

St Peter Port Radio maintains constant watch on 2182 kHz, H3E MF and Channel 16 VHF. Working frequencies are MF 1810 kHz, J3E and VHF Channel 78. Telephone number of St Peter Port Radio is 0481 20085.

A radio beacon in position (South) Breakwater Lighthouse, is continuous on a frequency of 285 kHz, identification signal 'GY', range 10 miles. The Radio Beacon is synchronised with the fog horn for distance finding. Blast begins simultaneously with 27 sec. long dash after 4 × GY identification signals. The number of seconds from start of long dash until blast heard (× 0.18) is distance from horn.

An aeronautical radio beacon near Pleimont Point is continuous on a frequency of 361 kHz, identification 'GUR' range 25 miles.

A link call service is available on VHF Channel 62.

Recorded weather forecasts can be obtained by telephone 0481 64033.

19 Herm, Jethou and the Great Russel

High Water and Tidal Data: See Guernsey.

Tidal Streams along the eastern shore more or less conform to the stream in the Great Russel as shown in the Tidal Atlas i.e. to NE + 4h 45m Dover (− 2h 45m St Helier) and to SW − 1h 25m Dover (+ 3h 30m St Helier). Around the northern and western shores the offlying shoals and islets occasion a number of diverse eddies and cross currents.

In the Percée Passage the stream runs SE for 9 hours from local LW and NE for 3 hours from half tide down.

Herm, originally Crown Property, now belongs to the States of Guernsey and is at present leased to a tenant. As the island has a rocky coast, with wide sandy bays (including the famous shell beach), it attracts many visitors, and there is a stream of boats between it and St Peter Port during the holiday months. The island is well worth seeing and has a good anchorage. There is an hotel, a tavern, and a café.

Jethou, with its two satellite islets (attached to it below half-tide mark), Crevichon to the NW and Grande Fauconnière to the SW, is still Crown property and privately leased.

The Passe Percée

The Passe Percée, called and pronounced colloquially 'The Pershee', is the passage from the Little Russel to the Great Russel between Herm and Jethou and is navigable at all states of the tide.

The approach to the Percée which is most often used lies between two groups of rocks to the SE of Bréhon Tower, both marked by beacons. The northward one Petit Creux (dries 3m3) Red post, topmark C, and the southward one is Alligande (dries 6m1) Green post topmark A (*Fl (3)G 5s*). Pass between these beacons (nearer to Alligande) on the transit Vermerette, Yellow post topmark V (*Fl (2)Y 5s*), and the White patch on the end of Herm pier, leaving Godfrey (dries 4m0) Green post topmark GB ½ cable to starboard. (The passage is narrow at low tide when marks should be kept dead on.)

When north of Epec, Green post topmark E (*Fl G 5s*), bear to starboard on the transit Vale Mill, and associated building (the tallest tower on NE Guernsey), open twice its width S of Corbette, Yellow post topmark white disc, to leave Gate (Percée) Rock W Cardinal beacon (*Q (9) 15s*), ½ cable to port.

An alternative approach to the Percée is to the northward of Bréhon Tower, half a mile to the NE of which stands Corbette beacon already referred to. In order to clear the sunken rocks to the N of Bréhon Tower keep this beacon well down to the Herm Pier, and then passing quite close to the S of the beacon keep it open of the Vale Mill, as earlier described, to pass between Vermerette and Epec beacons. The lead of Vale Mill open of Corbette 308° passes close SW of the Gate Rock. To ensure clearing it when covered a detour of about 50 metres can be made SW of the line. The southerly spur of Gate Rock, which is covered above half-tide, is absolutely sheer to 8m2 deep on its S side and has one part of it flattened rather like an old-fashioned milestone with a hole some inches in diameter through the top. Legend has it that in prehistoric times this was a gatepost, as there are still in existence some ancient field gates in Guernsey consisting of two stone posts

Herm, Jethou and the Great Russel

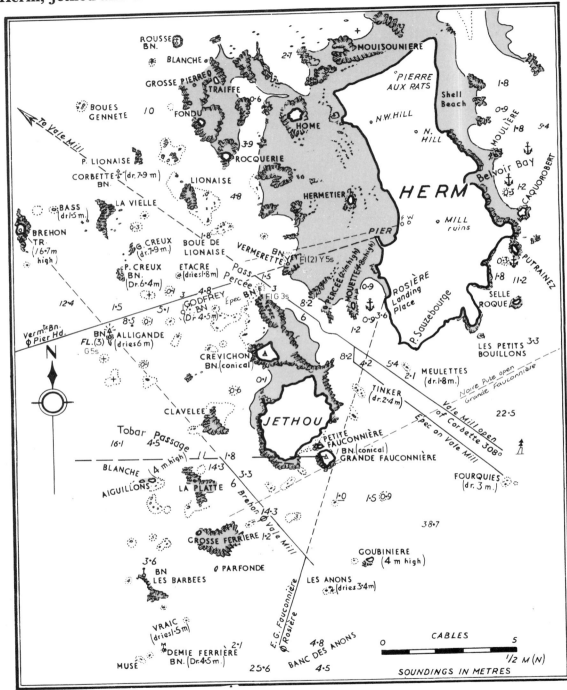

Herm, Jethou and Great Russel: (Based on British Admiralty Charts Nos. 807 and 808 with the permission of the Controller of HM Stationery Office and of the Hydrographer of the Navy.)

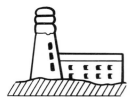

19.1. Vale Mill, on Guernsey, the principal landmark. From SE.

19.2. Corbette Beacon with Vale Mill open twice its own width S of beacon leads through the Passe Percée.

19.3. Vermerette beacon on N of Passe Percée. *(Fl (2) Y 5s)*

19.4. Epec Beacon on S of Passe Percée. *(Fl G 5s)*

with holes in the tops for a spar to pass through. As, even today, the LWS outline of Herm includes this Gate Rock and also an area of beach and rocks on its west side nearly as large as the island itself the opinion is held by some that it was a boat mooring in ancient times when the sea level was lower—or perhaps the islands higher.

After leaving the Gate Rock to port a second big rock, Mouette, 5m high, will be seen to the eastward. Between this and the Rosière landing steps is the anchorage, but to enter near LW a wide sweep must be made to avoid the shoal which extends 1 cable east of Gate Rock. Herm Harbour is ¼ mile north. Both are described later.

Continuing on the transit through the Percée, there are no outstanding rocks between Rosière and the S Point of Herm (Pointe Sauzebourge); but half a cable to the S of this are the Meulettes (dry 1m8), and 2 cables to the SW of these are the Tinkers (dry 2m4) (near the NE of Jethou). To pass between them keep Gate Rock beacon open just W of Vermerette beacon. When St Martin's Point comes open of the Grande Fauconnière you are well clear to the SE of both of these.

Rosière Anchorage and Herm Harbour

Below half tide the anchorage off the Rosière steps is well sheltered from every side except S. The holding ground is indifferent and at local high water there is a SE going tide which is quite strong at Springs, rendering the anchorage uncomfortable even in a light breeze from this quarter, until the sands to the northward dry out. If remaining in the anchorage at night remember that it would be tricky to navigate the Percée in darkness, if this should be necessitated by a change of weather.

Herm Harbour, 3 cables N of Rosière landing is very small and dries out so that it can only be used by yachts above half tide when there is about 1 metre depth. As a rough guide, when the Vermerette Rock is just awash there is about 1m of water at the pierhead.

19.5. Petit Creux beacon, N side of approach from westward.

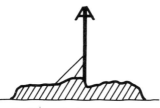

19.6. Alligande beacon, S side of approach from westward. *(Fl (3) G 5s)*.

19.7. Gate Rock beacon YBY *(QkFl (9) 15s)* E side of Passe Percée.

19.8. Vermette beacon at the NE end of Percée Passage.

19.9. The Percée Passage at LWS with Herm harbour in the foreground and Jethou, Crevichon and St Martin's Point beyond.

19.10. Gate Rock W cardinal beacon with Rosière anchorage behind.

There are a few visitors' buoys (with stern lines to the quay) and chain on the beach for boats prepared to dry out. Water and provisions are available and there are no harbour dues!

There are leading marks with white drums, the upper and more easterly being situated at the south end of a long field. The drums are very close together, so that the slightest deviation from their transit makes a considerable difference to the yachts' position. The drum leading marks which are lit (*FW*) should not be used for entering the Passe Percée near low water, because they are almost striking marks for the Etacre and rocks W of it, which would be dangerous at that state of the tide.

Guernsey yachtsmen often return after having had dinner in Herm, with the aid of these lights and the lights on Alligande, Vermerette, Epec and Gate Rock beacons, but strangers are not recommended to make this passage at night.

East Coast of Herm

The east coast of Herm is fairly clean up to Belvoir Bay (a mile from the S Point of Herm), the only rocks being very large and all more or less attached to the coast with the exception of La Selle, or Saddle Rock, an islet which has a clear passage inside it. Having passed the Meulettes, keep St Martin's Point just open of the Grande Fauconnière until Belvoir Bay

19.11. The anchorage off Rosière Steps.

19.12. Herm harbour showing white patches at the end of the jetty and leading marks for the final approach.

opens up to the northward of Caquorobert, a big square rock 15m high close to the shore.

In fine weather Belvoir is a good spot to spend a night round about Neap tides. Here all is clear sand though shallow. Anchor opposite the middle of the south side of the small steep bay on a line between Caquorobert and Moulière. (The rock on the north side of the bay). This anchorage will give about 3m on a really neap tide, but of course dries out on big Springs. One cable E of Moulière will give about 2m1 even at LAT but will be in the tide.

If the wind is NW, there is another good anchorage just S of Putrainez, which is the big slug-shaped rock sticking out from the land between the Saddle and Caquorobert. The south side of this is clean quite close to with about the same water as the other anchorage.

To the north of Belvoir Bay the numerous rocks and strong currents make it inadvisable to explore without local knowledge on board. This also applies to the west coast of Herm.

As a point of interest Caquorobert is said to mean Robert's helmet, and to have been so named by the monks of Mont St Michel to whom this island was given by Robert, Duke of Normandy, father of William the Conqueror.

The Tobars Passage

The Tobars Passage is between the south of Jethou and the Ferrières. Coming from the Little Russel enter about 1½ cables N of the Blanche Aiguillon Rocks (1m2 and 4m0 high), the NW corner of the Ferrières. At this point you are S of the leading marks, but steer with the white beacon on Grande Fauconnière over the south slope of Jethou. This leads south of Clavelée (just west of Jethou) and N of La Platte. When Vale Mill comes into line with Bréhon Tower keep the marks dead on until Noire Pute (Great Russel) opens up to the E of Grande Fauconnière. Then alter course on this line to pass $\frac{1}{2}$ cable E of Grande Fauconnière.

Notes. (1) There is a boue awash at LWS 2 cables south of Grande Fauconnière.

(2) The leading marks of the passage (Vale Mill transit Bréhon Tower) are almost the striking marks for the rocks Les Anons (dry 3m4) SW of Goubinière. Cross striking marks are Goubinière on with Noire Pute.

The Great Russel

Entry from either N or S presents no difficulty in good visibility, as this Russel is practically devoid of covered rocks except along its NW side, that is to say the Humps. By keeping St Martin's Point open to the S of Jethou all those rocks to the N of Noire Pute group are cleared.

South of the Humps, the outlying rocks are:-

(1) Noire Pute, a large black rock a mile east of Herm, 2m high and marked with a pole beacon (*Fl (2) WR 15s*). There are boues which extend up to a cable on its northerly side.

(2) Goubinière, a large loaf-shaped rock 5m high, 4 cables SE of Grande Fauconnière, with Les Annons (Dry 3m3) 2 cables to the SW.

(3) The Fourquies which dry 2m3 and over which the ebb tide runs like a mill race. It is marked by a N Cardinal buoy (Q) one cable to the north of the rock. The Vale Mill on with either the south of Herm or the north tangent of Jethou clears it to the NE or SW respectively.

At night, the red sector of Noire Pute light covers all dangers on the E coast of Herm and Jethou.

The east side of the Great Russel is quite clear, being bounded by the Bec du Nez, (the north point of Sark), (*Fl(4)WR 15s*) and the island of Brecqhou, with its outstanding islet, La Givaude, 11m high, which is clean up to 2 cables away.

The biggest overfalls in the Great Russel lie between Brecqhou and the Lower Heads S cardinal buoy (*Q(6)*) + *LFl 15s*). There are four or five patches, the more easterly ones being the worst. The overfalls to the east of Sark right out to the Blanchard buoy can at times be as bad if not worse. These are not places to be with a lot of wind on either strong flood or ebb.

20 Sark

Heights above Datum: St Peter Port. MHWS 9m0. MLWS 1m0. MHWN 6m7. MLWN 3m5. On the east of Sark at Creux Harbour the rise is stated to be 0m6 higher MHWS, 0m3 MHWN.
Tidal Streams near middle of Great Russel. The NE stream begins +0440 Dover (−0250 St Helier) and the SW stream begins −0125 Dover (+0330 St Helier). (See Notes below)

Situated about 7 miles east of St Peter Port this island is a part of the Bailiwick of Guernsey and thereby is to a certain extent under Guernsey law. Nevertheless it has its own administrative body, the Court of Chief Pleas, and also a Seigneur, some of whose feudal rights have not been altered since the time of William the Conqueror.

It is considered by many the most beautiful of the Channel Islands, and though small (about 3 by 1½ miles) its coastal scenery certainly has a dramatic quality not found elsewhere in these islands, and the visitor's pleasure is undisturbed by motor traffic, cars not being allowed on the island.

Perhaps its most startling feature is La Coupée, a place where the whole width of the island narrows to a knife-edged ridge of cliff, in places only a few feet wide, which has been built up and widened to carry the precariously perched, and only, road joining the two portions of the island—Sark and Little Sark. Standing on this one-cart-wide causeway at a height of about 75 m one can see sheer down to the sea on both sides at the same time. Even at sea level the width of the island here is only ½ cable. From this point there is a pathway down on the west side to Grande Grève Bay, but the east side is practically sheer and scalable only by expert climbers.

Another spot which has to be seen to be believed is the Creux Harbour, which gives one the slightly unreal impression of a film set. It is a tiny rock-bound cove in the middle of the east coast protected by a pier and sheltered outside by grass-covered islands, the Burons. As the cliffs surrounding the harbour are nearly sheer, a tunnel has been bored through the solid rock leading to the bottom of a valley which runs up to the middle of the island. Just to the north of this old harbour the new jetty, in Maseline Bay, has been built which is joined to the same valley by another tunnel.

To complete the spectacular, on the west coast the island of Brecqhou is separated from Sark by the Gouliot Passage, which is only 70 metres wide, a clear cut gash between high cliffs.

The water round Sark is deep and most of the above-water rocks are quite sheer; but most are covered at high water. The tides are very strong and the range great, which produces bad overfalls in some places. Even in fine weather these are best avoided at spring tides. The positions of the principal races are marked on the chart.

Note

A tidal stream atlas may be referred to for direction and rates of the main streams off Sark, but the scale is too small to show, even by hair lines, the streams and eddies close in to the coast. For this information the Author has consulted Mr R. C. Adams, who is an authority on the Sark tidal streams, and he has generously provided the summary which appears on page 125. He says there can be no set rules or precise times as there is so much variation between spring and neap tides, and particularly on the east coast times and heights are also influenced by prevailing meteorological conditions.

Sark

The East Coast (N to S). On the east coast there are three precipitous and grass-capped islets with navigable passages between them and the island. The two northerly ones, Petite Moie 14 m high and Grande Moie 25 m high, are close together and immediately visible on rounding the north of Sark. The third isle, the Burons 16 m high, exactly opposite the Creux Harbour, will be hidden by Pointe Robert, on which the lighthouse stands, until the Pécheresse Rock is passed.

The north point of Sark named Bec du Nez may be passed on the N and NW sides at a

20.1 The Noire Pierre near low water. The Burons just open of Pointe Robert with this rock in the gap clears dangers NE of Sark. The rock may be passed on either side.

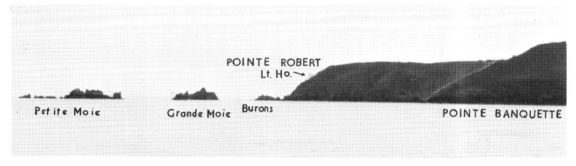

20.2. The Burons just clear of the land.

20.3. The passage between Grande Moie and Pointe Robert. Keep rather to land side of the centre of the passage.

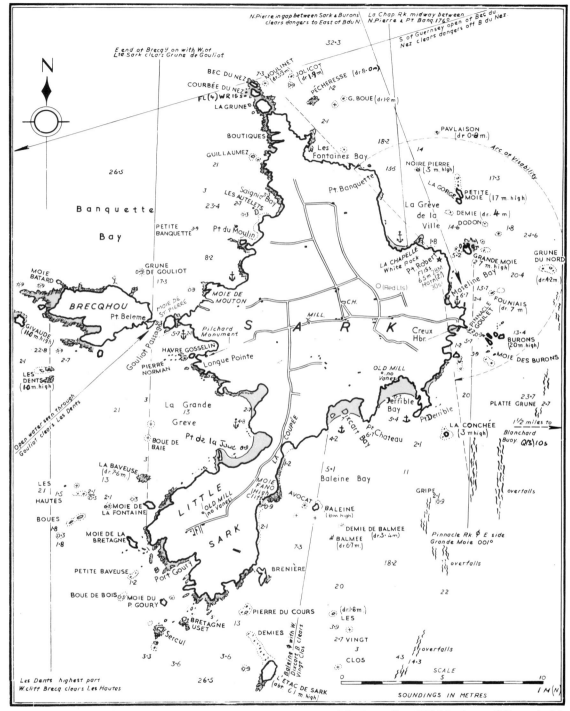

Sark: (Based on British Admiralty Chart No. 808 with the permission of the Controller of HM Stationery Office and of the Hydrographer of the Navy.)

20.4. Maseline harbour with Founiais beacon in the foreground.

NOIRE PIERRE

20.5. Looking N from a position off Maseline Bay and just inside Founiais beacon.

distance of 1 cable. Three cables to the E of it is Pécheresse (dries 8m), which has several boues around it. Moulinet (dries 3m3) and Jolicot (dries 2m) lie NW between it and Bec du Nez and Grande Boue (dries 1m8) is 1½ cables E of it. To clear to the N of all these keep the South of Guernsey open of the Bec du Nez.

To the SE of Pécheresse are the Petite Moie and Grande Moie already mentioned. Three cables NW of Petite Moie is Noire Pierre, 3m0 high, a black slab-shaped rock. Keep Guernsey open until the whole of the Burons have just opened clear of the land. At this point the Noire Pierre will come into the gap. Keep this mark, on leaving Pavlaison (dries 0m8) a cable to port, and pass either inside or outside Noire Pierre, which is quite clean, as also is the land opposite to it (Pointe Banquette).

After passing Noire Pierre keep the E side of the Burons in the middle of the Grande Moie passage in order to pass inside Demie (dries 5m), a rock just S of Petite Moie.

The passage between Grande Moie and Pointe Robert is 140 metres wide but looks much narrower, owing to the height of the cliffs. It has a depth of 6 m MLWS, but there is a group of boues (awash at MLWS) which stretch out from the Grande Moie for about a third the width of the passage. The rest of it is quite clean.

apart, the striking mark for both of which is the west side of the Burons on with Point Derrible. Baleine anywhere on the Coupée and just south of it also puts you on them.

To the south of La Brenière the only rocks outside L'Etac are a patch of shingle, sand and boues known as Les Vingt Clos (curiously enough there are only six of them marked). The northern boue dries 1m8 and the southern is awash at LAT. To pass between these and L'Etac (which is quite clean on its E side) keep Baleine on the W point of Dixcart Bay. To clear round outside keep the E side of Grande Moie just open of Sark. To clear the Vingt Clos on the south side keep the south of Guernsey open S of L'Etac.

It should be noted when navigating on the east side of Sark that the principal overfalls lie between Point Robert and the Blanchard whistle buoy just over 2 miles to the SE, and there are extensive overfalls east and south of La Conchée Rock. The Blanchard rock is nearly $\frac{1}{2}$ mile WNW of the buoy, and at LAT there is only 1m2 over it and weed extends to the surface.

The West Coast (North to South)

The whole of Banquette Bay, which extends from the Bec du Nez down to the island of Brecqhou, is entirely devoid of rocks except within about a cable of the shore with the exception of Grune de Gouliot (with 0m9 of water at LAT), which is 1½ cables from Brecqhou and 3 cables NW of the Gouliot Pass. Marks: E end of Brecqhou on with W side of Little Sark clears well to the E of it.

The island of Brecqhou has on its W side La Givaude, 11m high and on its SW side Les Dents, 1m high. The highest peak of Les Dents is at its most southerly end and is quite clean on the S side. Open water seen through the Gouliot Passage clears Les Dents from the SW.

The Gouliot Passage

This has 3m3 of water at LAT, and a reputed speed of 7 knots at flood on Springs. It is entirely clean on both sides with the exception of a spur which sticks out from the SW corner of the Moie de St Pierre. To clear this see the Bec du Nez (N point of Sark) in the centre of the passages.

20.8. Bec du Nez showing in the centre of the Gouliot Passage.

Sark

On the west side of Little Sark a large patch of boues, Les Hautes Boues (two dry up to 2m1), extends for half a mile. La Pointe de la Joue, on with the south of La Coupée clears to north of all these boues with the exception of two which dry 0m3 at LAT, and are $3\frac{1}{2}$ cables W by N of Pointe de la Joue. The exact marks for these two are not easy to describe, but the west point of the Moie de la Fontaine and the east end of Moie de la Bretagne (two islets close to the west of Little Sark) puts you about on both of them. The highest point of Les Dents on with west cliff of Brecqhou clears to the west of Les Hautes Boues.

The SW side of Little Sark from Les Hautes Boues to L'Etac should not be explored without local knowledge on board.

Harbours and Anchorages

Sark possesses no harbours sheltered from all winds. Creux harbour is tiny and dries out entirely at LWS. In fine weather yachts may lie alongside the northern end of the outer quay at the top half of the tide (depending on draught), leaving the steps at the S end free at all times. There is about 4m at the pierheads at half tide. Those prepared to take the ground can do so along the northern end of the harbour, rafting up as required. Anchorage off Creux harbour is prohibited, as indicated by the red barred anchor sign on the pierhead.

The Maseline jetty offers a deep water alongside berth for strictly limited periods when not in use by ferries. Two visitors' buoys (orange with white tops) are provided NW of the pier or yachts may anchor inside the mooring lines for local craft.

The Sark Harbourmaster keeps listening watch on VHF Channels 16 and 13 when attending at ferry times and whenever possible appreciates visiting yachts calling to confirm anchorage position.

There are telephone booths and water at both harbours with washing facilities between, and tunnels lead to the road up a hill to the scattered village. In the island there are four licensed hotels, two banks, a telephone service via Guernsey, post office. Many small shops. Petrol, paraffin and diesel oil are obtainable. There is a daily commercial boat service a.m. and p.m., except Sundays, when commercial traffic is prohibited.

On the east side of Sark there are many other anchorages in settled offshore winds. North of Pointe Robert is La Grève de la Ville, where a yacht can anchor 1 cable N or NW of La Chapelle Rock, out of the tide and on good holding ground in sand. When the afternoon sun is casting shadow over the high cliff the anchorage looks somewhat forbidding, but it is sheltered from the prevailing wind between south and west and has a landing.

In Baleine Bay there are several anchorages protected from W to N, notably in Derrible Bay or Dixcart Bay. In severe westerly gales the wind comes round the ends of the island as well as gusting down from the heights. Anchorage close in under the lee of the shore in La Grève de la Ville with good ground tackle may be safe, but landing by dinghy is adventurous and the yacht rolls day and night in a spectacular fashion, especially when the wind veers towards NW. However, in these conditions the visitor can count on having the whole anchorage to himself.

On the west side of Sark there are several anchorages in easterly winds in Banquette Bay to the north and La Grande Grève to the south.

Havre Gosselin, to the SE of the Moie de Gouliot, is deep and good anchorage in fine weather with clean bottom. There is a landing and water is clean right up to the cliffs on the north side. The south side of the harbour is guarded by a row of rocks, the westerly end of which is Pierre Norman, which covers at HW Springs. If covered keep the Pilchard Monument (a high tower on the cliff above Havre Gosselin) to the north of the southern spur of the harbour to clear north of Pierre Norman.

By Night. The lights on Sark are Pointe Robert lighthouse (*Fl 15s 65m 28M Horn(2) 30s*) on the east side, and Bec du Nez (*Fl (4) WR 15s 8M*). The Blanchard Whistle buoy (*Q(3) 10s*) lies 2 miles E of Creux Harbour. Fixed white lights of low power (about a mile) are exhibited from the ends of Creux and Maseline jetties.

On the west side the nearest lights are (*Noire Pute (Fl (2) WR 15 secs)* the Lower Heads buoy (*Q (6) + LFl 15s*) south of Herm and St Martin's Point (*Fl (3) white sector*) on the SE of Guernsey. Accordingly, when anchoring off Sark, and intending to stay the night, the position of any light which can be seen should be noted in case of change of weather that may necessitate leaving during darkness.

Inshore streams round Sark

Contributed by Mr. R. C. Adams

The tides around Sark vary all round the coast.

On the east coast at the Pécheresse the tide starts running SE at HW and runs in that direction for 9 hours until after half flood when it turns NW for about $2\frac{1}{2}$ hours. *Note:* The SE tide starts at the Pécheresse or just N of it and runs all along the coast as far as the *Founiais* and turns with the NE tides of the *Déroute* (the offshore passage on E side of Sark) and as far out as the Grande Moie to put the *Conchée* just showing inside Burons and nearly one mile outside *Pavlaison* running more northerly the further N it goes until joining the tides coming down the Great Russel. There is a counter current of less strength inside the Greve de la Ville.

In the GOULET PASSAGE the tide runs about the same as the *Déroute* but it is also always a little earlier in changing either ebb or flood.

At the CONCHEE the SW stream starts running at half ebb and continues running until nearly or about LW depending upon the type of spring tide, whilst at the *Pierre du Cours* it runs SW from half ebb until nearly one hour after LW when it changes and runs in an E direction until half flood, then NE till half ebb.

Inshore taking a line from *Brenière* to Baleine and Derrible Bay it runs in a SW direction from HW until about LW but not with great force except at the Points.

The tide in the *Vingt Clos* and E of L'Etac runs about the same as the *Pierre du Cours*.

On the west coast at the BEC DU NEZ the tidal stream starts running to the W a little before HW or even one hour before HW on a big spring tide and runs towards *Brecqhou* curving to the westward as it approaches the tide coming up the Gouliot Passage; it meets the stream coming between *Givaude* and Brecqhou then runs to the NE. While right inshore it runs in the opposite direction.

In the GOULIOT PASSAGE the tide runs about the same as in the Great Russel, whilst immediately N of Gouliot it starts running N before LW and runs right up to the Bec du Nez where it meets the SW tide running down the Great Russel and keeps on running in that direction until nearly HW. It runs with great force from half flood until one hour before HW.

21 Jersey

High Water, St Helier: −4 h 47 m Dover. **Heights above Datum:** MHWS 11m0. MLWS 1m3. MHWN 8m1. MLWN 4m1.
Depths: All harbours except St Helier and St Catherine Bay, dry out.
Yacht Clubs: Royal Channel Islands Yacht Club (at St Aubin), St Helier Yacht Club and St Catherine's SC.
Admiralty Charts: 3655, 3656, 1136, 1137, 1138, 3278.

Although all harbours in Jersey are tidal, with the exception of St Helier and St Catherine, the island has a beautiful sea coast which offers many sheltered anchorages under suitable conditions. There is a good marina at St Helier and among the anchorages, St Aubin Bay on the south side and Gorey and St Catherine Bay on the east may be noted, and will be referred to later. Visiting yachts, especially those prepared to dry out, will find much interesting navigation and be assured of a pleasant stay in Jersey. The unusual range of spring tides, sometimes over 12 metres, which run in certain places at 4 knots and over, need attention, and the Admiralty Tidal Stream Atlas should be studied. The principle is to use the tides to advantage and to avoid unnecessary battle against them.

All visiting yachts coming from foreign ports, must clear Customs and Immigration authorities either at St Helier or Gorey, and yachtsmen are not allowed to land anywhere in the island until this formality has been completed.

Approaches to Jersey

Because of the rotary nature of the tide, the approaches to Jersey can be considered separately under the following headings:
1. From the North: (A) for St Helier, (B) for Gorey.
2. From the North-West: (A) for St Helier, (B) for Gorey.
3. From the South-West.
4. From the South and South-East: (A) for St Helier, (B) for Gorey.
5. From St Helier to Gorey and the Violet Channel.
6. From the East.

1. Approach from the North
This approach probably by way of the Race of Alderney at or before High Water Dover (+4 h 47 m St Helier) has only two formidable reefs to avoid. These are the Paternosters or Pierres de Lecq and Les Dirouilles, both reefs several miles to the north of Jersey.

(A) **If bound for St Helier** steer for Banc Desormes YBY W. cardinal buoy (*Q (9) 15s*), just over 4 miles WNW of the Paternosters. At a speed of 5 knots, this course from Alderney should give a fair tide and an extra knot until +5 h Dover (−2½ h St Helier) when the tide sets hard to the east. Assuming that the vessel has arrived at the buoy some 4 miles NNW of Grosnez Point, NW corner of Jersey, (*Fl (2) WR 15s 19/17M*) a course should be shaped southward to pass at least 1 mile west of Corbière Lighthouse (*Iso WR*

21.1. La Corbière Lighthouse looking E to Noirmont Point. Note also Lookout, Chimney and old semaphore tower.

10s 18/16M Horn Mo(C) 60s Radio Beacon), allowing for some easterly set of tide. In heavy weather it is well to keep west of the Rigdon Bank to avoid rougher seas.

When about 1 mile due west of Corbière Lighthouse, the course may be altered to round Corbière, keeping the same distance off to avoid the detached reefs. In calm weather if the lighthouse balcony does not appear to be above the high land the distance should be sufficient, but all vessels should guard against a NE set which may take them too close to the out-lying reef. Rounding Corbière Lighthouse by night, do not alter course to the eastward until the Fixed Red Light on the high ground behind the lighthouse is open clear E of Corbiere's occulting light. Note that, having rounded Corbière, yachts must pass through a red sector of Corbiere Lighthouse before reaching Le Fret Point. Until HW St Helier (-4 h 47 m Dover) the flood tide runs easterly along the south coast at a rate of between 1 and 3 knots, according to the range of tide. To approach St Helier after local HW will mean stemming the tide as it ebbs westward, and this adverse factor may require the use of the engine or the advantage of a fresh and fair wind. There are rough seas off La Corbière in strong winds.

It is advisable to reach certain positions on the passage to Jersey at certain states of the tide. An example of this, described briefly, is the punctual arrival in the Race of Alderney at HW Dover ($+4\frac{1}{2}$ h St Helier) or even an hour earlier, the arrival at a position west of Grosnez not more than five hours later and the arrival off Corbière Lighthouse six hours after HW Dover ($-1\frac{1}{2}$ h St Helier) when a fair tide will be continued up to St Helier for the next hour, and the maximum strength of the stream, which causes overfalls off Corbière and especially off Noirmont Point, will be avoided.

To maintain an average speed of 6 knots over the ground, it may be found necessary in light or contrary winds to increase sailing speed by the use of the auxiliary engine before reaching Jersey waters. Without this speed, it would be wise to be prepared for a much longer time, say another five hours, on the journey, or to put into Guernsey, or even make for Gorey. Before describing these alternatives let us continue the approach to St Helier Harbour from Corbière.

Keep a good $\frac{1}{2}$ mile south of Corbière and sail 097° between Pt. Le Fret and Passage Rock BY N. cardinal buoy, *(VQk),* in position 9 cables SW of Le Fret, marking entrance to the Western Passage. Alternatively, it is merely necessary to steer to pass about 2 cables

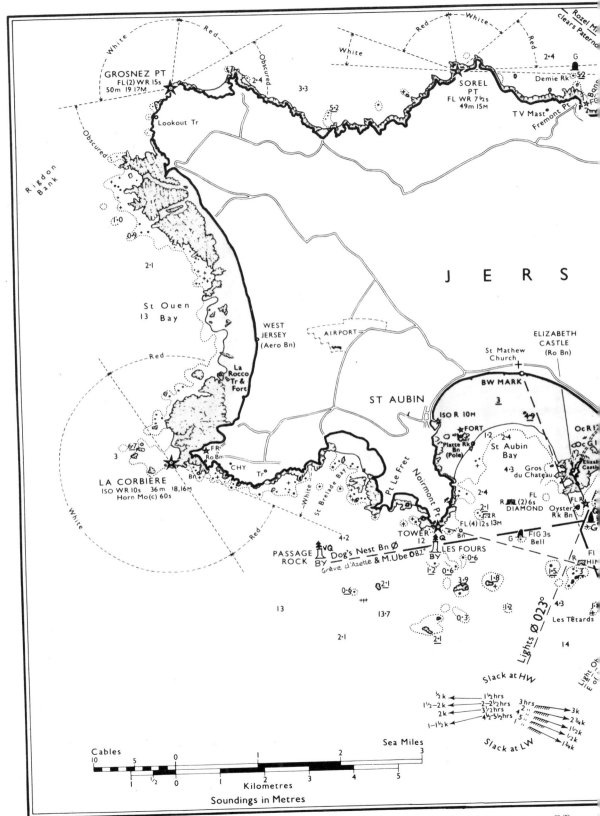

Jersey: (Based on British Admiralty Chart No. 3367 with the permission of the Controller of HM Stationery Office and

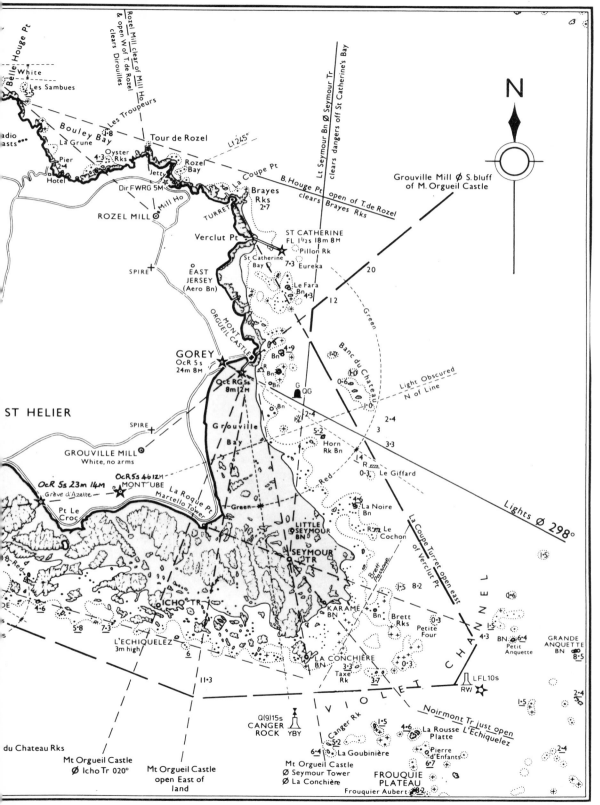

N

Belle Houge Pt

White
Les Sambues
5·5

Radio
Masts...

Bouley Bay
La Grune
Pier
2·4
Hotel

Les Troupeurs
1·8

Oyster
Rks
4·3

Dir FWRG 5M

Tour de Rozel
Rozel
Bay

Jetty

ROZEL MILL
Mill Ho

TURRET

SPIRE

EAST
JERSEY
(Aero Bn)

Rozel Mill clear of Mill Ho
& open W of T de Rozel
clears Dirouilles

Lt 245°

Coupe Pt
Brayes
Rks
2·7

Verclut Pt

St Catherine
Bay

Lt Seymour Bn Ø Seymour Tr
clears dangers off St Catherine's Bay

B. Houge Pt open of T.de Rozel
clears Brayes Rks

Grouville Mill Ø S. bluff
of M. Orgueil Castle

ST CATHERINE
FL 1½s 18m 8M
Pillon Rk
7·3 Eureka
Le Fara
Bn
4·3

20

Green

12

MONT ORGUEIL CASTLE

GOREY
OcR 5s
24m 8M

OcR RG 5s
8m 2M

ST HELIER

SPIRE

GROUVILLE MILL
White, no arms

OcR 5s 4·6 12M
MONT UBE

OcR 5s 23m 14M
Grève d'Azette

Pt Le
Croc

La Roque Pt
Martello Tower

Bn 4·9
R
Bn
Bn

G QG

Bn
2·4

Grouville
Bay

Green

Banc du Chateau
1·0
1·0
0·6
1·0

Light Obscured
N of Line

2·4
3

3·3

5·2
Horn
Rk Bn

14
R
0·3 Le Giffard

Red

4·6
La Noire
Bn

R Le
Cochon

LITTLE
SEYMOUR
BN

SEYMOUR
2 TR

ICHO TR

L'ECHIQUELEZ
3m high

6

11·3

Brett Passage

La Coupe Turret open east
of Verclut Pt

Lights Ø 298°

1·5

VIOLET CHANNEL

1·5 8·2

1·5

0·6

1·5

KARAME
BN

Bn
0·3
Brett
Rks

Petite
Four

BN 6·4
Petit
Anquette

GRANDE
ANQUETTE
BN
8·5

4·3

LA CONCHIÈRE
BN

3·3
Taxe
Rk
3·7

LFL 10s
RW

2·4

1·5

Q(9)15s
CANGER
ROCK YBY

0·3

Canger Rk

1·5
5·2

Noirmont Tr just open
La Rousse L'Echiquelez
Platte

du Chateau Rks

Mt Orgueil Castle
Ø Icho Tr 020°

Mt Orgueil Castle
open East of
land

Mt Orgueil Castle
Ø Seymour Tower
Ø La Conchière

6·4
La Goubinière

4·6

Pierre
d'Enfants
6·7

2·4

FROUQUIE
PLATEAU
Frouquier Aubert 8·2

4·6
7·3
5·8

5·8
7·3

Red

DE

(...drographer of the Navy.) When navigating it is preferable to use the Admiralty Chart itself, this being on much larger scale.

21.2. Noirmont Point. Note also German watchtower.

south of Pointe le Fret and Noirmont Point Light Tower (black tower with white band (*Fl (4) 12s 13M*). There is a race off Noirmont Point and a BY N. cardinal buoy Les Fours (*Q*) 3 cables south of it. Leaving this buoy to starboard the next leading marks should be picked up, to the left of the four prominent blocks of flats. These are the Dog's Nest (white pillar beacon, 4 cables SE of the Breakwater end) in line with the red daymark on the tall, white light-structure of La Greve d'Azette Lt. (*Oc W 5s*) in line with Mont Ubé Lt (*Oc R 5s. 12M Radio beacon*) at 082° T.

This line leaves Pignonet S cardinal beacon, Les Grunes du Port red can buoy and Diamond Rock red can buoy (*Fl (2) R 6s*), to port, and Ruaudière green conical bell buoy (*Fl G 3s*) to starboard. The turn into the inner roads occurs just before reaching East Rock green conical buoy (*Q G*), 2 cables W of the Dog's Nest and when the Oyster Rocks RW beacon, 2 cables SW of the breakwater end, comes abeam. (See St Helier Harbour, pages 135–6.)

(B) **If bound for Gorey**, a course should be set to pass between the Paternosters and the Dirouilles. The marks to clear the Dirouilles on the west side are Rozel Mill just clear of the Mill house and open W of the Tour de Rozel, 171° T. If these cannot be distinguished it would be wise to steer for Sorel Point Lt. Ho. (*Fl WR 7.5s 15M*), and when about 1 mile offshore to alter course ESE towards the Tour de Rozel. The latter is a conical white-washed rock (see photograph 20.4) on the coast just over 1 mile from the NE corner of Jersey. Between Sorel Point and the Tour de Rozel lies the bluff promontory of Belle Hougue, which should be passed at least a half-mile offshore to avoid Les Sambues Rocks (dry 5m5). There is little else to bother about on this north coast as long as a vessel keeps $\frac{1}{2}$ to 1 mile offshore. The TV mast in position bearing 117° from Sorel Point at distance 13 cables is a useful additional aid. At night it has three vertical tiers of *Red lights*, of which the topmost lights eclipse for *1 sec* after a *Flash of 1 sec* at elevation 232 m. There are other smaller masts with single red lights at night above Belle Houge Point and Vicard Point to the east. This part of the passage on a sunny day presents most beautiful scenery. The deep water has a dark blue colour and the white surf breaking at the foot of brown rocky cliffs gives a gentle contrast of colours. Beyond this are green and brown fields with patches of heather and purplish granite rock.

21.3. Tour de Rozel, with white-washed conical rock. It lies between Rozel and Bouley Bay.

At the NE corner of the island are the Brayes Rocks NE of La Coupe Pt., which should be passed ½ mile to the north on a line Belle Hougue Pt. open N of Tour de Rozel 290° T until Mont Orgueil Castle (see photograph 21.14) opens to the east of the white house on the land end of St Catherine's Breakwater, when the course is altered to pass 1 cable off the end of the Breakwater (*Fl 1.5s 13M*). A strong tide causing broken water can be expected over the Pillon rock (covered 1m0 LAT) and the Eureka rock (covered 3m4 LAT), but there should be no danger except at Low Water Springs.

On rounding the breakwater, Seymour Tower comes into view 4 miles to the south. This square tower (line sketch 20.10), though apparently 1 mile off La Rocque shore, dries like most of the surrounding rocks. Three cables to the north of Seymour Tower is a rock named Little Seymour which is marked with a beacon. These two Seymours in line 184° T lead to the south along the east coast until the green conical buoy (*QG*) 4 cables SE of Equerrière Rock beacon (topmark E) has been passed and the leading marks into the Port of Gorey can be picked up—see Gorey Harbour, pages 137–8.

2. Approach from the North-West

(A) **For St Helier.** If sailing from St Peter Port, Guernsey, commence the passage an hour before LW by the shore. With an average speed of 5 knots set a course to pass 2 miles W of Corbière Lighthouse, but see tide maps for set of stream. When in position 1 mile W of Corbière proceed to St Helier in the same way as described in 1 (A).

21.4. La Coupe Point. Viewed from NW. Brayes Rocks can be seen off the point, and St Catherine's Breakwater with white light tower is on the left. The sentry box, pillar and globe barely show in the picture, but they are situated at the summit of La Coupe, ¾ inch to the right of the inner end of the pier.

Jersey

(B) **For Gorey.** Shape a course for Grosnez Point, allowing for tidal streams as shown in the tide maps. On the flood tide the passage along the north coast of Jersey can be speedy and pleasant. If set near to the Paternosters, keep the Tour de Rozel shut in with Belle Hougue on a bearing of 111° T. If identification of these marks is in any way doubtful it will be best to make for Grosnez Point, giving the Paternosters a wider berth. Keep ½ to 1 mile offshore till the Tour de Rozel is passed, then proceed as described in 1 (B).

3. Approach from the South-West

Set a course to pass 2 miles S of Corbière Lighthouse at about half flood and from this position sail on to the St Helier leading marks—Dog's Nest white pillar beacon in line with the red day marks on the tall white light structure of La Grève d'Azette 082° T, passing between Noirmont Point Light Tower and the Les Fours N. Cardinal buoy and from there as described in the latter part of 1 (A).

4. Approach from the South and South-East

(A) **For St Helier.** The visitor is advised to shape a course to pass not more than ½ mile W of Demie de Pas Light Tower YB (*Mo(D) WR 12s 14/10M Horn (3) 60s Radio Beacon*) and to avoid the reefs lying southward of St Aubin's Bay. Demie de Pas is 1½ miles SSE of St Helier harbour. Four cables to the west of St Helier harbour is the historical Elizabeth Castle, from which a breakwater runs SSE to shelter the harbour entrance. On the end of the breakwater are painted BWVS—see photograph 21.5. This breakwater kept end on will lead between Demie de Pas and Les Tetards and east of the Hinguette Rocks, marked by a red buoy (*Fl (4) R 15s*) on their east side, but at low water, when half a mile off the breakwater, the correct leading marks should be picked up. They are the BWVS patch painted on the sea wall, in line with or between the two heads of the Gros du Château Rock (which lies a cable west of Elizabeth Castle) 341° T and are shown in photograph 21.5. The latter marks give a course parallel to and 1½ cables west of the approach keeping the breakwater end on. They avoid the reef running west from the Dog's Nest, marked by a green conical buoy (*QG*).

Course should be altered as soon as the leading marks on the northern part of Albert Pier come into line—see St Helier Harbour, pages 135–6.

(B) **For Gorey.** Coming up to Jersey from the south, by day, a course can be set for Icho Tower (round, top half painted white, see 21.11), which will be sighted somewhere below the high ground of the east of Jersey.

Icho Tower is built on a rock 2¼ miles east of Demie de Pas and 1½ miles to the westward of Seymour Tower, a square white tower about 1 mile seaward from the SE corner of Jersey. Two miles to the northward of Icho Tower and on a hill is another round white tower, Grouville Mill, elevation 60 metres, which makes a useful landmark on the east side of the island.

In thick weather or at night, a passage to Gorey should not be attempted, and course should be altered to pick up the Demie de Pas Light Tower and to make for St Helier.

Icho Tower in line with Grouville Mill 353° (is a useful leading mark up to within, say, 2 miles of Icho, when the course can be altered NE toward La Conchière Rock (2m bent iron pole Bn) whence follow instructions for the Violet Channel (page 133).

This detour towards the Icho Tower is to make sure that the course is well to the west of La Frouquie Plateau. The highest rock of this plateau, the Frouquier Aubert, dries 8m2, and is just over 2 miles SSE of La Conchière. It is marked by a S. cardinal buoy (*Q6+LF 15s*) approximately 6 cables to the SW. Another rock 11 cables southward of La Conchière, on the west end of La Frouquie Plateau, La Goubinière, (dries 5m and has no beacon). To pass west of this rock and the Canger Rock, 1 cable north of it, Mont Orgueil (Gorey) Castle must be kept completely open west of Seymour Tower and La Conchière, 351° T. The Canger Rock (dries 3m), marked by W cardinal buoy (*Q (9) 15s*) lies 1 mile southward of La Conchière and with it forms a 'gateway' into the Violet passage.

With experience, in good weather, the yachtsman can shape his course from the Minquiers or Chausey more to the east than Icho tower; but the eastern safety limit for the approach to the Violet channel is the transit, Mont Orgueil castle full open west of Seymour Tower and La Conchière.

21.5. Elizabeth Castle and breakwater and Platte Beacon which are left to port when entering the inner roads. When approaching from S or SW keep the end (BWVS) on with Elizabeth Castle to lead between Demie de Pas and Les Tetards and east of the Hinguettes. This transit must be left before approaching the rocky patch W and SW of Dog's Nest, except after half flood. Gros du Chateau Rock is seen left of the breakwater. This is the outer leading mark which, on with the BWVS mark on the distant sea wall bearing 341° clears the Dog's Nest rocks at LW.

5. **St Helier to Gorey, via the Violet Channel**

NE Stream begins approximately +4 h 30 m Dover (−3 h St Helier) and the SW Stream at −2 h Dover (+3 h St Helier).

Weather and visibility permitting, a daylight passage between St Helier and Gorey through the Violet Channel is possible at all states of the tide provided that the vessel can make good her course possibly against a very strong stream. At times other than near High Water there would be little sea room under sail to tack against an adverse wind, and as the direction of the tide changes hour by hour and also to some extent according to the exact locality, the stranger in these waters should be constantly on the watch for set, so that headings can be adjusted to make good the course required.

While there should be no difficulty in following sailing directions in clear weather and preferably at neap tides, it is recognized that the navigation on the south-east of Jersey is considered by strangers to be exceptionally difficult, and a visiting yachtsman may well be advised to have a pilot or local yachtsman aboard to point out the marks on the first occasion when he makes the passage.

The best time to set out from St Helier to Gorey is on the last half of the flood, say −2 h 30 m St Helier or +5 h Dover to arrive at the Violet Channel just before High Water.

After leaving St Helier Harbour leading marks (see St Helier Harbour) set course keeping Gros de Château rocks in transit with the BWVS mark on the sea wall until

Jersey

Demie de Pas bears east. Then make good, allowing for tide, about 112° T, to pass about 2 cables south of Demie de Pas, and hold this course, keeping Noirmont Point (photograph 21.2) open to the south of Demie de Pas, until Mont Orgueil Castle (photograph 21.14) opens east of the land.

Then steer for a position about midway between La Conchière (2m bent iron pole beacon) and the Canger W cardinal buoy (*Q(9) 15s*), with the Violet buoy RWVS (*L Fl 10s*), two miles further on, bearing 085° true. Make good this course until just short of the buoy, when alter course for Petite Anquette beacon (topmark PA) on a bearing of 045° true. Maintain this course for about 4 cables until the transit La Coupe Turret (see over the land end of St Catherine's breakwater) is open east of Verclut Point on a bearing of 332° true.

Steer on this transit leaving to port Le Cochon red can buoy, Le Giffard red can buoy, and La Noire (*E* cardinal) and Horn (red bucket topmark) beacons, until Gorey leading marks are picked up.

The reverse passage through the Violet Channel requires the use of the same marks, and is best made to arrive at the Violet Channel at low water or half an hour before to get the benefit of a fair tide. At this state of the tide La Rousse Platte (1.6 miles SE of La Conchière) and other rocks of La Frouquie Plateau will be uncovered.

Brett Channel. Near HW (St Helier) an alternative passage about 1 mile inshore of the Violet Channel can be taken by yachts and ships of light draft. This may be used with local knowledge and passes 4 cables east of La Conchière Rock and 1 cable west of the Brett Rock beacon (see 21.7). From St Helier the 6 miles to La Conchière might be sailed in the hour before HW St Helier so that even at neap tides, sufficient water and a fair tide can be assured. On the north-going passage there are some overfalls near Brett Rock, which need cause no alarm at the right state of the tide.

The passage from St Helier to a position S of La Conchière is the same as for the Violet Channel. Then steer to bring Icho tower close south of La Conchière until St Catherine's Breakwater Lighthouse (5 miles northward) and Karamé Rock beacon (topmark K (6 cables SSE of Seymour Tower) are in line. Do not allow the tide to set the vessel north of a line Icho Tower/Conchière until the marks are clearly identified.

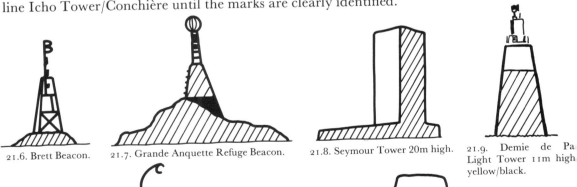

21.6. Brett Beacon. 21.7. Grande Anquette Refuge Beacon. 21.8. Seymour Tower 20m high. 21.9. Demie de Pas Light Tower 11m high yellow/black.

21.10. Conchière Rock. 21.11. Icho Tower as seen from seaward.

From this position steer 028° for about 1 mile to pass 1 cable west of Brett Rock (dries 3m) beacon (Topmark B). Continue on this course until La Coupe Turret open E of Verclut Point at 332° is reached about 4 cables east of Cochon buoy (red can), when course may be shaped for Gorey Harbour. The reverse passage Gorey to St Helier by the short cut can be made before High Water (St Helier), but an adverse tide of $2\frac{1}{2}$ knots should be expected at Springs until past La Conchière, when a fair tide is found.

6. From the East

The two likely approaches from the east are:
  (A) from the direction of Carteret and
  (B) from the direction of Granville via the passage between Le Boeuf Tower and Le Sénéquet Light.

  (A) **From the direction of Carteret.** There are many reefs with little water over them between Les Ecrehou and the Normandy coast, so that this passage should not be attempted at Low Water.

  South of Les Ecrehou the Ecrevière Bank must be cleared by passing outside the S cardinal bell buoy established at its SE corner (*VQ (6) + LFl 10s*). By night, Sorel Point Lt shows red over the Ecrevière bank and white up to $\frac{1}{2}$ mile to the south of it.

  Strong tides run SE on the flood and NW on the ebb. About 1 mile to the east of Mont Orgueil (Gorey) Castle lies the Banc du Château, on the Middle bank of which the least depth is 0m1. At MLWS a detour to the north should be made to close Grouville Mill (white, on hill) with Mont Orgueil Castle 230° T. Continue on this transit until 6 cables off the Castle when La Coupe Turret lies just open of Verclut Point at 332° T, when bear to port to bring this transit astern and continue on this course until Equerrière Rock beacon bears W, when course should be altered to the S, leaving to starboard the green conical buoy (*QG*), until Gorey leading marks are picked up. (See Gorey Harbour.)

  (B) **From the direction of Granville**. The easiest route is probably via the passage between Le Boeuf N cardinal Tower and Le Sénéquet Lighthouse (*Fl (3) WR 12s 13/10M*), passing between the E and W cardinal buoys on either side and close to the Bas Jourdan E cardinal whistle buoy. From Bas Jourdan make good a course of 290° T passing 2 miles north of Les Boeufs and Grande Anquette (9m high white refuge Bn) and thence on to the Gorey leading marks, which lead S of the Banc du Château.

  From Gorey to Granville this course reversed is probably the most practicable to avoid the many changes of direction required to travel through the Violet Channel. It can also be negotiated at night in fair weather, if necessary. Given clear visibility, of about 12 miles Le Boeuf Tower and rocks may be left to the east, passing between them and La Grande Arconie Rock (dries 3m0), on a stern transit of St Catherine's breakwater end lighthouse on with La Coupe Turret at 315° T. Least water is 1m8 over Basse Occidentale des Boeufs (2 miles W of Boeuf Tower) which can be avoided by a $\frac{1}{4}$ mile detour to W around it.

Harbours and Anchorages

St Helier. The leading marks through the inner roads from south of Oyster Rocks beacon to the entrance of St Helier Harbour consist of a white patch (front) on the outer angle of Albert Pier (the long west breakwater) and a white lattice structure with an orange patch (rear) at the esplanade end of the breakwater at 023° T. By night (*Oc G 5s*) (front) and (*Oc R 5s*) (rear) lights, (192 metres) apart.

21.12. St Helier Harbour entrance. The entrance to La Collette Yacht Basin is on the right leaving the dolphin to starboard and the red buoy to port.

Traffic signals are exhibited from the Control Station on the head of the Victoria Pier (starboard hand) which is equipped with VHF Ch 14. A fixed or flashing green light permits entry into harbour and a fixed or flashing red gives permission to leave. Entry and exit is prohibited when both lights are exhibited. It is essential that Port Control signals should be obeyed, but quick flashing Amber lights on NW and NE sides of the station permit power-driven craft up to 25 metres to enter or leave at 5 knots or under contrary to signal lights displayed. Such craft should keep to their starboard side whenever practicable while passing between the pierheads and transitting the commercial harbour.

The marina, situated at the N end of the harbour, is open approximately 3 hours either side of HW. Depth gauges and light signals show clearly when entry and exit are possible. Green light for entry; red light for exit; red and green lights together—marina closed. Visitors' berths for craft of draft up to 1m8 are on the inner pontoons E, F and G. Berthing for deeper draft vessels is available on request. A scrubbing pad is situated in the NE corner.

When entry into the marina, or the port, is not possible, yachts should proceed into La Collette Yacht Basin situated on the starboard hand immediately before the harbour entrance, passing between the green (*QG*) and red (*QR*) channel buoys and securing to one of the holding pontoons. The old harbour dries and is full of local boats; berthing only on request.

Facilities at St Helier are excellent. Petrol and oil are available at the fuelling berth on the South Pier of the main harbour, but access is limited by draft near LW.

Water and electricity at marina pontoons. If not handed over from a Port Control dory on arrival, Customs and Immigration forms should be obtained from the marina office and, when completed, posted in the box provided. The St Helier Yacht Club, above the fuelling station on South Pier, is hospitable and local advice may be obtained.

The town is an exceptionally good shopping centre and there are many excellent hotels and restaurants. A choice of several chandlers, chart suppliers and repair yards. The marina shop stocks a wide range of provisions and everyday needs.

There are good air connections and passenger services by ferry and/or hydrofoil to both UK and French ports. A good bus service serves all parts of the island.

St Aubin. This harbour is situated 2 miles west of St Helier across St Aubin's Bay, and is the headquarters of the Royal Channel Islands Yacht Club. The harbour, which dries out 6m8, is very full of boats and moorings but either side of HW short stay berths may be found alongside the northern or southern jetties. Diesel is available at the end of the north arm. The entrance is marked by small channel buoys. By night, approach in the white sector of the north jetty light. There are many drying moorings to the north of the

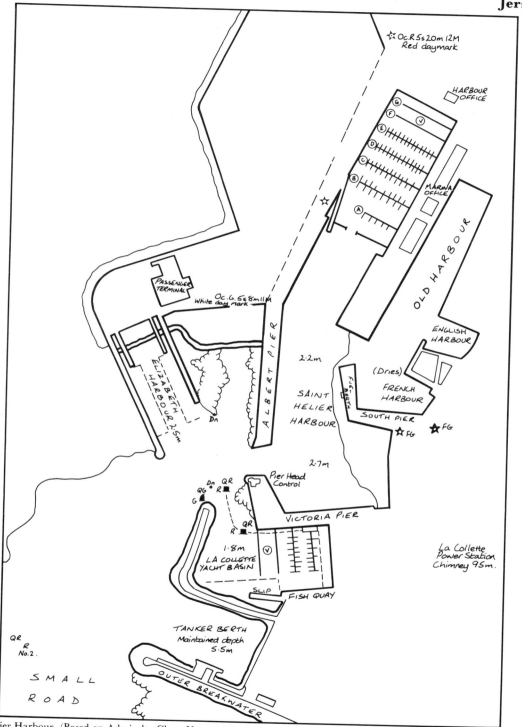

St Helier Harbour. (Based on Admiralty Chart No. 3278 with the permission of the Controller of HM Stationery Office and the Hydrographer of the Navy.)

Jersey

Fort but a deep draft yacht will have to take soundings to find a suitable depth, according to the state of the tide, in which to anchor east of Platte Rock pole beacon. The anchorage is good, being open only on its south side although it is a long distance from the harbour. The R Channel Islands YC have a visitors' moorings with one ton concrete sinker in Belcroute Bay. The minimum depth is stated to be 1m4 MLWS. Note that the stream runs south along the shore from half flood to low water St Helier.

21.13. St Aubin Fort which dries out at LAT.

Gorey. This is a charming little town, or large village, on the east side of Jersey, nestling under Mont Orgueil, on which stands the castle dominating the harbour and its approaches. There are hotels, restaurants and several shops. Gorey Yacht Service Ltd. provides diesel, petrol and water from the end of the pier, as well as shipwright and engineering services, winter yacht care, chandlery, clothing etc. Gorey is the only harbour, other than St Helier, where Customs can be cleared. Some yachtsmen prefer it to the larger port. There are vedettes in summer to Carteret and to Portbail and when entering, the pierhead should be given a wide berth.

When approaching Gorey keep a distance of 1 cable outside all local beacons until the leading marks are identified. These are Gorey Pier lighthouse on with the rear lighthouse

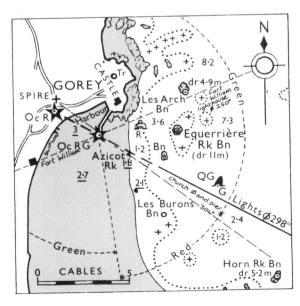

Gorey. (Based on Admiralty Chart No. 1138 with the permission of the Controller of HM Stationery Office and the Hydrographer of the Navy.)

(with rectangular white surround with vertical red edges) at 298° T. The green conical buoy (QG), 7 cables off the pierhead and Ecureuil beacon (G triangular top mark) left close to starboard. If the rear mark is difficult to pick out in daytime, the transit Gorey church on with the white patch on the end of the pier, 304° T may be used instead.

At low water entry to the harbour is impossible, and the flat Azicot Rock (dries 1m8) which is almost on the leading marks 2 cables from Gorey pierhead, may be avoided by a detour to the north, where temporary anchorage may be found while waiting rise of tide.

From the NE a short cut can be made by day, passing close SE of Les Arch (BW letter A) Beacon and, with sufficient rise of tide, making straight for the pierhead, remembering to give the rocks under the NE side of the pierhead a berth of ½ cable.

21.14. Mont Orgueil Castle just north of Gorey Pier affords a conspicuous landmark. There is an anchorage in offshore winds and neap tides near the white mooring buoys.

21.15. The light structure at the end of Gorey pier is the front leading mark. The rear mark is an oblong white light structure with vertical red borders between the two white houses on the left.

Jersey

By night. Approach in the green sector of Gorey Pier Light (*Oc RG 5s 12M*) in transit at 298° with the rear shore light (*Oc R 5s 8M*).

Harbour and Anchorage. As Gorey Harbour dries out the only position where a deep keeled yacht can remain is alongside north of the fuel berth, shown in photograph 21.16. There is about 1m8 at half tide. The Port Authorities prefer yachts from foreign countries to report here for Customs, and in any case this is necessary to obtain instructions from the Harbour Master if wishing to remain there or elsewhere in the harbour, which is often very crowded. Call Channel 74 or telephone 53616. The Port Control Office is on the pierhead. Other possibilities are: (a) 8 sets of moorings inside harbour which dry at half tide or earlier, (b) visitors' buoys which dry at low water, (c) a deep water mooring outside the harbour on the States of Jersey Hippo Buoys. Although the harbour may be crowded in bad weather, refuge can usually be found somewhere within it and yachts which can dry out should move well up the harbour to find the best shelter.

The outside anchorages are suitable only in offshore winds and reasonably settled weather. As the sands dry out 2 cables off the pier at LAT the state of the tide and the draft of the boat are the principal considerations, and soundings should always be taken. At MLWS there is 1m3 and at MLWN 4m1 above the LAT chart datum, which makes a great difference. At neaps a shallow draft yacht can anchor near or even just inside the pierhead, but clear of the fairway and the rock ledge marked by E cardinal BYB beacon. East of the pier there are several moorings for shallow draft local craft and usually room to anchor just north of them, clear of the rocks when LW is 2m0 above LAT datum. A small jetty or drain runs out from the steps, which facilitates dinghy work. At spring tides yachts of say 1m8 will have to anchor about 2 cables off the pierhead just north of the leading line but no more west than the States buoys.

St Catherine Bay. Situated rather over 1 mile north of the prominent Mont Orgueil Castle and ½ mile south of La Coupe Pt., and made conspicuous by its long breakwater on the north side, St Catherine is easy to find and enter by day or night. It is protected from the north by the breakwater and from the west and SW by the land. The southern part of the bay contains many rocks, extending beyond and to northward of Le Fara E cardinal beacon which is south of the breakwater head. To clear these dangers when approaching from the south, keep the lighthouse at the end of the breakwater on with La Coupe Turret, which is conspicuous on a transit of 315° true. From north or east there are no outlying dangers, other than the overfalls in rough weather on two shoals 1½ cables from the breakwater head. The tide is very fast in the offing and there is an eddy along the breakwater.

When close to the breakwater follow it up on the south side, keeping within a cable of it and anchoring off about the middle of its length. The holding ground on mud or fine sand is good. There is a rock a cable south of the inner end of the breakwater. The breakwater lighthouse (*Fl 1.5s 13M*) enables the anchorage to be used at night, and it is often a most convenient one although uncomfortable in easterly weather. There is a sailing club and café but no other facilities other than buses to Gorey and St Helier. Landing on slipway at northern end of breakwater.

Rozel Bay lies on the NE coast of Jersey, under a mile west of La Coupe, and is sheltered from SSE through S to W. There is a small drying jetty on the west side against which a yacht can lay alongside. Approach from the north is made with the end of the jetty bearing 250°, leaving drying rocks NE of it to starboard. Anchor in 2 metres off the jetty. With

21.16. Gorey Harbour showing the fuelling berth ahead of the ferry and visitors' (drying) moorings in the foreground.

21.17. Rozel Harbour. *E. Bruce*

21.18. Bonne Nuit Bay. *E. Bruce*

sufficient rise of tide enter the harbour close to the end of the jetty leaving to port a rock, dries 5m5, marked by iron beacon with RW globe top. The entrance is only 18m0 wide. Rozel is a picturesque fishing village with hotel, restaurants and café. At night the white sector of a *F WRG* light leads into the harbour.

Bouley Bay. This wide bay on the NE side is a popular anchorage, which is easy to enter and is sheltered on west and south. There is a shoal Les Troupeurs (1m8 over) in approach

Jersey

on the NE and the Oyster Rocks (dry 4m3) 2½ cables NE of Etaquerel Fort, but the west half of the bay is clean beyond 200 metres of the shore. There is a jetty near the corner of the bay in the SW side and anchorage off it.

Bonne Nuit Bay. This pretty bay is situated near the centre of the north side of Jersey 1½ miles east of Sorel Point and close east of Fremont Point, ¼ mile off which there is the Demie Rock, marked by a conical green buoy. There is a stone jetty, which dries out, fringed by drying rocks at low water, in the SW corner of the bay and anchor NE of it. Approach in a SW direction leaving to port the Chevel Rock (dries 10m7) and rocks ½ cable north of it. At night there are two leading lights *FG* at 223° T.

Radio

Jersey Radio maintains a continuous watch on Channel 16 VHF and 2182 kHz MF.

The following frequencies are used:

VHF Channels 25 and 82.
MF Channels 3 (2104 kHz) and 6 (2534 kHz).

The following services are available at Jersey Radio.
  (a) Weather bulletin at 0645, 0745, 1245, 1845 and 2245 GMT.
  (b) Gale warnings upon receipt, after the next silence period following receipt and at 0307, 0907, 1507 and 2107 GMT.
  (c) Navigation warnings prior to weather bulletins and at 0433, 0833, 1633 and 2033 GMT.
  (d) Decca warnings on receipt, at three minutes past the next hour and one hour after that.
  (e) Link calls on Channel 25.

All broadcasts are made on Channels 25 and 82 VHF and 1726 kHz MF after initial announcement on Channel 16 and 2182 kHz.

Radio beacons are established at St Helier Harbour (Signal EC 287.3 kHz range 10M) and Corbière (Signal CB 305.7 kHz range 20M). Corbière is grouped with Cap Frehel and transmits in sequence at 2, 4 and 6 minutes past each hour. In poor visibility, the commencement of the Corbière fog signal, (C), coincides with the end of the 18 second dash of the radio beacon sequence. Each 1000 Hz pip (transmitted at the end of the 18 sec dash) heard before the fog signal represents a distance from the lighthouse of about 335 metres.

Aeronautical radio beacons are established at St Ouen Bay (Jersey West, Signal JW 329 kHz range 25M) and St Catherine Bay (Jersey East, Signal JEY 367 kHz range 75M).

22 Les Ecrehou and Plateau des Minquiers

Tidal Streams. The NNW stream begins +5 h 05 m Dover (−2 h 25 m St Helier), and S stream −0 h 40 m Dover (+4 h 15 m St Helier).

Admiralty Chart 3367.

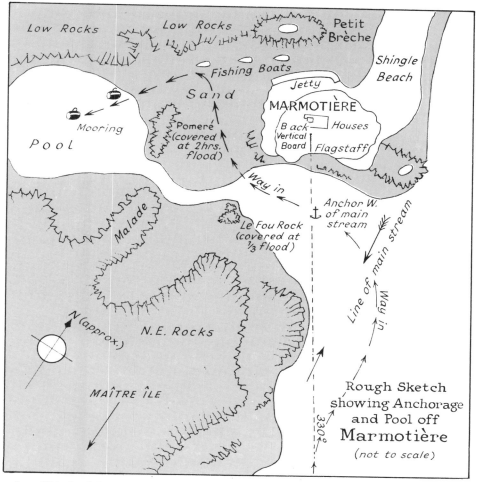

Les Ecrehou: This sketch is intended only to illustrate the anchorages described and the slight alteration of course necessary to avoid rocks NE of Maître Ile, which at low water touch the transit of the flagstaff and black vertical board.

Les Ecrehou and Plateau des Minquiers

Although Les Ecrehou and Minquiers are difficult, and regarded as dangerous to navigate without local knowledge, this book would be incomplete without mention of them.

The Ecrehou group of islets and rocks lies 5 miles off the NE coast of Jersey, and once formed part of the continent with Jersey. Maître Ile, some 600 metres long, is the largest, and in medieval times had a Priory where monks lived, sung masses for the souls of the dead, and tended a beacon for mariners. The ruins are still to be seen.

The only inhabited island is Marmotière just to the north of Maître Ile, which is a mere fistful of rock capped by a tiny cluster of stone-walled cottages. They are crammed close together, and look like a Grimm's Fairy Story village, with grey and red roofs, bright against the summer sky, and below them the craggy islet, completely devoid of vegetation, standing in the fast-running tide. It is difficult to imagine how the original inhabitants lived in such an inhospitable place, but the buildings are used now by a few lucky Jersey yachtsmen who lease them for use in the summer. The third island is Blanche Ile, which is connected with Marmotière by a long curving ridge of shingle covered at high tides and smoothed by the fast-running currents. The rest of Les Ecrehou is composed of islets, countless rocks, seaweed and sands, all in a compact group a bare 2½ miles long. Sea birds make their nesting places in the higher rocks, and lobsters, prawns and shrimps multiply in the channels between them. Les Ecrehou are well worth seeing, and there is a temporary anchorage in deep water south of Marmotière. Yachts prepared to take the ground can feel their way into shallower and more protected water and dry out at low tide.

Navigation in the approach and up to Marmotière is intricate, and should not be attempted at high water or at Spring tides. The tide is so strong that a yacht with a good breeze may be passing over the bottom at 10 knots, in restricted waters peppered with rocks. Furthermore, when bringing up, it may be difficult for the anchor to get a hold when the tide is pouring through the reefs at its maximum rate.

The Approach. It is best to plan arrival at half ebb; south and westward of Les Ecrehou the tide will then be running strongly to the north-west. Coming from the French coast a course must be set to pass to the southwards of the Ecrevière Bank, S cardinal buoy (*VQ (6) + LFl 10s*) then westward until the first transit is identified. From Gorey set a course southwards of Maître Ile until the first transit is identified. Eastwards of Maître Ile is a distinctive rock Bigorne (5m high) shaped like the horn of an anvil, see photograph 22.1. North-eastwards and beyond Bigorne are two large rocks, Grand Galère (4m), which is a long reddish coloured rock partially white with bird lime, and Sablonière (2m). At low tide these three rocks appear to be merged from the approach angle, see photograph 22.2.

The first transit is with Bigorne immediately mid-way between Grande Galère and Sablonière, bearing 022°, as shown in photograph 22.1. Keep closely to this transit, which will probably mean pointing well to starboard as the tide will be setting strongly to the north-west, until approaching Grand Noire and nearby rocks close to starboard when it is safe to keep slightly to the north-east until Bigorne is in line with the north side of the Sablonière, while Maître Ile will be clear to port. Four cables short of Bigorne the next leading marks will come in line bearing 330° and it is important not to continue beyond their line; both are on Marmotière Island, in front a prominent flagstaff on a whitewashed rock and, in rear, a vertical black board looking as though it was a chimney on the left-hand end of a cluster of houses. The tide will now be astern.

Until beyond Maître Ile it is important to keep close to the transit line which leaves close on the port side two rocks (drying 6m7 and 7m0) to the south-east of the island

22.1. Bigorne in the centre is the key rock in the approach to the Ecrehou with Grand Galère to left and Sablonière to right.

22.2. This photograph near LW shows how different is the picture when the rocks dry out and the groups merge with each other, but Bigorne remains clear in the centre for the first line of the approach.

22.3. The temporary anchorage at Marmotière. The picture is taken at LW with a number of week-end yachts from Jersey rafted on two moorings. At HW Marmotière is only a fistful of rocks capped by a cluster of stone walled cottages. The front leading mark is a white flagstaff (over a white patch on the rock below it) in line with black vertical board at 330°, but when passing the rocks off Maître Ile (shown on left of picture) it is best to open the board to east of the flagstaff. The entrance to the pool is on the left side of the picture and the Sound with its fierce tidal streams is to the right of the big right hand rock at Marmotière.

although there is room for a slight divergence to starboard without getting too close to Sardrière (dries 8m5). When abreast the northernmost islet of Maître Ile borrow a little to starboard, as shown on the sketch plan. Anchor close in to the pebble beach on the south side of Marmotière, or pick up one of the States of Jersey mooring buoys about 100 metres south-south-east of the flagstaff.

This temporary anchorage (see photograph 22.3) south-east of Marmotière is much used for day visits by yachts from Jersey; during low water it is usually quiet and it is easy to land by dinghy on the slipway. The main stream runs fast past the rocks E of Marmotière and Maître Ile, so a yacht should anchor out of this as close to the beach as soundings permit. At low water this allows ample room, yet as the tide rises the main stream moves closer in, so it is not likely to be a comfortable anchorage during high water. Indeed, anyone not thoroughly familiar with Les Ecrehou would do well to keep to settled weather for a visit, as it could be quite difficult to get out safely through the rocks in unfavourable conditions, especially at night.

Given good conditions, when the tide turns southwards just before low water, it will be favourable for clearing into deep water, so long as the visibility is a couple of miles or more.

The Pool. As well as the temporary anchorage south-east of Marmotière described above, there is the Pool two cables west-south-west of Marmotière, with room for two or three yachts to moor in 1m2, which means there will always be 2m on an average low water springs. There are some private moorings in the Pool, and enquiry in Jersey before leaving may enable a yacht visiting Les Ecrehou to borrow the use of one. But apart from these moorings, the holding ground is good, and the Pool is well sheltered except at high water.

There is enough water to make for the Pool when Pomeré is covered at about half tide. The track (see map on page 145) is round the south and west side of Marmotière to the line of fishing boats generally moored off the jetty slipway. Then steer south-west towards the mooring buoys about a cable away.

A yachtsman strange to these waters is advised first to settle in the temporary anchorage, and then explore by dinghy the passage into the Pool, especially noticing the bearings to clear Pomeré.

Plateau des Minquiers (Minkies)

Admiralty Chart 3656

This group of rocks is situated some 9 miles south of Jersey, and covers an area greater than Jersey itself. Unlike Les Ecrehou and Les Iles Chausey (Chapter 29) there are only about a dozen very high rocks on the whole plateau which never cover, and the only one worthy of the name of island is Maîtresse Ile, a narrow slice of rock about 300 metres long and 9m7 high. On this island there are a number of stone cottages built in the eighteenth century for men from Jersey to quarry rock. More recently they have been used by fishermen and some are now leased, as at the Ecrehou, to Jersey yachtsmen. The area around Maîtresse Ile is alive with low-water fishermen on the big March and September tides, who look for ormers (shell fish), and by bird watchers in the spring and early summer. An Anglo-French helicopter air/sea rescue landing platform is established.

At low water the whole Plateau des Minquiers is a maze of rocks and sands with shallow passages between them, and countless below-water rocks. The only island worth visiting is Maîtresse Ile. The anchorage here is to the SE of the island. At low water springs it almost dries out but at neaps there is about 2m on the States of Jersey buoy. Above half tide it can become most uncomfortable and at high water springs it is very exposed and boat-work at the slip can be dangerous. In parts the bottom is mud and soft sand so that when taking the ground no attempt to ship legs should be made. Local advice (if any is available) is needed here. However, it has not been heard that any boat has foundered in the anchorage and a visit in fine weather at neap tides is worth while, even if it has to be a short one.

The best deep water anchorage is $\frac{1}{2}$ mile WNW of Récif Le Coq Beacon, which can be reached with the aid of Chart No. 3656. It is very exposed but in good conditions the 1-mile passage to Maîtresse Ile slipway might be made by a reliable motor dinghy, though the streams are very strong.

The easiest approach to the Maîtresse Ile anchorage is from the north, timing arrival at about half flood, when the stream will be setting eastwards. If coming from St Helier the Demie de Pas lighthouse in transit with the power station chimney provides a good back mark to make the Demie de Vascelin green buoy situated 8 miles 175 from the lighthouse. Leaving this buoy 2 cables to starboard, bring Jetée des Fontaines de Bas RWHS pillar beacon (topmark F missing 1990) on with the flagstaff situated on the lefthand mound of Maître Ile, 161° true. If the beacon is difficult to see against the island, run in on the bearing of the flagstaff until the beacon becomes visible.

When about a cable short of Jetée des Fontaines, alter to starboard to bring Grune Tar white pillar beacon on a bearing of 200° true and make good this course until the two beacons on Rocher du Sud Bas come in line on a bearing of 165°. The southernmost beacon is a white pillar and the northernmost a red pole. (The two spherical topmarks missing 1990.) Proceed on this transit until the Demies pole beacon (topmark D missing 1990) comes abeam to port when, giving it a berth of at least $\frac{1}{2}$ a cable, alter to port to bring Rocher Blanc pole beacon with cross topmark, on a bearing of 081°. Steer on this line until the final transit of Rocher NE RW beacon on with La Petite Gauliot pole beacon with mitre shaped topmark, 018°, leads into the anchorage. A useful guide to the amount of water over the sandbank to the south of the Demies is that when the Demies rock is itself awash there should be at least 1m8 on the bank.

If proceeding southwards, leave the anchorage by the same route and recover the transit of the two Rocher du Sud Bas beacons 165°, diverting westwards to round the rocks themselves giving them a berth of about a cable. The same transit leads out towards the SE Minquiers buoy, but beware Les Sauvages shoal a few cables NW of the buoy.

22.4. The anchorage at Maîtresse Ile, which dries at LWS. The yacht is lying on the States of Jersey mooring.

PART IV
DIELETTE TO ST MALO
Introduction

Chart Datum: The chart datums in this part IV of the book correspond to the datums of the individual French Charts on which they or the Admiralty Charts are based. For most practical purposes the datums correspond approximately to those given in Admiralty Tide Tables Vol I. **Local Magnetic Variation:** The *Channel Pilot* states that abnormal magnetic variation, due to local magnetic anomalies, may be experienced within an area bounded by lines joining Cap de Flamanville, the island of Sark and Cap de Carteret.

The harbours of Goury, Diélette, Carteret and Portbail are included in the following part of this book, instead of Part II with those of the Cherbourg Peninsula, as they are visited more conveniently on the way to or from the Channel Islands, which have just been described.

The west coast of the Cherbourg Peninsula and the French coast to the south of it as far as Granville is inhospitable, as it is open to the prevailing winds, and from Cap Carteret southwards it is fringed by reefs of rocks which dry out high, and reach far seaward. Goury, which is ½ mile SE of Cap de la Hague, is approached through the Alderney Race, and is a tiny drying harbour. Diélette, which is just north of Cap Flamanville, is also a drying harbour, but provides an anchorage which is sometimes useful in offshore winds when waiting for a tide through Alderney Race. Carteret is a pleasant village with a harbour which is well worth visiting during a spell of fine easterly weather, though a visiting yacht must dry out. Portbail likewise dries out but is attractive.

There are no harbours on the 35-mile stretch of French coast between Carteret and Granville, other than Regneville and a few small inlets which are difficult to approach over the outlying ledges, and dry 8 metres or more. Granville itself, though it faces west and dries out in the approach, offers the visitor the splendid half tide marina of Port de Herél in complete security, with a pleasant French town conveniently at hand.

Immediately west of Granville lie the Iles Chausey, which should certainly be visited. They are of similar formation to the Ecrehou, the Minquiers and the other plateaux which lie off the Jersey coast, but they offer a good anchorage which is easy of access. Here is seen at its best the combination of islets, rocks and sands subjected to nearly the greatest range of tide in Europe.

The principal harbours in the SE corner of the Gulf of St Malo are St Malo itself with a marina wet dock, and in the Sablons Marina at St Servan. The River Rance provides a cruising ground of its own, offering many anchorages.

To reach the SE corner of the Gulf of St Malo is a matter of chart work (Chart No. 2669) and careful tidal calculations both for directions, rates and heights. The passages are not difficult in clear weather, especially near neap tides but can be horrid when it is thick. Several options are open.

From St Peter Port or St Helier the simplest passage lies west of the well-marked Minquiers to St Malo or to Grande Ile, Iles Chausey, but from St Helier the quickest lies east of the Minquiers through the Entrée de la Déroute to Grande Ile or the Déroute de Terre to Granville.

From the north the direct course is to follow the French coast southward in the Déroute de Terre. This passage can be very rough in strong westerly winds as it crosses shoals and uneven bottom close to a lee shore. Carteret cannot be left except near high water when the tide will be foul. The stream off Cap de Carteret will be strong but once south of Les Ecrehou it becomes much weaker. The line to follow on chart 2669 is given as Hatainville Sandhills shut in with Cap Carteret at 349°, but it is easier to keep Cap Carteret lighthouse itself on this stern bearing. The shallowest part lies when crossing the Banc Félés in 1m2 LAT, which gives 2m5 at MLWS and plenty of water at most states of the tide. The line leads to Bas Jourdan whistle buoy between the Boeufs and Le Sénéquet lighthouse, where the stream turns SW about HW Dover (+5 h St Helier) and south just over an hour later.

Continuing south after passing Le Sénéquet the bottom becomes very irregular and there are shoals 0m3 LAT and rocks. But the dangers are marked by buoys, except for one wreck, and with the aid of the chart and sufficient rise of tide there is no difficulty in reaching Granville or off the east and south of Iles Chausey to Grande Ile.

From Gorey the passages round the Boeufs have been referred to on page 138 and can be continued to Granville or Iles Chausey as described above or through the Entrée de la Déroute to St Malo.

A great help for navigation on the French coast are the numerous beacon towers and buoys, and the excellent lights, even for harbours of minor importance. If there is any ground for criticism it is that there are almost too many lights.

In other respects problems of navigation in the SE corner of the Gulf of St Malo are much the same as for the Channel Islands but, although the range of the tide is higher than in the Channel Islands, and in fact reaches its maximum in the Baie du Mont St Michel, the rates of the streams are generally less.

23 Goury

High Water: −4 h 20 m Dover (−1 h 05 m Cherbourg).
Heights above Datum: MHWS 8m1. MLWS 1m2. MHWN 6m5. MLWN 3m2.
Depths: Harbour dries up to 4m8. Anchorage outside 3m7 to 1m3.

This very small drying harbour snuggles among rocks on the west side of the Cherbourg Peninsula, little over ½ mile SE of Cap de la Hague lighthouse. The approach appears singularly uninviting when a yacht is being swept in a 9-knot stream past La Foraine beacon tower in the Race of Alderney. Indeed such strong tides running through a long approach among dangerous rocks would seem hazardous, while a position so exposed to any westerly winds might seem unlikely to offer good shelter. Yet the fishermen state that the Alderney Race, combined with the rocks, act like an outer breakwater, and even in a south-westerly gale the inner harbour is reasonably sheltered. The accompanying chart is based on the large scale French Chart No. 5631, '*Abords de Goury*', which also covers Omonville. Alternatively use the smaller scale No. 5636, covering whole coast from Nez de Jobourg almost to Cherbourg.

In the approach allowance must be made for the fierce streams in the offing and a leading wind or auxiliary power is needed. It should only be attempted for the first time·in good weather conditions and at the right state of the tide near neaps, consulting the *Pocket Tidal Stream Atlas*. The streams weaken inshore and the difficulties are nearly over when the leading marks have been identified with certainty and Diotret has been passed.

The best time for the approach is stated to be on the last of the south-going stream through Alderney Race to arrive south of La Foraine Beacon Tower at 5 hours after HW Dover, which is about half flood locally. Alternatively, on the last of the north-going stream arriving 1½ to 1 hour before HW Dover, which is about half ebb locally. See also Alderney Race Tidal Streams, page 91.

Approach and Entrance. Make good a position about half mile to SSE of La Foraine beacon tower, YBY, 2 cones points together. Owing to the strength of the athwartship stream it is necessary to keep La Foraine on the stern bearing of NNW as near as possible. When the right distance of ½ mile has been made good the large rock Gréniquet (1m8 high, and sometimes white at top) will bear about 110° distant ½ mile on the port bow, and other nearer rocks in the groups (see charts) may be uncovered. By then the leading marks (daylight only) will be identified as they will be less than a mile away and course can be altered to port on their transit shown on the large scale French chart as 066°.

The front leading mark is a narrow circular green beacon with a cone point upward on a rock called Hervieu, (dries 5m2) and the rear is a green pole (also with a cone point upward) on Jet d'Aval which dries 6m3. This line after passing very close to Bau Charlin shoal (1m6 LAT), leaves:

(a) Grios, dangerous twin rocks drying 2m9 100 metres to port, and

(b) Diotret, a rock drying 9m2 (the summit of which is always above water) 70 metres to starboard, or less.

150

24 Diélette

High Water: −4 h 35 m Dover (+0 h 12 m St Helier).
Heights above Datum: MHWS 9m7. MLWS 1m3. MHWN 7m4. MLWN 3m6.
Stream sets off the anchorage to the SW about −2 h 30 m Dover and to the NE +4 h Dover.
Depths: Harbour dries out, and the entrance dries about 2m1 off the end of the outer breakwater.

Diélette is a small artificial harbour situated some 11 miles south of Cap de la Hague. It is not a particularly good harbour, but the temporary anchorage can be useful in offshore winds when awaiting a fair tide through Alderney Race or along the coast. Yachts should only use the anchorage or harbour in offshore winds or settled conditions.

The Approach. From the southward the approach is easy. Cape Flamanville is a prominent headland with a signal station, and it is only necessary to follow the coast keeping a mile offshore to avoid off-lying rocks. A mile or so north of the Cape a conspicuous tower and extensive building into the sea off the mines will be seen. This tower is left to starboard, and then, a mile beyond, the harbour will be seen. There is a shoal with 0m5 to 1m5 water west of the southern breakwater, which need only be considered near low water or if conditions are rough. Streams in vicinity of the Dolphin are strong.

From the northward, after passing through the Alderney Race, the three shoals, Basses St Gilles, Les Huquets Jobourg and Huquets de Vauville must be avoided. This may be done either by keeping outside them, with the pitch of Pointe du Rozel (south of Flamanville) well open of Cape Flamanville or by going inside between the shoals and the coast; the passage is over a mile wide. In the outside passage allow for strong tides setting rather athwart the shoals, and for the inside passage remember that the tide turns early. The shore south of Vauville to within a mile of Diélette is clear, with a shelving sandy shore, but for a mile north of Diélette there are rocky ledges extending 4 cables seaward. In settled weather and an offshore wind there is anchorage SW of Vauville.

The Entrance. The harbour entrance dries 2m1, so that it can only be approached with sufficient rise of tide. The entrance is with the lighthouse on the outer pier (*Oc WRG 4s W 8, sectors W 072°–138°, R 138°–206°, G 206°–072°*) in line with a fixed light (*FR 11M intensified 122°–129°*) in the window of a white house ashore, at 125°. Approaching with the end of the inner pier just open of the outer one is quite accurate enough.

The water shoals about 100 metres off the pierhead. On close approach (at suitable tide only) alter course to pass about 25 to 50 metres off the outer pier. In the harbour the stream runs SE towards the old jetty when the stream outside is NE, and westward along the old inner jetty.

The Harbour. The harbour is filled with boats moored fore-and-aft with bows facing the entrance; the bottom being criss-crossed with mooring chains and ropes. A yacht can berth alongside the inner wall of the outer pier near its end where the bottom dries about 2m. There are steps near the end of the quay which are used by local boats and the best berth appears to be beyond the steps at the first or second ladder. There is a steel obstruction under the wall beyond the third ladder. Some 100m inside the end of the breakwater the

Diélette

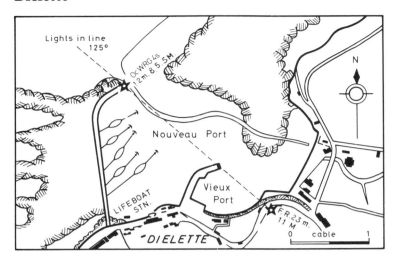

Sketch map of Diélette.

harbour dries out to 4 or 5m. The section inside the inner breakwater is the Vieux Port, also with small boat moorings, which dries even higher, leaving only one berth alongside the outer end of the breakwater.

The harbour can only be used in settled weather and an offshore wind. There is a surge under many conditions, and in westerly winds even the inner harbour may be untenable.

There is room to anchor temporarily in the entrance to the harbour, but the holding is poor on a bottom of thin sand on rock.

24.1. Diélette Harbour. Approach with the inner breakwater just open, or at night with the leading lights in transit (lighthouse on jetty, and light in white house with gable) until close to the entrance.

Anchorage. Outside. With offshore winds and in the absence of swell the anchorage outside, just E of the line of the leading lights, seems quite good, although the holding ground is stated to be bad, as it may be if there is a swell or sea. There is about 2m of water at a distance of rather less than a cable off the pier, and plenty of water farther out. At neap tides it is possible to anchor closer to the pierhead if soundings are taken, and the steps barely dry out.

Facilities. The village is small, but is on a main road with a bus stop opposite Hotel de la Falaise. There are three hotels, small shops and two garages. There is a Lifeboat Station. A baker is up the hill on the west side of the village, but bread can be obtained from the *épicerie*. Electricité de France have a large power station just to the south of the village.

25 Carteret

High Water: −4 h 36 m Dover (+0 h 6 m St Helier).
Heights above Datum: Admiralty Tide Tables, Vol I. MHWS 10m9. MLWS 1m3. MHWN 8m2. MLWN 3m9.
The stream near Cap de Carteret begins NW at −5 h 47 m Dover (−1 h St Helier) and to SE at HW Dover (+4 h 47 m St Helier), both streams attaining 3.8 knots.
Depths: The sands vary from time to time in position and height, in some years forming a bar drying 7m0. Of recent years there has been more water over the bar but a high sandbank has developed off the west jetty.

The fishing port of Carteret is an attractive place and a popular summer holiday resort for those who need no organized amusements. Entry and departure can be made only near HW, so that a visit to the Port usually entails a stay of either an hour or two or at least 12 hours. In westerly or SW winds the approach is generally rough, as the yacht is approaching a shallow lee shore, but in winds from N to E the harbour is sheltered.

Approaches and Entrance. The dark headland, over 76 m high, on which is the Cap de Carteret Lighthouse (*Fl (2 + 1) 15s*) usually shows up well in the line of sandy beaches and dunes along this coast. There are numerous fishing floats in the approaches.

To the east of the headland are some buildings, those sheltering behind the headland being the town of Carteret. On the coast to the ESE about a mile from Carteret Harbour lies the seaside resort of Barneville Plage, where a large red-roofed building on the shore gives a good line of approach from the west until the Carteret stone jetty can be seen, with a white light structure and red top (*Oc R 4s*) at its end. When the tide has risen high enough, steer east to leave the jetty end about a cable to port and pick up the leading marks for the harbour.

Outside Carteret it is slack water about 1 hour before local HW and arrival at HW −½ hour is the best time for approach. At spring tides in the absence of strong onshore winds entry over the bar presents no difficulties, but at neaps only light draft craft can cross it even at the top of the tide, and there is no water to reach the Petit Port (dries 8m8) beyond the second slipway. On the flood immediately before and particularly after HW the inshore stream sets strongly westerly across the entrance.

There is an eastern mole ½ cable east of the West Jetty the seaward end of which is marked by a green pole beacon (*Fl (2) G 5s*) (see photograph 25.2). The mole submerges at HW. The transit for entry which gives the best water over the sandbank (but this varies in position and depth) is this *East* mole-end beacon in line with the Life Boat shed, a long building with a large door at 007°, in front of which is a tall telegraph pylon at the top of the second slipway. On this transit there should be about 1m8 over the bar when ATT Vol. 1 gives a height of 8 metres. When the stones at the foot of the eastern mole-end beacon, referred to above, are seen to be awash, the tide has risen to 8m8 above datum.

An alternative transit is the eastern mole-end beacon in line with a large cream-coloured house with green woodwork and a Mansard roof over the Majestic Hotel. This is easier to identify and avoids the westerly running eddy, but it may cross the bar in rather less water than on the other transit.

When entering on either transit, the course should be altered as given in the diagram,

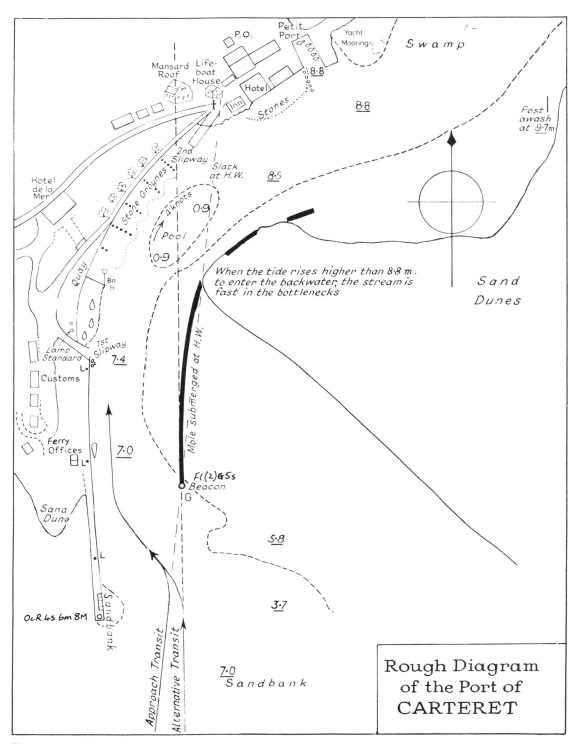

The positions of the sandbanks vary year by year.

25.1. Cap de Carteret from the NW.

MANSARD
ROOF

25.2. The west jetty and light structure which should not be approached closely. Towards the right is seen the starboard hand beacon marking the end of the nearly submerged mole and behind it the lifeboat house and the house with a mansard roof just to the left.

where the channel is shown about twice its actual width. A sandbank which bulges into the channel may exist off the jetty end, but soon after it comes abeam alter course towards the ferry offices from which *vedettes* leave for Jersey, Guernsey and Sark. When the eastern mole-end beacon comes abeam to starboard the best water lies within 10 metres of the West Jetty side and there are high drying sands extending off the west side of the submerged eastern mole.

The Harbour. Yachts berth and dry out alongside the jetty and quay. Berths lie between the ferry offices and the first slipway, but not too close to the latter where there is a small dangerous ledge. There are quay-side ladders S of the ferry offices. The harbour is used by only a few fishermen so there should be no difficulty in finding a berth. The HM operates from a small cupboard-like structure in a corner of the Yacht Club, opposite the Majestic Hotel. The jetty is rough so plenty of fat fenders are required and the bottom is uneven with numerous stones etc. The streams run very fast near HW on both ebb and flood, so bow, stern and breast ropes require careful attention until the yacht has taken the bottom.

Upper Harbour. Most local yachts are berthed above the second slipway and Petit Port, but this whole area is high-drying and generally suitable only for shoal draft yachts; it may not be possible to leave until the height of tide reaches some 10 m. The Petit Port is

Carteret

filled with local craft. Above Petit Port is a considerable area of level bottom with yacht moorings laid out. All these berths dry out completely.

Anchorage. In calm weather, it is possible to anchor in shallow water just over $\frac{1}{2}$ mile south of Carteret Harbour Light. Fishing boats sometimes anchor here while the smaller dories fish inshore for bait, but strangers should take soundings and anchor well outside the fringe of rocks which dry out over a long distance from the shore and the stream is strong.

Ashore. The town has all the usual shops one would expect. There is a bus service to Cherbourg and other places of interest. The restaurants in Carteret are excellent and accommodation can usually be found in the hotels for those who would like a spell ashore.

25.3. Carteret Harbour looking to seaward at low tide from the stone groynes above the first slipway. Several small craft are berthed beyond the beacon marking the end of the groyne; the first slipway is obscured beyond these, before a line of trawlers leading to the white vedette. On the left is the end of the east mole. *Keith Blount*

25.4. Inshore end of the western jetty, showing vessels dried out alongside. *H. A. Stevenson.*

Departure. It is not advisable to leave if it is blowing hard from the SW, because of the difficulties met with on a lee shore and since the falling tide will close the harbour and prevent return if the weather worsens. If bound north the navigator may leave at HW or just before. If bound south or for Jersey then it is best to leave as early as possible to gain distance before the tide starts running hard to the north.

25.5. Carteret. The 'pool' at low water.

26 Portbail

High Water and Chart Datum approximately as at Carteret.

Portbail is a delightful drying harbour for moderate and shallow draft yachts and has an active sailing school. The entrance is situated some 4½ miles SE of Cap Carteret and is approached by a passage over low reefs to seaward and sandbanks closer inshore. Due to continual gravel dredging within the fringe of outer rocks, the sand and gravel banks bordering the entrance channel have been appreciably reduced with resultant greater depths of water than those indicated on charts. It is nevertheless inadvisable to attempt entry (even with only 1m2 draft) more than, say, 1½ hours either side of HW. At springs 2 hours after HW the tide pours out and the jetty area dries out completely before ½ ebb. Vessels alongside are left high and dry. Portbail is not generally suitable without legs or bilge keels.

Approach and Entrance

French Chart No. 827 shows the harbour approaches and covers the coast north to Diélette and No. 826 also includes the harbour and the coastline south of it. Entry can be made with either chart aided by the following notes, but is not advisable in strong onshore winds.

Portbail is readily identified from far to seaward by a large, high, slightly funnel-topped, white water tower, standing close to the coast line westward of the small town and northward of the entrance channel. Approach from a SW direction and bring the water tower on to a bearing of approximately 025° and continue on it until a RW fairway buoy is identified. Steer for the buoy until it is 3 or 4 cables distant when course may be altered to bring the church at Portbail (photograph 26.1) on to a bearing of 042°. Then steer on this bearing for the church, allowing if necessary for a tide on the beam. The small town and church are some distance back from the shoreline and, due to the height of the land and sand dunes nearer the shore, the church tower is only visible over a narrow arc when seen from seaward. The church must not be confused with another church east of it. The fairway buoy will be left over a cable to port and the line crosses a 0m9 shoal and drying rocks with a head drying 5m3 a cable to starboard. By then the inshore buoys will be seen, Red to port Green to starboard, which mark the shallow bar. Steer midway between these. Then a straight stone training wall will be seen which, when covered (as it will be during the HW period except at dead neap tides) is marked by a line of balise poles. Leave the first two poles about 20 metres on the port hand and then keep closer to the training wall. Here the channel dries out at approximately 4 hours ebb. At the last but one balise alter course to starboard for the jetty end on which there is a beacon with a red can top.

The outer half of the jetty is a slipway sloping upwards from the river. On the inside of the jetty, mooring is reserved alongside the southern part for vedettes; then white marks show the section reserved for fishing craft, and a mark defines the northern section for 'Plaisance', with a ladder for access (photograph 26.2).

The rest of the area enclosed by a sea wall, except for the 70 metre wide entrance, has rows of moorings, some 12 in each row, where yachts dry out. The whole area is firm, generally fine sand, with almost 5m at MHWS in the centre.

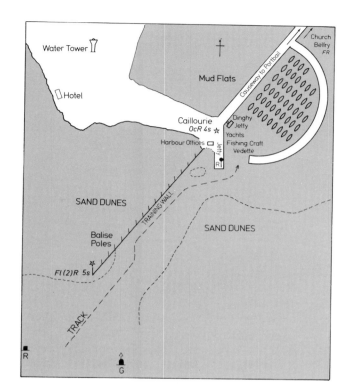

26.1 The end of the training wall at low water springs. The approach is made with the church bearing 042°.

26.2. Jetty and yacht harbour at Portbail. *E. Bruce*

Lights. The leading lights are (*Q*) (rear) in the church belfry (*Q*) (front) La Caillourie, while on the training wall is (*Q (2) R 5s*); but strangers would be unwise to attempt entry at night.

Facilities. The Harbour Office is close to the *vedette* booking offices, where *vedettes* leave for Jersey, Guernsey and Sark. The nearby Yacht Club is active during the season. There is a drying out berth for yachts alongside the jetty. From the jetty to the delightful little town there is a motor road on a raised causeway about ½ mile long. There is a restaurant in the town as well as the usual shops, P.O., *bureau de change* and, at the far end of the town, a garage.

26.3. The line of poles marking the submerged jetty.

27 Granville

High Water: −5 h 02 m Dover (−0 h 15 m St Helier).
Heights above Datum: MHWS 13m1. MLWS 1m4. MHWN 10m0. MLWN 4m5.
Streams 1½ miles off Pointe du Roc are rotary anti-clockwise. Just after local high water (−5 h 02 m Dover) the stream is NE, then it backs through N to W which it reaches about −1 h 30 m Dover, S at about +3 h Dover, E at about +5½ h Dover. The rate is a little over or under 1 knot. For tides offshore refer to tidal atlas.
Depths: Port de Hérel is a half tide harbour and the depth at the marina entrance is indicated by illuminated figures. When the tide reaches 6m55 the hinged marina gate drops giving 1m4 to pass in or out.

The avant port dries out and the wet basin (1½ hrs—HW—1 hr) is the commercial port used principally by the fishing fleet. A large marina for yachts (Port de Plaisance de Hérel) lies to the E of the Avant port. The marina is only a short walk from the centre of Granville, which has all the facilities of a good sized town and summer holiday resort.

The Approach and Entrance. The approach to Granville is rough in strong winds between west and NW, and is exposed to the SW though the seas will not be so high from this quarter. The near approach and marina entrance are sheltered by land from the north and east. In good weather or in offshore winds Granville is easy of access, granted sufficient rise of tide. If coming from the northward the quickest course lies between Chaussée des Boeufs and Le Sénéquet, and thence southward by the Déroute de Terre leaving Iles Chausey to the west. The passage might be difficult in bad weather off a lee shore or in fog, but in the ordinary way it does not present any difficulty because it is not usually made near low water as Granville marina has a half-tide sill. A longer but easier approach (except for erratic tidal streams) can be made by the Entrée de la Déroute passing west of Iles Chausey and then doubling back east to Granville. Coming from the west, whether from Iles Chausey or St. Malo, presents no difficulties given reasonable weather and sufficient rise of tide on arrival at the shoals off Granville.

The principal feature in the approach from the north is the Pointe du Roc, a prominent headland with a grey lighthouse (*Fl (4) 15s 23M*) and a signal station. Le Videcoq whistle buoy, YBY (*VQ (9) 10s*) marking a rock which dries 0m8, lies 3½ miles off Pointe du Roc.

The Pointe du Roc is fringed by reefs extending nearly ¼ mile. There is La Fourchie beacon tower red (*Horn (4)*) on the NW of the reef, but there are detached rocks 300 metres seaward of it. Despite the great range of tide, the streams 1½ miles off Pointe du Roc are moderate, attaining a rate of a little over a knot, though they are stronger inshore.

Once Pointe du Roc has been passed course may be set to the SE for the conspicuous BRB Le Loup light-tower (*Fl (2) 6s 11M*), given sufficient water over the rocks south of Le Roc. The long western breakwater of the Avant Port to Granville commercial basin will be seen to the eastward, and soon the principal breakwater of the yacht marina will open up beyond it. This breakwater bears the name Granville-Hérel in large letters and immediately above there are large illuminated numbers giving the depth over the sill at the marina entrance. White numbers denote metres, orange figures decimetres. The lowest figures exhibited are 1m4; 'O' denotes no entry. For yachts leaving the marina, illuminated numbers, though smaller than those outside, are shown on the inside of the breakwater near the entrance.

When the figures indicate the required depth at the entrance there will be plenty of

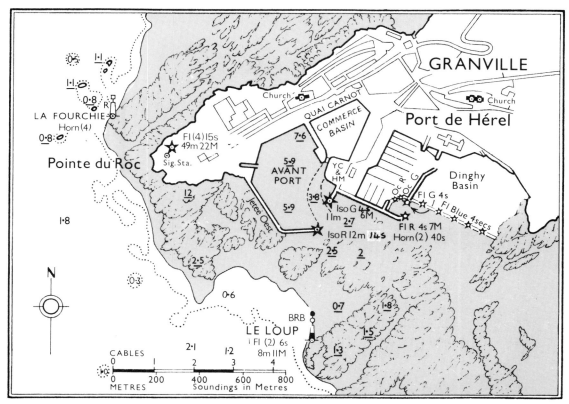

Granville: Dotted contour indicates the 1 metre line. (Based on French chart No. 5897 by permission of the Service Hydrographique de la Marine.)

water over the outlying rocks as it will be about half-tide. Proceed from a cable north of Le Loup tower, steering to keep the end of the Hérel breakwater in line with a conspicuous radio aerial on the skyline (bg 055°), and then skirting the end of the breakwater leave it about a cable to port. A line of crimson poles (*Fl Bu 4s*) marks the submerged sill of the dinghy basin. Before reaching these the entrance to the marina will have opened up between the de Hérel breakwater to port (*Fl R 4s*) and the S end of the secondary breakwater (*Fl G 4s*) to starboard. Bear sharply to port to enter, when the two beacons marking the gate of the sill at the marina entrance will be seen: red to port (*Oc R 4s*) synchronized with green to starboard (*Oc G 4s*). The distance between them is narrow. Between them the tidal gate opens at 6m55 above datum, leaving a minimum depth of 1m4.

Port de Plaisance de Hérel. This large marina has ten long pontoons with finger berths at right angles. The deeper berths of 2m5 lie at the southern end, the first east–west pontoon encountered on entry is marked for visiting yachts. The marina has all the usual facilities. There is a slip and grid in the NE corner and a re-fuelling point at the root of the visitors' pontoon.

The Granville Yacht Club has premises next to the Capitainerie at the marina. This is a

Granville

27.1. Point du Roc from south. Breakwater of Avant Port to commercial basin on right.

27.2. Marina breakwater showing tidal height recorder of Granville-Hérel.

27.3. The outer entrance to the Marina between the breakwaters with the tidal gate beyond.

27.4. Leave red beacon to port and green to starboard at narrow marina entrance. The tidal gate lies between the port and starboard pole beacons. The visitors' pontoon lies directly ahead.

27.5. Facing NE across northern end of marina for smaller yachts.

very active and hospitable club which also has moorings (mostly for light draft yachts) at Iles Chausey.

There is a sailing school in the dinghy basin. Facilities such as chandlers and sailmakers are convenient. In the town there are banks, hotels, restaurants, shops, P.O., casino as well as yacht equipment etc. Roguet in the Rue Le Campion (near marina) stocks nautical books and charts. There is a railway station and an airport. *Vedettes* leave for Chausey, Jersey, Guernsey and Sark from the east side of the Avant port.

Anchorage. In offshore winds the best position to anchor outside the harbour, while awaiting rise of tide, is $1\frac{1}{2}$ to 2 cables west of Le Loup beacon in 1m5 to 2m0 LAT. There is a reef of rocks extending about a cable SSW of Le Loup. The anchorage is exposed and in quite strong streams at springs, but at neaps a yacht may find enough water on the north side of Le Loup, or even get into the shelter of the breakwater ready for the marina gate to open.

28 Mont Saint Michel

Tidal Heights at MHWS stated to be nearly 1 metre higher than at Cancale, see page 175.
High Water: −0 h 10 m St Helier.
Depths: The bay dries out for some 6 miles seawards. Within the Cousesnon Channel, just west of Mont St Michel, a depth at high water of 2m9 was found on a 10m5 tide St Helier.

The whole of the coast on which Mont St Michel stands is tending to silt up and has been doing so for very many years. Much of the land between Mont St Michel westwards to the dunes of Cherneix has been reclaimed behind a polder and now forms exceptionally rich agricultural land. The authorities at Mont St Michel are concerned that if the silting continues it would result in the complete recession of the sea, leaving it by the end of the century high and dry amidst fields of waving maize. The Mount caters for one of the largest numbers of tourists of any place in France and it is felt that much of the attraction and ambience of the place would be lost in such circumstances. It is considered that a major cause of the silting is the existence of the causeway itself and a petition has been submitted to the French government for the causeway to be dismantled and removed as soon as possible. If and when this happens the entire situation in respect of visiting the Mount by sea may change critically.

However romantic it may seem to visit this historic Mount by sea the prudent mariner will give the matter considerable thought before venturing near the place. A very few diehards do visit by sea but they are either very well prepared or foolhardy. One of the well-prepared and intrepid visitors, who makes an annual pilgrimage by sea, Martin Richardson, has kindly provided most of the information incorporated in this section.

The following considerations must be taken into account before attempting a visit.

A very high tide is necessary before a visit is possible. For a yacht drawing only 1.4m it is necessary for the height of HW St Helier to be in excess of 10.4m, i.e. a coefficient in excess of 77. Atmospheric pressure can make up to a metre difference in the height of HW so this must be taken into consideration. HW Springs in this area occur in the early morning and evening which means that a winter visit is out of the question because it would be dark for much of the approach. In the summer, the morning tides are sometimes not high enough which limits the number of occasions when a visit is possible to some seven or eight a year. Obviously a visit should be made before the maximum Spring tide, for to attempt it at the top of Springs or with a falling coefficient would lead to the possibility of the yacht being neaped if she ran aground and was unable to extricate herself immediately. It should be emphasized also that a visit should only be attempted when the weather is set fair and the visibility is good.

The choice of yacht is also important. The yacht must be able to take the ground; legs are of no use. Bilge keels are satisfactory but even these can sink differentially due to the scouring action of the fierce currents; a yacht with a drop keel which can lie on its belly and particularly a catamaran would be satisfactory. On the approach the skipper must be prepared to take soundings (using his dinghy) without delay as there is little time to waste; consequently the dinghy must be inflated before starting the approach. At least two anchors are important because it is necessary to anchor the yacht facing seaward, i.e. facing the next flood tide, for the yacht must not be caught offering its transom, or particularly its beam, to the advancing tidal flow. The strength of the current can cause anchors to drag, conversely an anchor may be deeply buried making it difficult to recover. The flood tide is strong and advances at the rate of some 10 knots. The time between being able to walk around the yacht and it being afloat can be less than 30 minutes. Because of the turbulence the water becomes thick with sand and silt and turns the colour of café-au-lait. It is not too tempting in these circumstances to run the engine. Once the flood has run its course the ebb starts immediately, but for about an hour it falls quite slowly before receding more rapidly. It could be said, therefore, that there is virtually a stand of about one hour immediately after HW.

Approach

Due to the scouring action of the strong currents the channel is constantly shifting and even though a line of starboard-hand buoys is laid from time to time, these buoys can only provide a general indication of the area within which the channel meanders. It is always possible that the buoys may be dragged out of position by the strong currents and stormy weather.

The training walls are no longer as they used to be. The eastern training wall has been breached and the channel now runs to the east of it, alongside the causeway. The western training wall has been silted over.

So, being prepared for the above mentioned hazards you make course for the Island of Tombelaine. The approach will start from roughly 8–10 miles out on a SE bearing. Assuming the weather is fair and the visibility good, the lights on the Mount are conspicuous in the dark, and at dawn it is the only landmark to be seen. Tombelaine, however, can be picked out well before reaching it. In this area, at this time of tide, there is a strong easterly set which must be countered during the approach. It is best to contrive to arrive at Tombelaine about an hour to half-an-hour before HW so as to ensure reaching the Mount with sufficient time in hand to select a suitable anchorage before the ebb starts in earnest.

The first of the starboard-hand buoys will usually be found about $\frac{1}{2}$ mile W of the island. The line of buoys runs in a southerly direction, the last buoy being about a cable off the Chapelle St Aubert which is to the NW of the Mount. It is impossible to see the bottom and it is not feasible to select the channel itself. The edges of the channel can sometimes be quite steep, but generally the differences in height over the entire area are not great so that it is reasonable to follow the line of buoys even though they may not, in fact, mark the actual channel itself. More simply, it is probably sufficient to set course from a point about $\frac{1}{2}$ mile W of Tombelaine towards the western side of the Mount.

Anchoring

Having reached a point where you wish to anchor it is important, once the flood has eased, to sound around the yacht using the dinghy to be sure the bottom is reasonably flat and the yacht is not over the steep edge of the channel. It is also best to select the deepest possible position, which will probably be in the channel itself, so that there is less risk of the yacht being neaped by subsequent tides. To avoid the old silted training wall it is best to anchor north of a line running due W from the Chappelle St Aubert. Having selected the best position, lay out anchors fore and aft in such a way that the yacht takes the ground

Mont Saint Michel

28.1. Tombelaine, which should be left about $\frac{1}{2}$ mile to the eastward. Mont St Michel in the distance. *Combier Macon.*

28.2. Aspect of the Mount from the N; taken before the training wall was breached. *Combier Macon.*

28.3. Mont St Michel. Looking South.

168

Mont Saint Michel

General approach to Mont St Michel

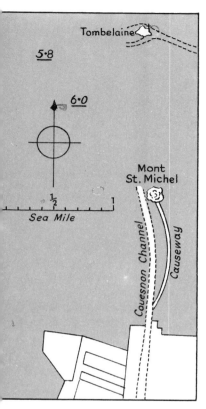

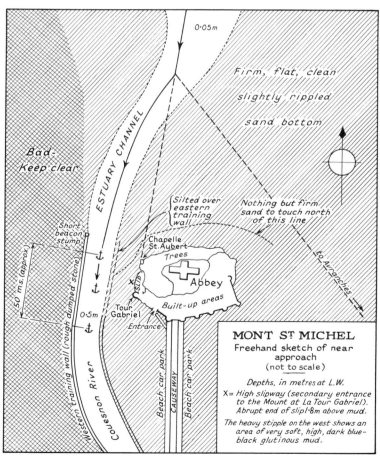

MONT ST MICHEL

Freehand sketch of near approach

(not to scale)

Depths, in metres at L.W.

X = *High slipway (secondary entrance to the Mount at La Tour Gabriel). Abrupt end of slip 1·8m above mud.*

The heavy stipple on the west shows an area of very soft, high, dark blue-black glutinous mud.

Mont Saint Michel

with its bows facing seaward. Once the tide has receded the stern anchor must be moved to the bows so that the yacht is ready to meet the next advancing flood tide with two anchors out ahead. It is necessary to follow this drill for every tide the yacht encounters.

One of the best places to anchor is about 100m or so to the NW of the Mount. The bottom to the west of the main channel is said to be too soft and variable in consistency to provide good standing. Even the sand on the east side of the channel tends to be very fine-grained and silty.

The navigator who still insists on attempting a visit may feel it is prudent to go to the Mount by land first in order to obtain the latest information and to make a survey on foot at low water. This would be particularly advisable if and when the causeway is removed.

29 Cancale

High Water: −5 h 02 m Dover (−0 h 15 m St Helier).
Heights above Datum: MHWS 13m5. MLWS 2m0. MHWN 10m4. MLWN 4m8.
Stream sets off Herpin Lighthouse to NW −5 h 15 m Dover and to SE +1 h 15 m Dover, and to S and N off Cancale N −6 h Dover, S +1 h Dover.
Depths: The harbour dries 5m8 at head of jetty.

Cancale: (Based on English Channel Handbook Misc. 679, with the permission of the Controller of HM Stationery Office and of the Hydrographer of the Navy.)

The small fishing harbour of Cancale is situated on the west side of the Bay of St Michel, 3 miles south of the Pointe du Grouin. The town consists of the seaside resort of Cancale with the fishing quarter of La Houle to its south. As the harbour dries out, the deep

Cancale

anchorage is exposed a long way offshore. It is not often visited by yachtsmen, however there are some better anchorages further north along the coast, see below.

The Approach

The main feature of the approach to Cancale is the line of rocks and ledges off the Pointe du Grouin, 3 miles north of Cancale, which project NE to Pierre d'Herpin lighthouse

29.1. Cancale (La Houle) Harbour near high water with fishing vessels alongside its east jetty.

(*Oc(2) 6s 20m 17M Siren Mo (N) 60s*) and beyond to La Fille buoy (*whistle*). There are channels between these features which require some care to navigate. Immediately E of Pte de Grouin lies the Chenal de la Vieille Rivière, between the Pointe and Ile des Landes, which offers a short cut when approaching from the westward. It is narrow, and at times the tide is strong. The best water is towards the Ile des Landes side as there are submerged rocks on the mainland shore at least as far south as the semaphore station. The wind here tends to be baffled between the land. Large scale French Chart No. 5644 is advised. With sufficient rise of tide it is possible to continue inshore passing between Pointe de la Chaine (off which there are rocks marked by a beacon) and Le Petit Rimain island.

Some may find it better to round La Fille buoy, giving it a good berth, and to leave all these potential dangers to the west. Plenty of allowance must be made for the tides. These are very strong in the vicinity—a good 5 knots or more at Springs—and set across the ledges. Course may then be set towards the Ile des Rimains, the outer of the three islands off Pointe de la Chaine, the prominent headland a mile N of Cancale. The island has an old fort standing on it and should be left $\frac{1}{2}$ mile to the west. Course shortly afterwards should be altered outside the oyster beds and then towards the harbour which will then be seen. The water will shoal rapidly and the bottom dries out at LW Springs south of the inner islands, named Le Petit Rimain and Le Chatellier. There is a rock awash at extreme LW situated about a cable SSE of Le Chatellier.

Anchorages and Harbour

The nearest anchorage to Cancale is S of Ile des Rimains and it is necessary to take soundings to find the best position. At Neaps a yacht can anchor nearer the harbour, but still seaward of the fish stakes referred to below. The tide attains a rate of 3 knots in the anchorage, which is only moderately sheltered even with an offshore wind, and over a mile from the harbour. Alternative anchorages are found NE of Pointe de la Chaine, or off Port Picain S of Pointe Chatry, or off the Anse de Port Mer N of Pointe Chatry. These anchorages are protected from the W only, and the tidal stream is strong except at Neaps. These embayments are filled by moorings but some may be available for the visitor.

If intending to enter Cancale (La Houle) harbour from off Ile des Rimains, look out for the fish stakes, stretching from the oyster beds S of Pointe de la Chaine across the approaches to the harbour, which can only be crossed near HW.

29.2. Facing seaward across the entrance from Rothéneuf. When entering near high water the beacon in centre is left to starboard.

The harbour which dries out 5m8 to 7m6, consists of a western jetty and an eastern jetty and is open to the S. Yachts can berth on the W side of either jetty. The eastern one is convenient, but is in frequent use by fishermen when there is enough water. There is a light at the end of the eastern jetty (*Oc (3) C 12s 12m 8M*). Minor repairs can be effected at La Houle. Water and fuel are available. There are plenty of shops, hotels and restaurants.

30 Rothéneuf

(Chart datum as for St Malo)

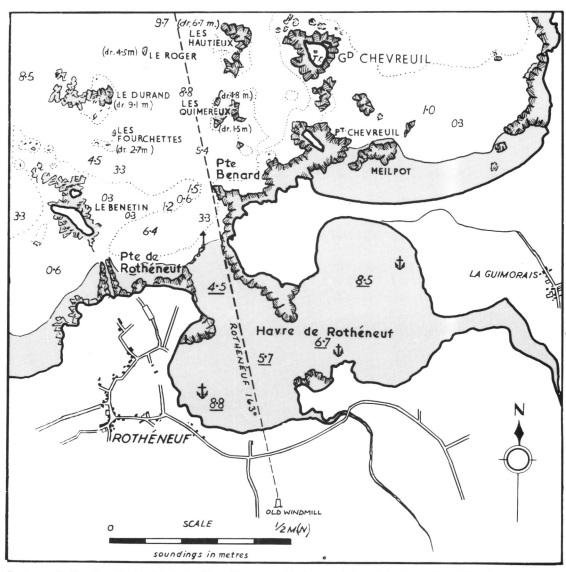

Rotheneuf: (Based on British Admiralty Chart No. 2700 with the permission of the Controller of HM Stationery Office and of the Hydrographer of the Navy.)

Rothéneuf is situated $3\frac{1}{2}$ miles E of St Malo and is a spacious natural harbour which dries out completely leaving a bottom of hard flat sand. It has a narrow entrance which is approached from La Bigne Channel, for which Admiralty Chart No. 2700 is advised. The approach lies between Le Roger rock (dries 4m6) on the west side and the reefs of Les Hautieux on the east (dry in places 7m8 and 8m0). The width of the channel here is only about 2 cables. Near HW all rocks are covered, but breakers can be seen on Le Durand (dries 9m1) which lies SW of Le Roger. There is a strong athwartship tide, attaining 3 to 4 knots at Springs and the approach when the rocks are covered may be regarded as difficult if not dangerous for strangers. There is however a fairly good transit of Pte Bernard in line with an old windmill which is partialy obscured by a copse of trees. This line must be left about 3 cables from Pte Bernard and a course taken a little to the west so as to pass half way between the point and the starboard hand beacon which marks the reef of rocks to the west of the entrance. The bearing of the transit is 163°.

Once notorious for its pirates, the harbour is an excellent one for yachts equipped with legs or for twin-keeled yachts or multi-hulls but can only be visited by deep-keeled yachts at high water. Many of the embayments around the harbour have been filled with moorings where the bottom is criss-crossed by chains and ropes (all the moored boats are held fore and aft with the bows facing the entrance to stem the fairly severe currents).

The village of Rothéneuf, with a small yacht club, is in the SW corner of the harbour, and provides the nucleus of a small seaside resort. There are shops, hotels, restaurants and a regular bus service to St Malo.

31 Iles Chausey

High Water: −5 h 01 m Dover (−0 h 14 m St Helier).
Heights above Datum: MHWS 12m6. MLWS 1m5. MHWN 9m7. MLWN 4m4.
Depths: The southern entrance of the Sound nearly dries out at LAT but at MLWS there is nearly 1m5. The northern passage dries 4m6 west of La Saunière.
Streams: See Admiralty *Pocket Tidal Atlas* for streams in the area between the Minquiers, Chausey and St Malo.

Les Iles Chausey form a group of islets and rocks, measuring some 6 miles from east to west, and 2½ miles from north to south. The plateau is compact, with few detached rocks outside the encircling line of islets and submerged reefs. Several navigable channels lead into or through the group, but the principal one is the Sound de Chausey, which is entered on the NW at the Grande Entrée, crosses a wide area of drying sands, and then deepens into a clearly defined channel along the NE of Grande Ile, where it provides the anchorage, and finally emerges into open water SE of the lighthouse.

At high water the Iles Chausey are seen as a group of islets and rocks rising from the sea, but owing to the immense range of tide, at low water land becomes the predominating feature—a vast area of islets, weed-covered rocks and sands, penetrated by narrow channels of water. The scene changes hour by hour as the tide rises or falls, and with its strange rock formations contrasting with the gentle colouring of the sands it is often very beautiful.

Grande Ile is the largest and the only populated island. Although less than a mile long, it is deeply indented and has a long sea-shore, with four sandy bays between five pronounced headlands, two of which are miniature peninsulas. It is composed of rock thinly covered by soil, on which have been built the lighthouse and the old fort near by, a large château belonging to the Renault family, a small church, the house of Marin Marie, the marine artist and sailor, a farm, two hotels, shops and a few other buildings and cottages. The permanent population numbers little more than forty, who live principally by fishing; but in the summer months there are streams of visitors who arrive by the motor boats from Granville.

Foreign yachts are not allowed to visit Chausey without having first made official entry into France at Granville or some other port.

The anchorage at Chausey is one of those which used to be regarded as difficult of access by strangers, but this reputation is unjustified and today it is so well beaconed that it is easy from the southward. Then again, although Chausey is subject to almost the greatest range of tide in Europe, the actual streams are not excessively strong, attaining rates of little more than are found in the Hamble River.

The Approach and Entrance. On the occasion of a first visit to Chausey, the approach is best made from the southward, as the leading marks for the northern entrance are not so easily picked up and much of the channel dries out.

The southern entrance to the Chausey Sound lies SE of Pointe de la Tour, the SE promontory of Grande Ile on which the lighthouse stands (*Fl 5s 23M Horn 10s*).

Rocks extend seaward from Pointe de la Tour for a distance of just over a cable, but are now marked by three RW beacons (with cones, bases together), but there is a rock awash at LAT about 50 metres SSW of the outer beacon.

Approach to the entrance is made from SSE, leaving the three RW beacons on the rocks

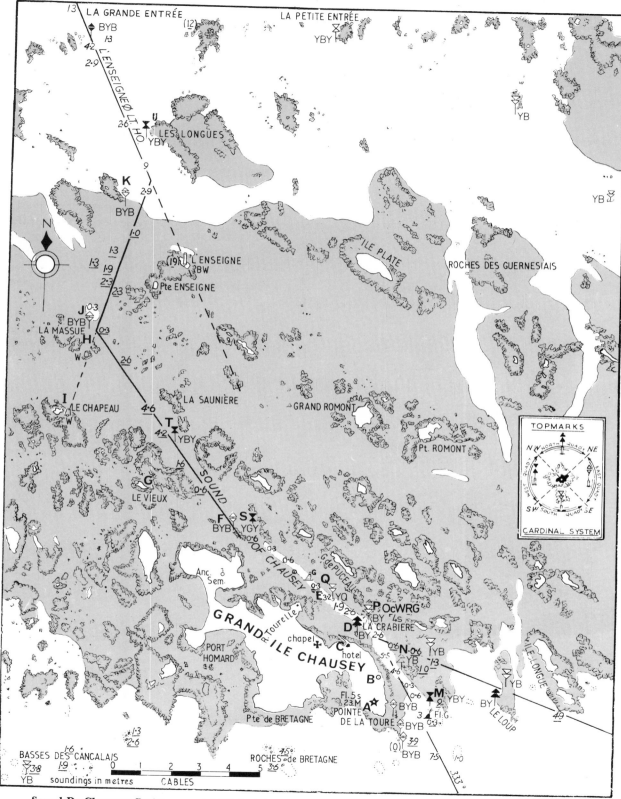

Sound De Chausey: Drying areas at LAT shaded, not drying white. (Based on French chart No. 829, by permission of the Service Hydrographique de la Marine.)

31.1. Approaching Grande Ile from the SE. The entrance is marked by three BYB beacons on the west side, of which two are shown.

to port and green buoy (*Fl G 2s*) to starboard. The transit is the BW beacon marked P on chart, with two cones points down which now has a tripod base and a light (*OC WRG 4s*) and the L'Enseigne BW beacon tower 19 m high on an islet nearly 2 miles away at 333°. Near LW L'Enseigne is hidden behind Grande Puceau islet but the passage is so well marked that no transit is needed. On the starboard side after passing the buoy there are two beacons, marked M (BYB 2 cones points together) on chart and N (YB 2 cones points up).

At LAT the transit crosses the edge of the sand to port which dries out and the channel is narrow and shallow, but at MLWS there is nearly 1m5 or 2m5 after an hour's flood and at neaps there is plenty of water.

When the yacht has passed the second starboard-hand beacon, the channel is deep and there are moorings for the vedettes. The anchorage will soon be seen to the northwest round the corner of the island, but the yacht has first to pass between a pair of beacons shown as D (marking the east side of the big La Crabière rock) and the tripod light beacon P (marking a rock on the north side). She then enters the Sound where the fairway runs approximately NW. On the starboard side there are rocks, the most southerly of which is marked by beacon Q. On the port side will be seen a landing slip and a small bay. Many boats and shallow draft yachts are moored there and dry out at low water, so they afford a useful indication of shallow water. Fishing vessels and a few yachts may be moored in mid-stream. The beacons are placed on the tops of rocks and should never be approached closely. There is over 1m9 at LAT as far as beacon Q but beyond that the channel soon shoals to 0m6 least water, and there is a rock which dries 0m3 on the west side of the channel about ½ cable NW of Q.

There is also an approach, with sufficient of tide, to the Sound off Grande Ile from the ESE with La Crabière (beacon D) in transit with Rocher Tourelle and the Semaphore at 292°. Borrow to the south temporarily to clear the rock (dries 4m9) south of Ile Longue. This transit crosses a shoal awash at LAT between a BY beacon (two cones points up) left to port and a YB beacon (two cones points down) to starboard and another broad stretch of sands which dries 2m3 at LAT but carries about 2m0 at LW neaps. See photographs:

31.2. On the east side of the entrance channel there is the conical green light buoy, the beacons on the two rocks (M) and (N) and the tripod light beacon (P) just to the left of the *vedettes* on moorings.

31.3. Here, the channel turns to NW between the light beacon (P) starboard and La Crabière rock (Beacon (D)) port. Most of the mooring buoys lie between the starboard hand beacons (Q and S). The picture is taken near LW.

31.4. Sailing through the Sound from southward, the next beacons are a pair at the northward end of Grande Ile. (F) is left to port and (S) to starboard. The course is then towards the island La Massue (H), leaving the beacon (T) to starboard. The transit after passing F is a stern bearing of beacon F in line with the lighthouse.

31.5. After passing the next beacon (T) the yacht crosses the shallowest part of the sound which dries 4m6. The best water is found on the direct line of (T) to the beacon (J) just north of La Massue.

Just before reaching (J), the chimney beacon on La Massue (see photograph 31.6) will come in line with a similar beacon on an islet named Le Chapeau, which is hidden in the above photograph by the island (G).

The transit of the two chimney beacons leads north of the slug-like island of L'Enseigne with beacon, and east of beacon (K) shown on the chart. Allow here for an athwartship tide.

Iles Chausey

31.6. The chimney beacon on La Massue. A yacht will leave this island to port, then, altering course on the transit of the chimney beacon and a similar one on Le Chapeau, she will sail towards L'Enseigne shown below, leaving it to starboard.

When L'Enseigne comes in line with Grand Ile lighthouse, come onto this stern transit of 156° leaving to starboard beacon (U) marking Les Longues reefs and leaving very close to port the rocks on the west side of the Grande Entrée. To give these rocks a wider berth keep the lighthouse just touching to the east of L'Enseigne.

31.7. L'Enseigne and associated reefs taken at half tide.

31.8. The Grande Entrée taken from north. The lighthouse is just open east of the L'Enseigne and to the left is the beacon (U) marking Les Longues.

31.9. Grande Ile as viewed from the Sound after passing La Crabière (beacon D). The chapel is in line with the tallest mast and the landing place is behind the boat under sail. *E. Bruce*

Northern part of the Sound. The northern part of the Sound dries out for a considerable part of its length, the shallowest part being west of La Saunière where it dries its maximum of some 4m6 at LAT. Thus it is navigable shortly after half flood until say ¼ ebb, when at Springs the water may be falling at a rate of as much as 1 metre in 30 minutes. The channel affords a useful short cut, and is not difficult when followed through on the first occasion from the south. The illustrations Nos. 6 to 8 and accompanying descriptions provide the simplest method of indicating the course.

By night. The general approach to Grand Ile is easy as the lighthouse light on the SE of the island *Fl 5s* has a range of 23 miles. On near approach bring the light on beacon P (*Oc WRG 4s*) on at 333° true and steer for it on 330° true leaving the light *Fl G* on the buoy close to starboard. Sufficient night visibility to identify the beacons at a short distance (say ½ cable) is required and it is probably best to anchor short of the beacon P (see Anchorages) as for strangers it can be difficult to continue up the Sound (with no further lights) and find a vacant mooring or anchorage at night unless there is good moonlight.

Other passages. There are many deep inlets among the islands, and another important channel named the Chenal des Roquettes à l'Homme. This is entered in the north at La Petite Entrée, and runs roughly SE and south, entering open water on the south through the Passe de la Conchée. This and the other inlets are beyond the scope of this book, but are mentioned as they provide interesting sailing with the aid of the large-scale French Chart No. 829, which is essential for their navigation.

Moorings and Anchorages

Owing to the great range of tide at Iles Chausey the state of the tide is the first thing to consider, and it is necessary to take soundings whether picking up a mooring or anchoring. At LW neaps there is 4m4 more water than shown on the chart at LAT. Thus there will be plenty of water at the moorings and much more room for anchoring in parts where the depth is inadequate near springs. The streams will be moderate at neaps and the Sound better sheltered.

At spring tides the deep water channel is narrow and ends at beacon Q. The NW current, which runs for about 9 hours out of the 12 from about +2 h Dover, attains about 3 knots. The anchorage will be uncomfortable in fresh or strong NW or SE winds if contrary to the streams, and very rough in gales from these directions. Yachts sometimes drag their moorings or anchors and it may be too rough to get ashore in a dinghy. The Sound is only fully protected under the lee of Grande Ile during gales between south and west, but the islets and rocks afford some protection from the NE (and the wind is across rather than contrary to the streams) and to a lesser extent from east.

There are a few deep water moorings in mid-channel between beacons P and Q which are used by fishing and other local vessels and yachts. Anchorage may be possible just NE of them and SW of the lobster boxes, but there is little room at springs and there is rocky bottom and weed in places if too near the lobster boxes. Use a trip line with the anchor.

Many yacht moorings have been laid in the reach NW of beacon Q, those in mid-channel having 0m6 and those at the sides drying LAT. Some are marked *privé* and others belong to the Granville Yacht Club or to its individual members. Nearly all are occupied at the peak of the holiday season and at fine week-ends, but at other times some may be vacant. Enquiries should be made before picking up one. Do not judge a mooring by the size or colour of its buoy as the holding power varies, the majority being for small yachts. Except near

Iles Chausey

spring tides it is possible with the aid of soundings to find room to anchor just clear of moorings in this reach. Rough landing at R Tourelle headland or at half tide or above at the slipway C.

During westerly winds anchorage may be found near the entrance, west and NW of beacon N, but the water is deep and the streams are strong. This is the easiest anchorage if arriving at night. The moorings nearby belong to the vedettes, but no objection is made to their use after the last has left for Granville provided the mooring is cast off *before* the first vedette arrives the following morning. Being in the fairway an anchor light is necessary. Landing west of beacon N or with rise of tide at the slipway.

Anchorage south and SE of Grande Ile is prohibited on account of telegraph cables.

Facilities. The Hotel du Fort has a good restaurant. The former smaller restaurant nearby has been converted into an hotel–restaurant with splendid views over the Sound. There is a shop, PO and telephone at the back. There is another small shop near the landing slip. Milk and vegetables may be obtained at the farm near Rocher Tourelle. Water appears to be rather a scarce commodity in the summer season but the restaurants may oblige customers. Vedettes maintain frequent communication with Granville on the mainland, except in bad weather.

32 St Malo

High Water: −5 h 15 m Dover (−0 h 28 m St Helier).
Heights above Datum: MHWS 12m0. MLWS 1m3. MHWN 9m3. MLWN 4m0.
Stream sets off the Cézembre to the eastward +2 h 20 m Dover and to the westward −4 h 25 m Dover.
Depths in Channel: Ample at any state of the tide.
Yacht Club: Yacht Club de Dinard. Yacht Club de St Malo.

St Malo is situated at the entrance of the River Rance. It is an important commercial port and tourist attraction; the town is also an historic one, founded in the sixth century, and is famous in maritime history. Yachts have a choice of entering the large marina of Port de Sablon at St Servan or of entering the main port through the sea lock, where there is a marina in the Bassin Vauban. The Yacht Club de St Malo is also here.

The Approach

For yachts passing W of the Minquiers, the course from the SW Minquiers buoy to St Malo is about SSE. Cap Fréhel 9 miles west of the entrance has a lighthouse (*Fl (2) 10s 85m 29M*) and semaphore station and can usually be seen from a considerable distance. When Cap Fréhel comes abeam, Ile Cézembre situated to the E of the entrance should be visible about 5 miles away. A lighthouse, Le Grand Jardin (*Fl (2) R 10s 15M*) will be seen ½ mile SW of Ile Cézembre and another, Les Courtis (*Fl (3) G 12s 9M*) to the W of Ile Cézembre with the prominent spire of St Malo in the background.

The course will bring the yacht close NE of a north cardinal buoy (*Q*) and ¾ mile SW of it a W cardinal buoy (*VQ (9) 10s*), both marking Le Vieux Banc. Both are left to starboard and the RW Fairway light buoy (*L Fl*) will soon come in view on a course of 130°. It is approximately 2 miles NW of the Grand Jardin lighthouse.

If the yacht is rounding the east of the Minquiers, using the Entrée de la Déroute, or through the channel east of Chausey, course may be set for the Grand Conchée Channel or the Chenal des Petits Pointus. Coming from Granville the yacht may use the Chenal de la Bigne. These last three channels converge on a course running NE–SW just outside Le Petit Bey where the bottom is very nearly at datum. However such is the range of tides in this area that the channel is readily passable at all times other than 2 hours each side of LW Springs. At neaps there are no problems.

Petite Porte Channel. Leave the Fairway buoy (*L Fl*) about ½ cable to starboard and steer on the lighthouse of Le Grand Jardin (*Fl (2) R 10s 15M*) on a course of 130°. The distant lighthouse of La Balue (*FG 25M*) on a hill beyond St Malo will then come into transit. This lighthouse is often difficult to see in daylight. Except at slack water allowance must be made for the stream which reaches almost 4 knots athwart the course. To avoid this strong cross tide in large part, the Decollé channel can be used.

St Malo

Continue on the transit of Le Grand Jardin and La Balue lighthouses until Les Courtis light (*Fl (3) G 12s 9M*) lies due W. Then steer S for a cable or a little more until the new transit, which is Les Bas Sablons lighthouse (*F G 16M*) (situated on the land just eastward of La Cité promontory on the E side of the river entrance, S of St Malo mole), on with La Balue lighthouse (*F G 25M*). If either or both of these lighthouses are difficult to pick out then it is best to steer to pass Le Buron tower (*Fl (2) G 6s 9M*) to starboard on a bearing of 129°. Opposite Le Buron, on the other side of the channel is a red lateral buoy (*Fl R 10s*). Some 2 cables later is another red lateral buoy (unlit) and then course is maintained, still with a cross tide, towards the end of the Mole des Noires, St Malo's outer harbour breakwater. When within ½ mile of the end of the mole there is a north cardinal light buoy (*Q*) marking the north end of the Plateau de la Rance. Three cables to the S is a S cardinal buoy (*Q (6) + L Fl 15s*) marking the southern end of the same reef. If bound for St Malo continue on the transit towards the end of the mole until 2 cables past the N cardinal buoy, then steer towards the middle of La Cité on the headland until the entrance locks of St Malo open up. Note that the sands on the S side of the entrance dry out at LW Springs and are marked by a green lateral buoy. If bound for the Rance leave the transit earlier in order to pass to the west of the Plateau de la Rance, keeping well to the west of both buoys.

By night the approach and entry to St Malo is almost easier than by day as the lights are excellent and the transits clear. La Balue lighthouse is fixed green, 25 miles, and Grand Jardin lighthouse (*Fl (2) R 10s 15M*). The transit is on a bearing of 130°. On a dark night it may be difficult to judge when to leave this transit, but this may be done when Les Courtis (*Fl (3) G 12s 6M*) and Grand Jardin lighthouses are equidistant and Les Courtis bears due W. Then steer south on to the transit of Les Bas Sablons and La Balue, both fixed green at 129°. This transit leads up the channel, leaving Le Buron Tower (*Fl (2) G 6s*) to starboard. On close approach the transit leads E of the Plateau de la Rance and when the N cardinal buoy (*Q*) at the north end of the Plateau lies due W, steer half way between the lighthouse at the end of the Mole (*Fl R 5s 13M*) and the S cardinal buoy at the south end of the Plateau (*Q (6) + L Fl 10s*). Hold this course until the leading lights, both fixed red, leading into the outer harbour come into line on a bearing of 071°.

None of the entries from the north are feasible at night as they are unlit.

Grand Port Channel. Although not so often used by yachtsmen, entry to St Malo by the Grand Porte channel is just as easy as the Petite Porte and is quicker when approaching from the west. The entry is made just south of Les Buharats port-hand whistle buoy No. 2 (*VQ R*) with Grand Jardin lighthouse true east. The leading marks are the Grand Jardin lighthouse in line with Rochebonne light (*F R 23M*), on the land 4 miles beyond, on a bearing of 089°. This course passes two port-hand buoys and quite close to a starboard-hand light buoy (*Fl G 4s*). Continue steering towards Grand Jardin until on the transit of Les Bas Sablons Lt and La Balue Lt, both fixed green, which as before leads to St Malo harbour.

By night follow the red leading lights of Grand Jardin (*Fl (2) R 10s*) and Rochebonne (*F R*) until the fixed green leading lights of Les Bas Sablons and La Balue come into line.

Decollé Channel. The advantage of taking the Decollé Channel is that except for the

184

32.1. Cape Frehel, 9 miles west of the entrance, is a prominent landmark in the approach. At night its powerful lighthouse, is sometimes sighted off the Minquiers.

32.2. Ile de Cézembre and rocks extending to Le Grand Jardin lighthouse.

32.3. Grand Jardin Lighthouse and beacon to be left to port, and BYB buoy and Le Buron tower to starboard. The lighthouse is erected on extensive reefs which bulge towards the fairway on the NW and SW of the lighthouse.

32.4. Le Buron light tower is left to starboard. There is a red Lt buoy on the opposite side of the fairway.

32.5. The Mole de Noires and the entrance channel to St Malo locks. A yacht should not turn to port until the lock gates are well open at the end of the mole.

St Malo

entry transit the channel is not beset by cross-tides or adverse currents to nearly the same extent as the Porte channels so far described. The disadvantage is that the channel is best not attempted until about half-tide, as otherwise any deviation from the entry transit could prove troublesome. If the channel appears a trifle awesome from studying the chart, comfort may be taken from the fact that it is sometimes used by the car ferries when they are late and avoiding the tides in the main channel. French chart No. 5645 is advised.

Entry to the channel is about ⅓ mile SW of the No. 2 port-hand buoy guarding Les Buharats. The course is 134° and the leading marks are two white beacon towers. The rear mark is the Amer de Roche Pelée and the front mark is on the rocks of Le Grand Genillet. If these two marks cannot be picked up it is better not to proceed although the course lies equidistant between two pole beacons, a port-hand one on Le Petit Pot de Beurre and a starboard-hand one on La Moulière. About a cable SE of La Moulière is another starboard-hand pole beacon, La Pierre aux Bars, and when this beacon comes abeam on the transit, course is altered to about 098°. From here on, the charts indicate a series of transits using mainly St Croix church and Le Cité at St Servan, but these are often difficult to pick up. It is perhaps more restful, and just as safe, to navigate to the south of the port-hand pole beacons and north of the starboard-hand ones for, once the passage between Le Petit Pot de Beurre and La Moulière has been safely accomplished, the rest of the channel is reasonably wide and free of dangers except for two rocks S of Les Traversins which must be left to starboard.

A course of 098° passes a cable or more north of Le Petit Genillet starboard-hand beacon and then close south of the port-hand Le Petit Buzard pole beacon. Then, after

32.6. The entrance to the locks. To the left are yachts at moorings on the north side of the entrance awaiting signals to enter the lock. Centre is the control office. Three red vertical lights prohibit entry and three green vertical lights permit entry. Above the control tower are displayed the lights controlling the approaches to the lock on both sides. Two vertical green lights with a white light offset to one side indicate that a large vessel is expected, has been given clearance, and all other vessels must keep clear. The waiting buoys on the left dry out at LW.

about ¾ mile, it passes no more than ½ cable north of the starboard-hand Rochardien pole beacon. When about a cable south of Le Mouille port-hand pole beacon, course should be altered to pass midway between Les Pierres d'Amourette port-hand pole beacon and Les Roches Bonnes starboard-hand pole beacon opposite Dinard beach. When close to and abeam the latter beacon, course should again be altered towards the starboard-hand beacon near the end of the Dinard north slip-way. Les Porceaux bank has been extending southwards and the deepest water between the two entry beacons to the Decollé channel from the Rance, lies well to the south and close to the beacon near the Dinard north slip.

La Grande Conchée Channel. The Grande Conchée channel lies between La Grande Conchée Fort and La Plate red-and-white light tower (*Q WRG sectored 9M*). Steer due S towards the E side of Le Petit Bey Fort which will pass between La Grand Conchée Fort and La Plate. A cable south of La Plate is a S cardinal buoy, and half a mile further south is the starboard-hand pole beacon of Les Pierres aux Normands. Another half mile further south is the starboard-hand light buoy (*Fl G 2s*) of Roche aux Anglais. Immediately after passing Roche aux Anglais buoy, the course should be changed to the SW to pass the port-hand buoy of Les Crapauds du Bey to port. A cable after passing this buoy, course should be changed again to due S and this held until the main channel is reached. The depths to the W and SW of Les Crapauds du Bey buoy are not much above datum. For absolute safety at very low Spring tides this channel should not be used for two hours either side of LW Springs, but it is quite safe to do so at LW Neaps.

Chenal des Petits Pointus. For those coming E about the Minquiers or using the Entrée de la Déroute the most natural approach to St Malo is the Chenal des Petits Pointus. The channel is entered some ½ mile W of the island of Les Grands Pointus and about 1½ cables E of La St Servantine starboard-hand buoy on a course of 203°. This course passes ½ cable W of the port-hand beacon Les Petit Pointus. The leading marks are the Villa Coppinger in Dinard to the right of the Petit Bey Fort. The former is not very easy to pick out in which case Dinard church tower can be substituted. Some ¾ mile past Les Petit Pointus beacon, the course comes abeam La Plate light tower (*Q 7m*) situated about 3 cables to the west and, to the south of it, Le Bouton S cardinal buoy lies about 2½ cables to the west. A further ¾ mile along this course the port-hand pole beacon Grand Dodehal will come

32.7. La Grande Conchée fort from the SE.

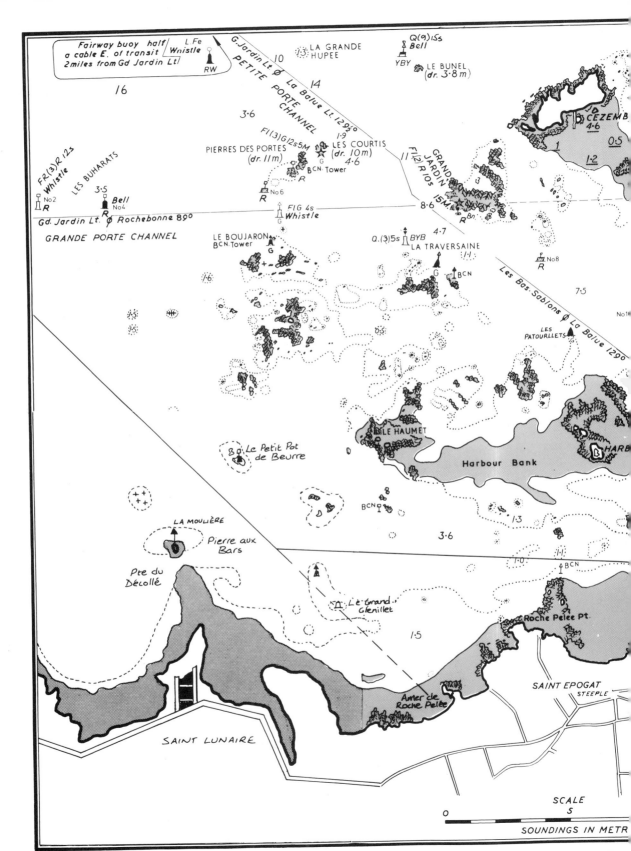

Fairway buoy half
a cable E. of transit
2 miles from Gd Jardin Lt

L Fe
Whistle
RW

G.Jardin Lt ∅ 10
La Balue Lt 129°

PETITE PORTE CHANNEL

16

Q.(9)15s
Bell
YBY   LE BUNEL
(dr. 3·8 m)

LA GRANDE
HUPEE

1·3

14

3·6

1·9

CEZEMB
4·6

0·5

1
1·2

FR(3)R 12s
Whistle
No2
R

LES BUHARATS

3·5

Bell
No4
R

Gd. Jardin Lt. ∅ Rochebonne 89°

GRANDE PORTE CHANNEL

Fl(3)G 2s 5M
PIERRES DES PORTES
(dr. 11m)

R
No 6
R

FIG 4s
Whistle
G

LES COURTIS
(dr. 10m)
G   4·6
BCN. Tower
R

GRAND JARDIN Fl(2) R 10s 11M 15M

3

8·6

R   Bn

LE BOUJARON
BCN.Tower
G

1·6

Q.(3)5s   BYB
LA TRAVERSAINE
1·1
G   BCN

4·7

Les Bas-Sablons ∅ La Balue 129°

7·5

No8
R

1·5
1·5

0·5

LES PATOURLLETS
G

ILE HAUMET

Le Petit Pot
de Beurre

Harbour Bank

HARB

+ +
+ +

BCN
R

1·3

3·6

1·0

LA MOULIÈRE

Pierre aux
Bars

1·1

BCN

Pte du
Décollé

Le Grand
Glenillet

1·5

Roche Pelee Pt.

SAINT EPOGAT
STEEPLE

Amer de
Roche Pelee

SAINT LUNAIRE

SCALE
S

0

SOUNDINGS IN METR

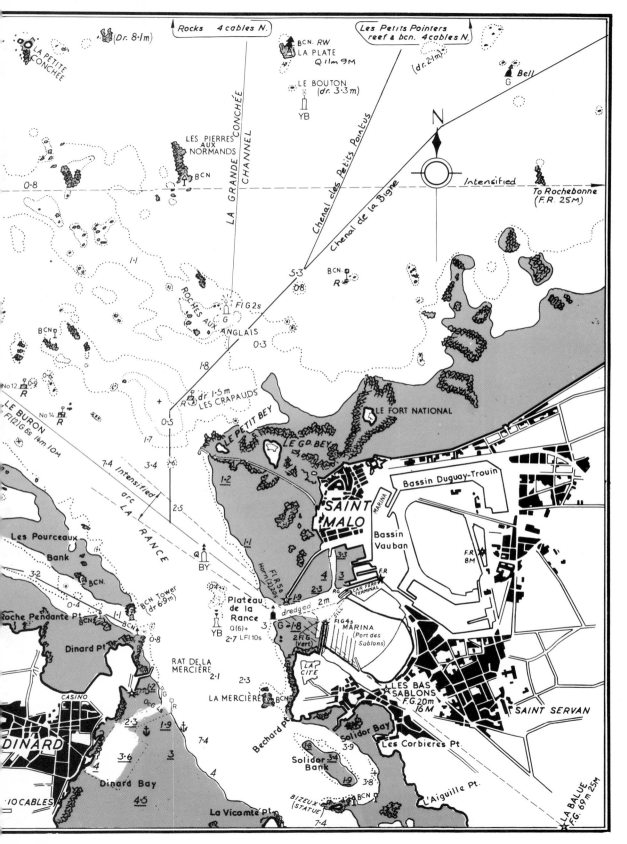

(Dr. 8·1m)

LA PETITE CONCHÉE

Rocks   4 cables N.

BCN. RW
LA PLATE
Q 11m 9M

Les Petits Pointers
reef & bcn. 4 cables N.

(dr. 2·1m)

LE BOUTON
(dr. 3·3 m)
YB

G
Bell

LES PIERRES
AUX
NORMANDS
BCN

LA GRANDE CONCHÉE CHANNEL

Chenal des Petits Pointus

Chenal de la Bigne

N

Intensified

To Rochebonne
(F.R. 25M)

0·8

1·1

ROCHES AUX ANGLAIS
Fl G 2s
G

5·3

0·8

BCN.
R

0·3

BCN
No 12 0·9
0·6
R
No 14 1·1
R

LE BURON
Fl (2) G 6s 14m 10M

7·4 Intensified

arc

LA RANCE

1·8

dr 1·5 m
R
LES CRAPAUDS

0·5

1·7

3·4

1·6

LE PETIT BEY

LE Gd. BEY

LE FORT NATIONAL

1·2

Bassin Duguay-Trouin

SAINT MALO

Bassin Vauban

F.R 8M

2·5

1·1

Les Pourceaux
Bank

3·2

BCN.

0·4

BCN Tower
(dr 6·9m)

1·1

BCN

Roche Pendante Pt

Dinard Pt.

0·8

a
BY

Horn (2) 20s

Fl R 5s

1·9

3·3

4   3

2·3 RG

F.R

CAR FERRY
TERMINAL

0·4

Plateau
de la
Rance
Q(6)+
YB 2·7 LFl 10s

3

G 1·8

dredged

2 m

Fl G 4s
MARINA
(Port des
Sablons)

2 Fl G
(Vert)

RAT DE LA
MERCIÈRE
2·1

2·3

LA MERCIÈRE

G

R

BCN

LA
CITÉ

LES BAS
SABLONS
F.G 20m
16 M

SAINT SERVAN

CASINO

G
R

2·3

1·9

DINARD

3·6

3

4

Dinard Bay

4·5

10 CABLES

Bechard Pt

Solidor Bank

1·8

3·9

Solidor Bay

3·4

Les Corbieres Pt.

1·9

3·8

L'Aiguille Pt.

La Vicomté Pt.

7·4

BIZEUX
(STATUE)

BCN

LA BALUE
F.G 69 m 25M

St Malo

abeam 2 cables to the ESE; here the course is altered to the SW, towards St Enogat church tower, so as to pass close to the port-hand Les Crapauds du Bey buoy which lies some 2 cables NW of Le Petit Bey Fort. Soon after passing this buoy, course can be altered to due S until the main channel is reached. The depths to the W and SW of Les Crapauds du Bey buoy are not much above datum.

Chenal de la Bigne. This channel is the one usually taken if coming from the direction of Granville. The channel commences close SE of the Basse Rochefort E cardinal buoy on a bearing of 222° with the Crolante white beacon off the Pointe de la Varde, in line with the W side of Le Grand Bey. This transit passes close SE of La Petite Bigne starboard-hand pole beacon. When La Bigne itself bears due N, course should be changed to 236° with the transit being La Villa Lonick on Pointe Bellafard in line with the Buron Tower. This

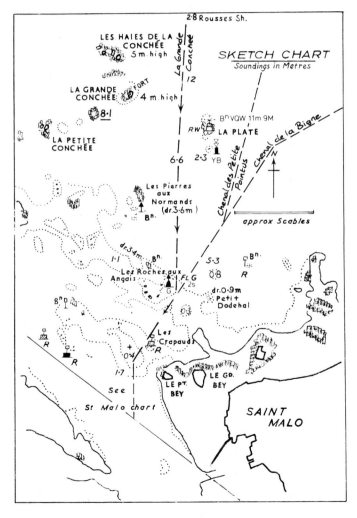

Sketch of the three N and NE channels.

32.8. The yacht marina at the end of the bassin Vauban. It provides long pontoons with water laid on. The hospitable Yacht Club de St Malo is the low building on the left centre.

32.9. Entrance to Port des Sablons Marina, leaving end of breakwater to starboard.

course passes 1½ cables NW of La Crolante white beacon and, after about half a mile, ½ cable SE of the Letruns starboard-hand bell-buoy. About ½ mile further on when La Plate and La Grande Conchée come into line, the course is once again changed to 222° on the St Enogat church tower. This passes 1½ cables NW of Grand Dodehal port-hand pole beacon, a cable SE of Les Roches aux Anglais starboard-hand light buoy (*Fl G 2s*) and close NW of Les Crapauds du Bey port-hand buoy. Shortly after passing the latter buoy, course can be changed to due S until the main channel is reached. Depths near the Crapauds du Bey buoy are not much above datum.

Port des Sablons. There is a large Marina NE of La Cité. To reach it, leave the main channel when S of a line joining the S cardinal buoy marking the south end of the Plateau de la Rance with the end of St Malo mole. The end of the mole should be given a wide berth and the area both N and SW of the dredged channel dries out. Anchorage in the dredged channel or in the approach as far west as the Plateau de la Rance is prohibited. There is temporary anchorage east of Plateau de la Rance, keeping east of the busy fairway, or in Dinard Roads where there are large white visitors' buoys. So keep in the main dredged channel until the north end of the Marina breakwater comes abaft the beam. The entrance to the Marina lies round the end of the breakwater on which there is a light (*Fl G 4s*).

The depth over the sill is indicated by illuminated numbers exhibited on a large panel at the north-east of the Marina. Three waiting buoys are provided close west of the Marina breakwater. These, unlike the waiting buoys to the NW of the dredged channel, do not

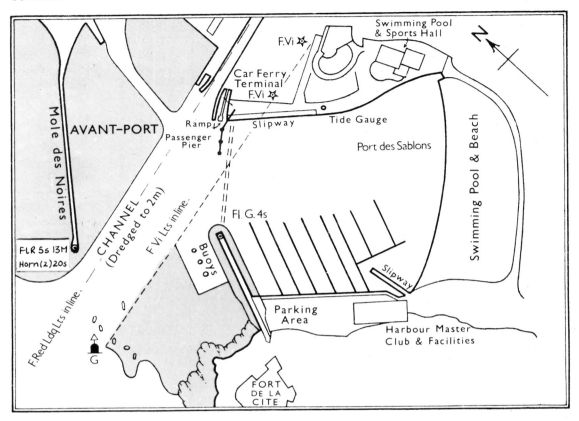

dry out but at low water they should be approached from the north as the dredged area is narrow.

The pontoon nearest to the breakwater on entry is reserved for visitors; depths are 2–2½m. The outer end of this pontoon can be uncomfortable if the wind is in the NW or N. There are finger berths at the pontoon for craft up to 15m LOA. There are also some berths on fore-and-aft moorings in the NE part of the Marina for craft up to 20m LOA.

The Marina has all the usual facilities, including a chandlery and a garage for fuel.

Vauban Marina. This involves locking in. The lock opens at intervals between 2½ hours before HW for the first entry to, or 2 hours before HW for the first exit from the port, until 1½ to 2 hours after HW, depending on the tidal coefficient. Yachts have the lowest priority on entry to the lock, after fishing vessels and port craft. They should proceed to the side of the lock where a lock-master's assistant will be waiting with a heaving line to pick up the yachts bow and stern lines. Once through the lock, a port-hand turn is made to the end of the Bassin Vauban where there is a Marina with all the usual facilities. It is here that the St Malo Yacht Club is situated. Yachts can also berth in the Bassin Duguay-Trouin at its W end near the Casino, but permission must first be obtained from St Malo Port Radio on Channel 12 VHF for the lifting bridge to be raised.

Regulating Signals. These are displayed on the N side of the entrance to the lock. Three vertical red lights prohibit entrance; three vertical green ones indicate entry permitted. At a higher level, above the control tower, are the international light signals controlling the approaches to the lock both from the landward side as well as in the outer harbour. These consist of two vertical green lights with a white light off-set to one side. This means that a large vessel is expected and has been given clearance to enter the lock, all other vessels should keep clear of the lock approaches.

Facilities. St Malo is an interesting historic town, with its thick masonry walls (almost entirely rebuilt since the last war) and heavy fortifications, it has a character of its own. Possibly because of this, it is a major tourist trap. It is a large city, stretching far beyond the confines of the ancient walls, consequently it has comprehensive facilities including yacht builders and repairers, marine engineers, chandlers and sailmakers. There are bonded stores from M. Hervé and French charts from Librarie Maritime in Rue Dinan. There are many hotels, restaurants, shops and supermarkets. There is a main line station and the Main Post office at the western end of the main docks (the Post Office inside the walls of the ancient city is referred to as the Post Office Intra Muros). There are bus services to all parts, air services from Dinard airport to Jersey and Paris, a car ferry to Portsmouth and *vedettes* to Ile Cézambre, Dinard and to Dinan via the Rance.

Dinard

Dinard was once one of the best known holiday resorts in France. It is no longer as popular as it was and is now rarely visited by yachtsmen from abroad. It has many hotels, restaurants, shops, a Casino and good bathing beaches. The Yacht Club is hospitable, to British yachtsmen at least, and has links with British clubs some dating back to Edwardian times.

Most of the area between Pointe de Dinard and La Vicomte Pointe dries out at Springs, and eastward of this shoal the streams are strong. There are moorings over most of the area but the outer line of mooring buoys does not dry out and contains some large visitors' buoys. They can be uncomfortable. At the N end of the bay there is a channel dredged to 1m marked, somewhat indistinctly, by poles, giving access to an area dredged to 2m used as a mooring area by the Yacht Club. Alongside the quay in front of the Yacht Club is the only bulk re-fuelling facility in the whole St Malo area. It can be reached above about half tide.

Vedettes run to St Malo every half hour, there is an Airport and a railway station.

33 La Rance

The Rance is an attractive river and a visit to Dinan is well worthwhile. The river has been dammed by a barrage, the Usine Maremotrice de la Rance. This dam incorporates a tidal electric generator. At HW the level of water above the dam is retained for some 2–3 hours to allow the level of the sea to fall. Water is then allowed to escape through the turbines until the level above the dam is no less than 4m above datum, a figure set by law. Often the level above the dam at LW is as much as 7m above datum, the actual level depending on the requirement of electricity for the grid. The same procedure is followed on the flood. The level in the river is retained at no less than 4m until the sea rises sufficiently to allow the upstream flow to be started. The levels of water in the river can also be adjusted by pumping.

Because the full range of tide is not used, the strength of the currents in the river, except in emergency, are normally not excessive and are less than before the dam was built. There are also long periods of slack water. The level at LW is published daily for the day following in, for example, the St Malo edition of 'Ouest France'. This, incidentally, is the authority used by the dockmaster of the Vauban Marina at St Malo for posting on his notice board.

The accompanying diagram shows a contour 2m above datum but, with experience, it may be found that the areas where it is safe to anchor are larger than shown. For example, when the level is 4m above datum the slip at St Suliac can still be used by dinghy. Relatively deep draft vessels moored not too far off the end of the slip do not touch bottom.

The Barrage Lock

This lock opens from 0700–2100 hours every hour on the hour whenever the tide level at St Malo is greater than 2m. When the tide level at St Malo is less than 2m, the lock does not open for a period approximately from LW St Malo to LW + 3 hours 20 minutes.

This means that during the summer months there is usually one Spring tide per month when the lock opening is affected for a few days at LW. Otherwise the lock opens regularly each hour.

The lock will also open on the hour between the hours of 2030 and 0430 provided the lock-keeper is given two hours notice by telephone (99 46 21 87). There are no lights in the river.

Instructions governing the use of the lock can be obtained with some difficulty in the lock itself or at the marina offices in St Malo and Dinan. Among other things, the instructions refer to those wishing to ascend the lock making their presence known to the lock-keeper 20 minutes before the hour. The reason for this is that the sequence of lock opening starts at 20 minutes to the hour by the closing of the upstream gates. If there are no vessels descending and no craft indicating their intention to ascend by 20 minutes to the hour, then the sequence does not begin. However during the sailing season there are usually many craft wishing to use the lock, both up and down, there is consequently no doubt about the sequence beginning and yachts may enter from seaward without any prior indication. The seaward end of the lock is crossed by a lifting bridge. Yachts with masts must move to the upstream end of the lock to allow the lifting bridge to be lowered. There are chains and ropes hanging down the side of the lock to assist mooring.

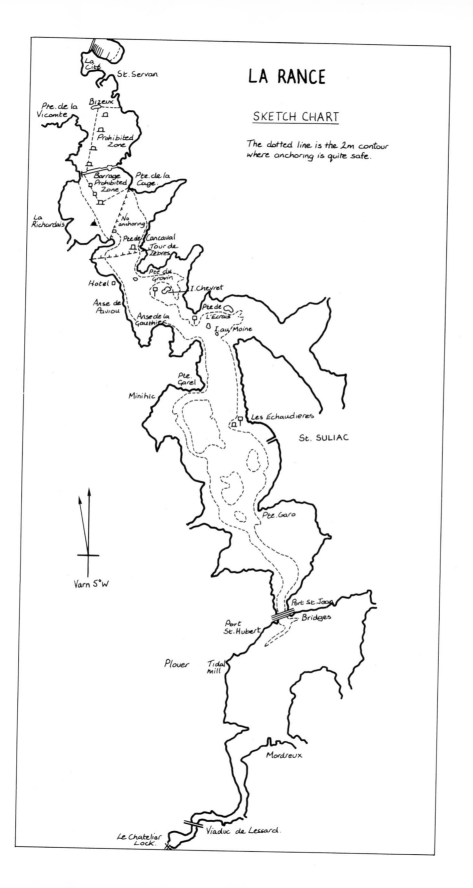

LA RANCE

SKETCH CHART

The dotted line is the 2m contour
where anchoring is quite safe.

La Cité
St.Servan
Bizeux
Pte.de la Vicomte
Prohibited Zone
Barrage Prohibited Zone
Pte.de la Cage.
La Richardais
No anchoring
Pte.de Cancaval
Tour de Zebres
Pte.du Grovin
Hotel
I.Chevret
Anse de Paviou
Pte.de L'Ecrois
Anse de la Gauthier
I.au Moine
Pte. Garel
Minihic
Les Echaudieres
St. SULIAC
Pte.Garo
Varn 5°W
Port St.Jean
Port St.Hubert
Bridges
Plouer
Tidal Mill
Mordreux
Le Chatelier Lock.
Viaduc de Lessard.

La Rance

Yachts wishing to descend from the Rance should enter the lock by 20 minutes to the hour.

There are waiting buoys both above and below the lock. When ascending it is expected that yachts, once the green light shows, will enter the lock without delay so that the lifting bridge can be lowered and road traffic resumed with the minimum of interruption.

Signals. Above the control tower there are signals indicating the opening and closing of the lock gates. A black ball hoisted indicates the upstream gates are open; a cone indicates the downstream gates are open. Do not enter from downstream, however, until the lights on the west side of the lock gates turn to green.

There are also signals in the middle of the barrage indicating which way the water is flowing through the turbines, if at all. A white cone over a black one, points up, indicates a flood stream; a black cone over a white one, points down, indicates an ebb stream.

Prohibited Anchorage and Prohibited Zone. Anchoring is prohibited for a mile S of Pointe de la Cage aux Moines on account of submarine cables.

The prohibited zones are well marked by strings of buoys, both above and below the dam. All movement in these zones is prohibited because of the danger of craft being sucked into the turbine intakes.

The Rance to St Suliac.

For the deepest channel give Pointe de Cancaval and its starboard-hand pole beacon a good berth. On rounding the point, steer to pass the port-hand beacon tower, Tour des Zebres, fairly close to and then steer due S towards the opposite bank. Then follow reasonably closely the line of mooring buoys off the Anse de Pariou and the Anse de Gauthier. Then steer towards the Ile au Moine. When a cable short of the Ile au Moine and due S of the port-hand pole beacon on Pointe de l'Ecrais, change course to steer on the end of Pointe Garo. This course passes to port the beacons and beacon tower on Les Echandières. The Bay of St Suliac then opens up.

Anchorages and Moorings There are visitors mooring buoys at Richardais just upstream of the lock, where there are plans to construct a marina. There is a landing slip, a store and a restaurant as well as a small shipyard. On the bank opposite Pointe Grouin is a hotel where some pontoons have been put out for the benefit of customers. Again, as in all the embayments on the river there are large white buoys for visitors, usually forming the outside line of moorings. The same is true of the Anse de Pariou and the Anse de Gauthier where there is also a thriving shipyard. The area behind Ile Chevret is filled with moorings but a place to anchor may be found. There are moorings also S of Pointe Garel and an active slip where dinghies may land if visiting Minihic, half a mile up the hill, where provisions may be obtained and where there is a restaurant. Opposite this embayment on the east bank is St Suliac. This has a harbourmaster and numerous buoys which can be picked up and for which a charge is made. There is plenty of room and depth of water to anchor outside the moorings, the best position probably being in line with the slip. St Suliac has a general store, P.O., baker, butcher, crêperie and an excellent restaurant, 'de la Grève', at the top of the slip. Water can be obtained from a hydrant near the HM's office on the front. Showers at the camping site; doctor above the bakery.

33.1. The approach from northward to the lock on the River Rance. The last of the yachts leaving from the river has left the lock and the cone point downwards has been hoisted to indicate that the seaward gates are open.

33.2. Tacking up the River Rance and approaching the Pont St Hubert and over head high tension cables.

La Rance

St Suliac to Le Chatelier Lock

Upstream from St Suliac, the channel is marked by a series of port-hand buoys placed within easy distance of each other. The best water is about 50m to starboard of these buoys. At the starboard-hand turn opposite the village of Mordreux there is a starboard-hand buoy where it is important not to make a short cut. There are two road bridges and power lines across the narrows between Port St Hubert and Port St Jean. The air draught is 22.8m at HW Springs.

Half a mile above Mordreux the channel is marked by poles and occasional small red and green buoys. The Viaduc de Lessard has an air draught of 18.9m at HW Springs. Shortly above the viaduct is Le Chatelier Lock.

Le Chatelier Lock.
At the downstream end of the lock is a swing bridge which opens with the downstream gates. The lock opens from 0800–2000 hrs whenever the water level at St Malo is greater than 8.5m. The lock then operates on an 'as required' basis for a period of about 4½ hours starting about 45 minutes after HW St Malo (unless this involves operating for less than an hour).

If the water level above the lock is low following a period of drought then the lock opens only once in each direction every hour between the times indicated above and, indeed, if

33.3. Dinan Marina.

198

the drought is severe there may be difficulty getting through the lock at all. Any of the harbour masters at St Malo or St Suliac will advise.

Mooring lines are provided in the lock.

Anchorages and Moorings. There is deep water for anchoring in the narrows crossed by the two bridges and also just above the narrows where there are moorings. There are plans to construct a marina behind the tidal mill which already has a sill, to be called Plouer Marina. Upstream from here the river dries out at low water.

Just above Le Chatelier Lock is a small marina with depths of some 2m + on the outer pontoons. There is a small café here only, but a good restaurant can be found about a mile up the road to Dinan which is 3 miles away, and if required, a taxi can be obtained through the lock-keeper. It is also possible to anchor in a pool between the lock and the marina (although this now seems to be discouraged).

Le Chatelier to Dinan.

Above Le Chatelier Lock the river is canalized and well marked. There are two shallow patches of only 1.5m, although some of the rest of the canal is quite deep. At Dinan along the left bank of the canal, pontoons have been laid out with short fingers at the upstream end where the canal widens near the bridge. All the usual marina facilities are available.

Dinan

Dinan is a delightful, medieval, walled town with an interesting history.

In the port area there are many restaurants, a butcher and baker and an embryo general store. Fresh milk can be obtained at the farm on the bank opposite the marina although there are plans to create an extension to the marina in this area. A narrow street climbs up to the town itself where there are many shops, a supermarket, P.O., banks, restaurants, etc. Even if draught considerations prevent a yacht proceeding above Le Chatelier by the canal, a visit to Dinan, by taxi if necessary, is well worthwhile.

The canal above Dinan with links to the Vilaine River, has a safe depth of 1.2m although some rehabilitation work is taking place. Near the first lock on the canal, about $\frac{3}{4}$ mile above Dinan bridge, is a large open-air swimming pool which is easily reached by dinghy.

There is a *vedette* from Dinan to St Malo nearly every day.

Acknowledgements for previous editions

For contributions and help in the first edition of this book, published in 1956, I gratefully acknowledge my debt to the following: Captain C. Stewart, Extra Master, for Christchurch and other advice and to Mrs Stewart for drawing the charts; to the late Mr A. J. Barber for the sailing directions and transits for Guernsey, Herm and Sark; to Lieut.-Colonel H. A. Stevenson for Jersey and Carteret; to Mr D. P. Richardson for Les Ecrehou, and Mr V. R. Richardson for Mont St Michel; to my own family and amateur crews who accompanied me on many happy voyages of minor exploration.

Additional information for the following four editions was gratefully received from Mr D. Russell Anstey (Poole Harbour), Dr J. C. Bulstrode (Guernsey and Herm), Mr J. M. Robson (Sark and Goury), Mr M. Gilkes (Goury), Mr John Marriner (Minquiers) and Lieut.-Colonel H. A. Stevenson (N. E. Passage to St Malo), Mr R. Yeabsley (Christchurch), Mr J. C. H. Tucker and Commander Erroll Bruce RN, Rtd. (Guernsey), Pilot B. Ching (Jersey), Monsieur B. Lefevre (President of the Yacht Club de Cherbourg), and Mr V. R. Richardson for Portbail, Monsieur Noël Laurent for particulars of Port des Sablons at St Malo, Mr R. C. Adams for his authoritative information on the inshore streams around Sark, and Mr C. Huggins who sent information on Granville Hérel and changes in other harbours. While useful comments were received from Mr Dennis Hall and many other yachtsmen. I wish to acknowledge with thanks the help of the Queen's Harbour Master, Portland, and the Harbour Masters and Authorities at Poole, Weymouth, St Peter Port and St Helier, as also the managers of the various marinas.

I am also most grateful to Dr C. Segel with whom I cruised for over three years in his *Sequel*, revisiting, checking information and taking new photographs of most of the harbours. I am indebted to Mr Alan H. Irving for bringing the original chart drawings up to date and converting them to LAT datum and metric units as well as for adding a number of new ones.

The charts in this book are largely based on Admiralty charts by permission of the Controller of HM Stationery Office and the Hydrographer of the Navy and reference has been made to the *Channel Pilot* and *Tidal Stream Atlas* by permission of the same authorities. Some of the charts are based on French charts by kind permission of the French Service Hydrographique de la Marine. Photographs, other than my own, are acknowledged individually.

Altogether I have had wonderful co-operation in making these editions as useful as possible for which I am very grateful.

K.A.C.

Buoys and Beacons IALA Buoyage System 'A'
The combined Cardinal and Lateral System (Red to Port)

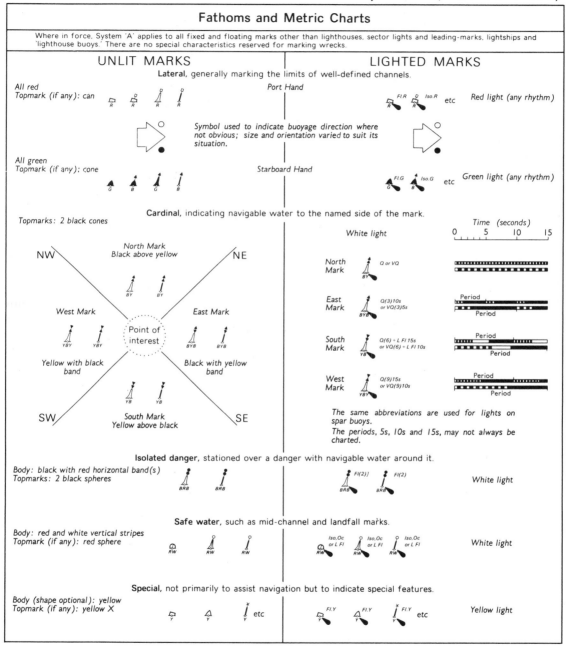

Fathoms and Metric Charts

Where in force, System 'A' applies to all fixed and floating marks other than lighthouses, sector lights and leading-marks, lightships and 'lighthouse buoys.' There are no special characteristics reserved for marking wrecks.

UNLIT MARKS | LIGHTED MARKS

Lateral, generally marking the limits of well-defined channels.

Port Hand

All red
Topmark (if any): can

Red light (any rhythm)

Symbol used to indicate buoyage direction where not obvious; size and orientation varied to suit its situation.

All green
Topmark (if any): cone

Starboard Hand

Green light (any rhythm)

Cardinal, indicating navigable water to the named side of the mark.

Topmarks: 2 black cones

White light

Time (seconds)
0   5   10   15

North Mark
Black above yellow

NW   NE

North Mark   Q or VQ

East Mark   Q(3)10s or VQ(3)5s   Period

West Mark   East Mark
Yellow with black band   Black with yellow band

Point of interest

South Mark   Q(6) + L Fl 15s or VQ(6) + L Fl 10s   Period

West Mark   Q(9)15s or VQ(9)10s   Period

SW   SE
South Mark
Yellow above black

The same abbreviations are used for lights on spar buoys.
The periods, 5s, 10s and 15s, may not always be charted.

Isolated danger, stationed over a danger with navigable water around it.

Body: black with red horizontal band(s)
Topmarks: 2 black spheres

Fl(2)   White light

Safe water, such as mid-channel and landfall marks.

Body: red and white vertical stripes
Topmark (if any): red sphere

Iso,Oc or L Fl   White light

Special, not primarily to assist navigation but to indicate special features.

Body (shape optional): yellow
Topmark (if any): yellow X

Fl.Y etc   Yellow light

Abbreviated from the book edition of British Admiralty Chart No 5011. With the permission of the Controller of HM Stationery Office and the Hydrographer of the Navy.

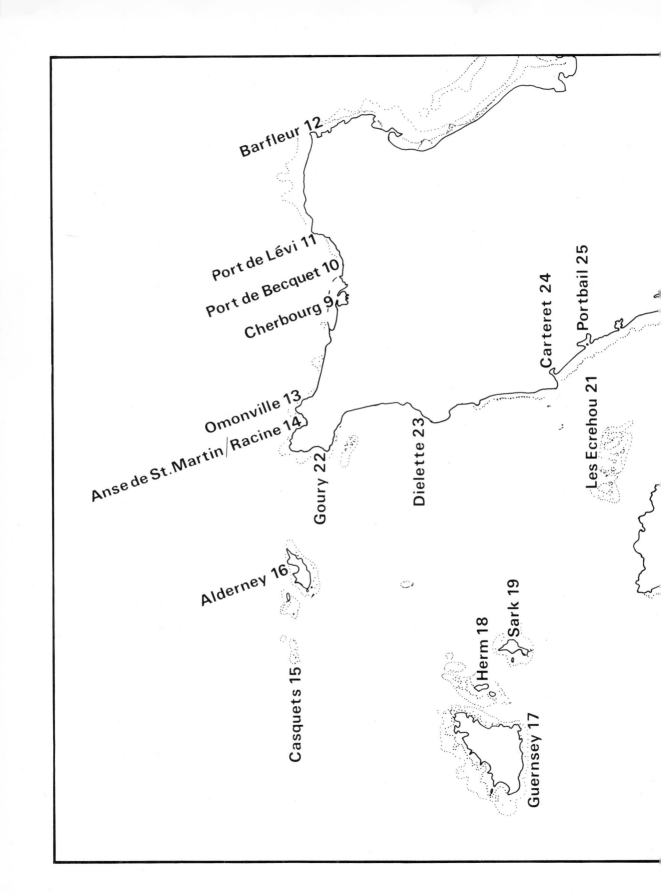

Barfleur 12

Port de Lévi 11
Port de Becquet 10
Cherbourg 9

Carteret 24
Portbail 25

Omonville 13
Anse de St. Martin/Racine 14

Dielette 23

Les Ecrehou 21

Goury 22

Alderney 16

Sark 19
Herm 18

Casquets 15

Guernsey 17